The Charlatans
We Are Rock
Lessons in pop survival

John Robb

EBURY
PRESS

This edition published in Great Britain in 1998

1 3 5 7 9 10 8 6 4 2

Ebury Press
Random House, 20 Vauxhall Bridge Road, London SW1V 2SA

Random House Australia Pty Limited
20 Alfred Street, Milsons Point, Sydney, New South Wales 2061, Australia

Random House New Zealand Limited
18 Poland Road, Glenfield, Auckland 10, New Zealand

Random House South Africa (Pty) Limited
Endulini, 5A Jubilee Road, Parktown 2193, South Africa

Random House UK Limited Reg. No. 954009

A CIP catalogue record for this book is available from the British Library

ISBN 0 09 186568 9

Cover design by Mokom
Plate design by Dan Newman
Cover photograph by Chris Floyd

Printed and bound in Great Britain by Mackay's of Chatham plc

Papers used by Ebury Press are natural, recyclable products made from wood grown in sustainable forests.

Introduction

'The thing you've got to understand about the Charlatans,' Jon Brookes once mused to Q magazine, 'is that we don't want to rock. We just wanna *roll*.'

'I was sitting on a train, thinking you've either got talent or a pretty face, but the Charlatans have got both, so we're lucky, ha ha ha . . . er . . . don't take that too seriously . . .' Tim Burgess.

They seemed to burst out of nowhere, ready formed and custom made for the relentless rush of pop energy that was the Madchester/baggy/scallydelic (delete as applicable) pop explosion.

In fact they had roots that went back deep into the Midlands mod and 1960s garage band scenes, and members of the band had already released records and struggled in small-town outfits out of sync and out of fashion. Far from being bandwagon jumpers they were already playing the same sort of sounds that were being banded about by their Manchester cousins.

I decided to write this biography after the success of my Stone Roses book; it was like taking the story of British pop in the 1990s beyond the band that was the catalyst for the whole era and on into the safe hands of the next wave of bands. The Charlatans were the most interesting of these, their music sound-tracking the changeover from baggy shuffle to a more traditionally infused rock & roll. Whilst others fell by the wayside, this band just got better and better. You follow the Charlatans through the 1990s and you get the story of pop through the decade, the rise and fall of baggy, the rise and fall of Britpop.

I was also fascinated by their roots, which dig deep into punk rock and post punk and through the mod scene of the 1980s, roots that I understand well as I grew up with the same influences.

British youth culture is a fascinating and intense scramble of styles and tastes, and making sense of this ongoing argument of taste is only possible if you were there. You've got to have argued the arguments, downed the drugs and bought the records to understand the intensity of the love of pop culture in the UK.

The Charlatans were born from these roots and, in turn, they hand over this love of pop to their fans, the next generation seeking the purity and exhilaration of great pop. They burst on to the Manchester scene in 1989 and of course I was there at each gig, and every twist and turn in the plot, recording everything for *Sounds*, the now defunct music paper that was always on the cutting edge for what was going on in rock & roll until it was bought by a new publisher and ridiculously shut down in 1992.

I interviewed the band when they started, speaking to Tim Burgess when he looked like a five-year-old kid, just when they were breaking and then at key points over the next few years, even accompanying them to Los Angeles on their first American tour. Being from Manchester gives you a good perspective on these things; you get plugged into the rush of energy when the city backs a band.

This is a story of a band that has too often been forgotten by the pundits, left out at the punch by the sudden flash-floods of success by rival outfits. The Charlatans themselves have just got their heads down and built up an audience that leave them as one of the biggest British bands of these times, a success sometimes overshadowed by their personal disasters. But the band themselves have never given up on their solid bond with their fans, and now, in the closing years of the millennium, there is massive confidence in their camp that they are about to deliver, crossover in the same sort of way that R.E.M. did all those years ago.

The Charlatans is a story of sheer bloody perseverance. How the hell they survived the pop free-for-all of the 1990s is detailed in here somewhere.

John Robb
Manchester 1998

Roots

THE MOD SCENE

At the heart of all British pop culture is the mod ideal. The sharp-as-fuck street swagger, the hip soundtrack, the neat freak clothes, cool lingo and fast drugs, it's been the spine and the backbone of every youth culture ever since it appeared.

The early punk bands were superannuated mod outfits, complete in paint-smattered mod gear: the Clash were hypa mods and Cook and Jones of the Pistols were scruffy mods with a love of the Small Faces and the Who; the hippies were mods with long hair, gone off on a long and winding road of dope, losing the plot; the skinheads were nasty post mods with the look tightened up to an impossibly brutal total; and the casuals were a modern mod equivalent who ironically became the mods' style enemies in the mid 1980s. You can catch a whiff of the mod ideal in Oasis, the Charlatans, the Stone Roses and quite definitely in Ocean Colour Scene. Rave culture had a smattering of mod style about it; it's everywhere in British youth culture – wherever you look the blueprint is the mod ideal.

Mod culture is the most diagrammatically apolitical of all British youth cultures, instead of dressing naaasty and spitting in the face of convention, the mods aimed to dress better than the boss, be sharper and smarter looking. Some of the snaps of them dressed in their finest make them look like parodies of city gents complete with copies of the *Financial Times*. These were working-class boys on the make – the idea was to use the system instead of bucking it and maybe, despite all their hi jinks and anti-authoritarian poses, mods were small 'c' conservatives at heart. They were shocked by the decay of the old orders and were the new, sharp and angular breed come to put things right.

The clothes/pop/drugs equation was a matter of life and death; to be a mod was a 24-hour experience, a full-on thing. The scene started in the 1950s, and some muffled accounts have it as the bastard offspring of the ted scene, where some working-class boys got into Italian clothes and sharpened up their act. Whilst teds retained the same look with few variations and became rockers, mods ran through a whole gamut of fashions and changes which were greatly influenced by the continent. Their modern-day equivalent would be the scally, baggy, football-terrace look. Instead of sharp shoes the row is now over trainers and labels.

The mods and rockers were at each other's throats and by the mid 1960s they were embroiled in press-hyped running battles. On British beaches on bank holidays, there was a confusion of the rioting and glorious stupidity that the British have revelled in since records began. Pre football hooliganism this was the excuse for booze-stained yobbery, as pent-up frustration and a sheer visceral search for kicks combined.

As the 1960s panned out the mods slowly turned into hippies or skin-heads, or just grew up and settled down. The whole movement went underground for ten years, only to be sparked back into action in the post-punk mish-mash of styles culminating in the highly influential *Quadro-phenia* film conceived by the Who.

Punk had reignited the youth culture debate by putting the first genuine pop culture on the streets for years – a rumbling, anarchic celebration of youth and energy that quickly soured and fell in on itself.

In theory punk was the year zero that wiped the rock & roll slate clean; in practice the rallying call of 'no future' was being heeded a little too literally. What followed was a smash and grab raid on whatever youth fashions could be dimly remembered from the past. There were rockabillies, skins, teds, mohicans, mods, rockers and scooter boys, and sometimes in mad, fucked-up little towns a mixture of the whole lot. Quite often they were all fighting each other and occasionally they were mixing and matching, swopping records and fighting the common cause of boredom.

Each scene, although diagrammatically opposed, was actually incredibly similar, fired by a love of freaky clothes and hard-to-find records; they thrived on the sense of outsiderdom.

At the core there were always some terrifically anal scenesters sup-porting a fistful of bands that really mattered. The passion generated was fierce, and the bands built up committed and intensely loyal partisan audiences. Scene life was about wearing the right shirt with the right socks and the right shoes.

Whatever the style, details were all. Especially in mod, a youth culture that was fanatical over the minutia of total detail.

Mod was enjoying its biggest revival since its heyday of the early 1960s, sparked by the energy of punk and ignited by the Who's aforementioned homage to mod culture, *Quadrophenia*, passing through the conduit of the Jam.

Overnight for about a month everyone seemed to turn into a mod. The punks got sharper, parkas were everywhere as were 1960s suits, and there was a definite two-tone flavour to some of the kids and a scooter boy element to the others. It was bizarre but a museum culture had been resurrected and was back on the streets. It brought with it a whole bunch of its own bands, the 1979 bands like the Chords, the Lambrettas and the Purple Hearts, heavily influenced by the Jam and, like most of the scene, in the shadow of Paul Weller.

The 1979 bands instantly attracted prejudice from the original mods and the new mods who were hooked upon the 1960s; they couldn't possibly lend their support to anything as gross as a band formed after 1969, and retreated into their own nether world of ancient music. This made it difficult for the new breed of bands, as with an already dwindling scene cut into two, there was far less support for their take on the big beat. Which was a shame, because bands like Makin' Time were really rather good.

By the mid 1980s the scene had split into two definite camps: some became mod purists while others got more into the scooter scene. Then everything died down again and got back to being a tight and loyal underground scene, kept alive with brutally idealistic fanzines, the main one of which was run by a key player in this story, Eddie Piller's *Extraordinary Sensations* named after a Purple Hearts' song.

Mod itself was still flaming in London and crept into the spill-over towns spinning out from the deathly-dull suburbs that surround the big hungry capital. Places like the home counties commuter belt and just beyond were the heartland of 1980s modernism. Enthusiasts kept the flame burning, running clubs, printing jagged fanzines and talking speed-driven bullshit with the sort of idealistic fervour that makes the very heart of pop music a viscious magnet for anyone with a lust for life.

GOING UNDERGROUND . . . MOD IN THE MID 1980S

It was an intense and wired scene.

Fanzines raged about clothes, styles, haircuts and bands. The letters pages were crammed with excited missives from all over the country, each talking about the scene in some provincial backwater as the number of mods imploded or exploded. Sometimes the whole town would have 'turned casual' and the disappointed correspondents would be one of the last handful isolated pockets of modernism in the town, fighting a rear-guard action to keep the faith. Similar to all intense hardcore scenes there was a mixture of dogged determination, stunning elitism, small-town boredom and intense pride. Being a mod in the early 1980s was a rite of passage and a way of life.

The mod scene was a tight knit community and was serviced by many long-forgotten bands. The post-punk revival mod scene was hooked around bands like Long Tall Shorty, featuring Tony Perfect who had been in the socialist skin punk band the Angelic Upstarts – Long Tall Shorty would eventually become the Rage who were one of the key mid 1980s mod underground bands, along with the Scene, the Moment, the Direct Hits, the Jetset, and, of course, Makin' Time. These bands would make up the new mod spearhead, replacing the tail end of the 1979 bands like the Cigarettes, the First Steps (who apparently featured a member of the Cure), the Directions (who donated a member to the near-miss band Big Sound Authority), and the Killermeters, as well as Rhyl's Seventeen (a favourite with the Stone Roses), who went on to form the Alarm. Others included the Crooks, who mutated into Blue Zoo; Graduate, who became the execrable

Tears For Fears; and Guns For Hire, who became Department S (remember 'Is Vic There?').

There was a myriad of supporting fanzines, like *The Countdown List*, which was Eddie Piller's follow-up to *Extraordinary Sensations*. It was newsy and packed tight with information, enthusiastically backing bands in an exploding scene. They shared the commentary with Jake S. Lingwood's enthusiastically buzzing *Smarter Than U*, and Mark Johnson's *Phoenix List* and column in *Scootering*, the magazine that joined the mod and scooter scenes.

Scooter clubs had been in existence before there were any mods and their existence was vital for many kids who joined up and made friendships across the country that cross-fertilised many unlikely groups of people.

In the early 1980s a young Steve Harrison, later to be manager of the Charlatans, would be on his scooter meeting up with the likes of the young Stone Roses Ian Brown and John Squire, and even members of eventual grebo bands like Pop Will Eat Itself were around on the scene hooking up with the pre-Manc-scene Mancs – it was a new underground network forging friendships and connections that would last through the years.

The mod fanzines frothed about the Prisoners, the legendary Medway band that provided members for the James Taylor Quartet and saw their records go for sky-high prices in the United States when it was too late. Over the years they have acquired a deserved legendary status. The Prisoners played a fired-garage mod rooted in the 1960s, although they seem to have one foot planted firmly in the mod scene and the other in the Medway scene along with groups like Billy Childish's Thee Milkshakes, garage purists who probably thought that rock & roll died the day the Beatles left Hamburg (too true if you compare the speed-freaked fabs with their later art school wankery of *Sergeant Pepper*), and would go on to carve out a several-decade run as perhaps the premier Brit underground garage band.

The scene was fairly all encompassing, and overlapped into other young idealists building pop empires. The fanzines would touch on the likes of Whaaam records, run by the TV Personalities whose witty and cynical take on 1960s pop music would obviously find aficionados in the mod scene.

The TVPs themselves were inspiring a young Alan McGee to put on his own gigs and start up a label called Creation Records whose pretty off-the-wall first ten releases were given a confused review reaction in modzines. McGee was building his operation around the swinging 1960s ideal, pop art clashing with bowl tops and slipshod jangly guitar workouts; he was trying to find a fierce contemporary edge to his whole schtick and even then was raving about a band who had two warring brothers and built their pure pop around a massive engine room of churning guitars and feedback – the Jesus & Mary Chain.

If this whole scene sounds like a complex and confusing sprawl of personalities, idealists, cranks, weirdos and full-on music nuts then that's because that's what it was. It was people with huge record collections, many opinions and a taste so refined that one shirt button in the wrong place could kill a conversation.

It was into this enthusiasm-fired world that Makin' Time were making their first tentative steps.

MAKIN' TIME FOR MAKIN' TIME

Makin' Time were formed in Willenhall, a Black Country town on the edge of the M6 next to Walsall, not the most glam of roots in terms of pop. They started by playing pure blues from the godlike Sonny Boy Williamson through to Buster Brown. The choice of a blues root for a mod-soaked band isn't that odd when you consider the huge influence the blues had on the nascent British mod scene, along with the backbone of soul and a flavour of jazz.

The original line-up of Makin' Time was put together in 1982; a basic 4-piece band, they went through eight different members in their brief tenure. The band was built around a twin vocal thing and was described by bassist Martin Blunt as being 'rhythm and soul'.

At school Blunt wasn't the driving force that he would later become in his bands: 'I was always the one that fell asleep at the back of the class!'

Like many others, the dreamers and the rebels, the lippy eccentrics and those that keep schtum, plotting away, Martin left school to go straight on the dole. 'I was totally insecure and kept getting kicked back all the time. I spent two years on the dole! I'd try to do things and then get knocked down, my dad spent the last eight years of his working life on the dole and that put a lot of pressure on everything!'

The dole experience made Blunt decide to be serious about his bands, and there was no question of anything he was involved in being just a hobby. From the start Makin' Time strived to be more creative than many of the bands that hogged the circuit making it easy for themselves by playing cover versions and pandering to the inherent conservatism of the mod revival. A pundit at the time remarked that 'unlike most rhythm and soul bands I have seen Makin' Time don't rely on playing cover versions'. It was a commitment to creativity that gave the band a chance of breaking out of the closed circuit.

The danger with all revived youth culture is its slavish dependency on the past, as trapped in the wreckage of a different time many people find it difficult to adapt the tried and tested ways to the present. At least Blunt's band were putting new tunes together, and in the context of their scene this was quite radical.

Vocalist and organist Fay Hallam was 16, whilst guitarist and other lead vocalist Mark Gouden was a relative veteran at 21, whilst Martin Blunt and drummer Neil Clitheroe were 19. Forming out of a mutual love of the music the band were less of a gang of mates drifting into bandom than people fired by their interest in the music. Before Makin' Time they had played in an R & B band, but got the new band together to 'go for a commercial sound'.

Makin' Time, like all young bands, wasn't without its teething problems, and after a short amount of time playing the blues Fay quit because, as she told the excellently on-the-case *Look Sharp* modzine, 'I got bored playing the same three chords.' It was a mini crisis and it would need a bit of diplomacy to get over.

Martin, as ever the backbone of any band that he was playing in, persuaded her back into the fold by lending her a Brian Auger album and pointing out a new direction that the band could follow. Fay was blown away: 'It changed my life,' she later explained.

She rejoined the group and started contributing her own songs, adding to the stockpile that Martin and Mark had piled up. Their influences were pretty varied, as whilst Martin was digging Stax and Atlantic, Neil, typically for a drummer, was fired up on Keith Moon, while Fay was still clutching her Brian Auger album and quoting David Greenfield, the great keyboard player for the eternally criminally under-rated Stranglers, as key influences. They were also dropping classic names like 1960s band the Creation (the band which Alan McGee got the name for his label from; the name of his group, Biff Bang Pow, came from one of their songs) and the Action.

Working the Midlands circuit Makin' Time built up a discerning following and made the occasional foray south to London, hampered by the crap money that London venues get away with paying desperate new bands to come down south.

At a rare show at the legendary 100 Club (only their fifth ever gig) supporting mod R & B band Fast Eddie they were spotted by Eddie Piller, one of the two men behind Countdown records.

Piller was pretty well known on the mod scene, and in a 1984 article on the mod scene in *Sounds* he proclaimed himself the 'ace face'. He certainly had the right roots as his mother used to run the Small Faces fanclub. With an ear tuned early to the possibilities of pop Piller was fascinated by the punk explosion but being too young he didn't get full-on into punk and instead opted for the more familiar territory of mod c/o the Jam. Quickly he became a mod fanatic and a key player on the early 1980s scene with his *Extraordinary Sensations* fanzine. From writing about the music it was an obvious step to releasing it, setting up Well Suspect and releasing records by bands like Long Tall Shorty and the Purple Hearts.

In 1982 he set up Countdown, a label dedicated to the third wave of mod, a third wave of bands like Makin' Time, the Jetset and Direct Hits. The label was set up with Terry Rawlings (soon to become one of the key players in Makin' Time's mini career), Jon Cook and Maxine Conroy. Countdown wasn't just a label but a whole scene machine, and also published a newsletter, a flysheet detailing the latest developments on the scene.

Rawlings had a long mod pedigree going back years to when he would holiday on a caravan site next door to the slightly older Paul Weller. 'I remember Weller had a homemade target T shirt!' he recalls.

He started work as a press boy at Decca, the label famous for not signing the Beatles but still ending up as a symbol of 1960s pop with its nostalgic look.

'Decca was like an old Etonian building,' remembers Rawlings, 'it was literally the same as it was in the 1950s and 1960s, and you were always surrounded by great pictures of the Stones and other bands of the time. They could have filmed a 1960s film in there.'

It wasn't always that hip though.

'I used to work under Jonathan King in 1979 . . . it was a bit of a joke as you might expect; the sort of bands that were on the label were Woolly Rhino and Isla St Clare and of course the Smurfs. The only cred record they put out was an EP in 1979 with stuff like the English Birds [Ron Wood's first group] on it.'

From there Rawlings followed fellow press boy at the office, Gary Crowley (now a top indie radio DJ), to the *NME* where they both penned reviews. 'It was Danny Baker that got us on the *NME* as he was from the same part of town that I was from,' he says. Soon he started work on graphics, later moving to Sire records where he touched up the sleeves for bands like Talking Heads and the Ramones, making their sleeves ready for the British market, changing catalogue numbers and details like that.

At Sire he met up with Maxine Conroy who would eventually become the third partner in Countdown Records. They met when Rawlings gave her the artwork for an album called *The Beat Generation And The Angry Young Men* in the company of Eddie Piller.

Whilst all this was going on, the second wave of mod was breaking – the so-called 1979 bands were bursting out of the mod revival scene, the biggest like the Chords, Secret Affair and the Purple Hearts seeing some chart action, although many of the groups would barely last a year.

As the 1979 bands petered out they were replaced by the third-wave groups, who appeared in the unlikely vacuum created by the collapse of the scene, a scene that had by now gone totally underground after mainstream fashion moved off into new romantic and whatever other piffle 1980s pop was providing.

For people like Rawlings and Eddie Piller, it didn't matter about the way fashion was going; the pair of them were true believers, Piller's Well Suspect label putting out compilations of the 1979 bands and others that followed. Well Suspect struggled along on a low budget and a lot of enthusiasm.

'Eddie came into money somehow and moved the label into a little office in Dagenham,' says Rawlings. 'We used to go down there on a scooter every day and there were nine railway bridges, like humpbacked bridges and the journey was murder,' laughs Rawlings. 'Well Suspect was putting out tail end of mod compilations – bands from Southend that you'd never heard of and some better known stuff like Merton Parkas who had some unreleased stuff to release. Other bands included Long Tall Shorty, who I was managing at the time, also the Small Hours, Directions, Purple Hearts – it got worse after that!'

By now they had decided to relaunch the label as Countdown after Stiff records promised to bail the label out, making Countdown a subsidiary of the legendary indie label.

Stiff had used smart marketing and resurrected the careers of several eccentric pub rockers in the midst of the punk explosion. People like Elvis Costello and Ian Dury, Wreckless Eric and Larry Wallis as well as the Damned could all thank Stiff for their idiosyncratic A & R and the knack for selling the weird to the straight. The years of eclectic post-punk activity and some quite considerable successes had paved the way for Madness, their biggest money-spinner yet, but by the mid 1980s Stiff was past its peak although it was still involved in the music business, and Countdown was one of the labels that it was helping out.

Rawlings had got the vital hook-up. 'I got Stiff interested, I was doing artwork there on stuff like Tracey Ullman and Tenpole Tudor – in fact I'm in a Tenpole Tudor video dressed as a viking in a galleyboat! When I was working there I got to know the boss Paul Conroy who is now the head of Virgin Records.'

With Conroy's help they upgraded the Countdown label and moved into new offices in Old Street, London. The first band they worked with were Boys Wonder who played a pre-Manic Street Preachers-style glammy power-pop punk, dressed in hypa mod clothes with mad bits of tape stuck over their eyebrows. They also used to wear washing-up gloves and they did a great cover of Paul McCartney's 'Live And Let Die'; they were a really cool band but never seemed to break out of their London following, and eventually became Corduroy and carved out quite a different career for themselves. Countdown were on the lookout for a real, full-on Mod outfit, and the night Eddie Piller put on Makin' Time supporting Fast Eddie, he was sure he had found something.

The 100 Club is legendary. Originally a jazz venue in Oxford Street, London, a whole heap of 1960s legends and punk rockers cut their teeth there. When Makin' Time played it they were playing their most high-profile London show to date, and it was the sort of place where things could really happen for the band.

Eddie Piller was instrumental in bringing the band down to London, and had first picked up on them in the weirdest of circumstances. 'When I was about 18 I went on holiday to Ibiza and I met this mod girl called Karen

Smart, and she was raving about this great mod band that came from the Midlands where she lived. I told her to send me a tape when she got back home again and she did, and that was the Makin' Time tape and it was great.'

Impressed, Piller went up north to Birmingham to check them out and bonded instantly. 'They were really cool. At the time there were all these sort of mod bands like Nine Below Zero and Fast Eddie who I managed – great bands but not quite proper mod bands. But Makin' Time were like a proper mod band; they had the scooters and went on the runs, the lot . . . Martin's brother was massively into all that scooter scene, and I went on a lot of scooter runs with him.'

Can you imagine the excitement of the young mod scenester who was trying to get some sort of action going in the early 1980s, a time when the scene's leaders had died out? What they needed was a cool band to rally the troops around; finding the Prisoners was one thing, but discovering this bunch of purists up in Brum was another. 'They were the first band that I could relate to, not just on the level of the music but with clothes and scooters and stuff,' recalls Piller.

He saw the band as a 'classy pop band' to counter the rawer and more aggressive Prisoners whom he had also signed to his label, and got them down to London where he signed the group. He put them into the studio with the Truth's Dennis Greaves and got them to record what was planned to be their debut single, 'Honey' and 'Feels Like It's Love'. The single was never released though; the tracks were recorded just before the Stiff Records takeover of the Countdown label and when Stiff boss Dave Robinson heard them he turned the songs down and decided to put the band in for a longer session that would see them recording their debut album with different producers.

Also on the scene now was Will Birch who became the group's manager. Birch used to be the drummer in the Kursaal Flyers (and was the original drummer in Dr. Feelgood) the Southend-based spivvy-looking pub rock band whose late 1976 hit 'Little Does She Know' was a huge top 10 hit that seemed to set the group up from major success until punk rock came along and drowned them. Rawlings acknowledges Birch's involvement, 'Will Birch was really important because of his knowledge of power pop through being in the Kursaal Flyers and the Records; he knew about quirky pop music. It was his idea to do "Pump It Up". He came from the Stiff Records thing. He was intrigued by Makin' Time, the way that they were a really misshapen band, the way that they weren't quite right.'

Rawlings clocked the dynamic of the band, of which he saw Martin as being the natural leader. Not that he always had things his own way. 'Fay didn't say a lot but when she did speak she got listened to. Martin came as a package with her, they were going out with each other at the time. She was a force to be reckoned with; she was a bit formidable, she would stamp her mark on things, but ultimately you could tell it was Martin's lot . . .'

Makin' Time were put into the studio again to record their debut single, and this time 'Here Is My Number' was recorded, with Will Birch overseeing things and Pat Collier producing. Collier was already known to the record label, having his office upstairs from Countdown Records; fresh from producing Katrina And The Waves he was at the very beginning of a long and fruitful production career. Once a member of the Vibrators, he was now making his way as a producer and had worked with a whole heap of bands.

Makin' Time, being no mere slackers, fired up the enthusiasm of their producers who left the band in the studio to record the whole of their debut *Rhythm And Soul* album which was released on 24 June 1985 along with their debut single 'Here Is My Number'.

The single was tantalisingly close to being a hit as Piller recalled. 'It was that summer that Katrina And The Waves had their massive hit with "Walking On Sunshine" and Makin' Time were the same sort of thing, but better, and we got a lot of radio off that. The single seemed to be number 103 in the charts for weeks. It seemed to be bubbling around for ages. It was a very exciting time, it was the first record that I'd put out that had done something after years of bedroom records!'

The band were at last now part of the pop game and to their new label bosses they seemed very green and innocent, as Rawlings remembers, 'They were really naive, they came down from Wolverhampton and we gave them money to buy clothes. I think it was 500 quid which was a lot of money in those days. They didn't know what to spend it on. Instead of spending the whole lot like most people would have done, they bought one thing each! And came back with the change and their receipts, they were so honest, bless 'em!! They were quite scruffy, Martin was about the smartest; he seemed more mod than the others.

'The album cover we had to compile from two photographs because we could never get them all to look right in the pictures. I think one of them had a digital watch on which was totally wrong for that sort of picture. We signed them for the music more than the clothes,' he exclaims as his mod purism shines through. 'The other thing that I remember was that they couldn't agree on nothing!'

Makin' Time went out on tour with their new-found stablemates, Californian ska band the Untouchables.

The second single, the already recorded 'Honey', backed with 'Take What You Can Get' was produced by Mick Lister and Dennis Greaves, the frontman from the Truth and Nine Below Zero. The sleeve was designed by Rawlings who had also designed the Truth's sleeves.

Countdown was buzzing because as well as the Prisoners and Makin'

Time they also had the Kick, and the bands were sent out on package tours much in the same tradition as the Stiff package tour.

The band were by now deeply into the new mod underground, a scene optimistic fans were pointing to as a groundswell of enthusiasm that could well launch the next mod revival but which would ultimately peter out.

'The bands were trapped by the times,' says Rawlings, 'they were too late for the original scene and too early for the 1990s, when it's all come back into fashion again. It's like a forgotten episode in music and Stiff didn't have enough money to push the bands, they were too busy spending it on racehorses!'

Despite being short of money, Countdown worked its roster hard, and the Prisoners' Hammond-driven garage mod was begging to build up a cult following. The band were to have a profound effect on Martin Blunt, as Rawlings remembers, 'We found the Prisoners; they were Martin's absolute heroes because of the Hammond – I think he always felt that the Farfisa keyboards in Makin' Time were too weak-sounding. I think the Prisoners gave Martin the idea for the Charlatans. The other band that he loved was the Truth.'

By the mid 1980s the new romantic bands were ruling the pop charts, and the underground was dominated by the likes of New Order and the fast-rising Smiths, by now the mod bands seemed quaint and from another time. It's strange that by the 1990s they would seem bang up to date again, but then that's the sort of weird tricks that pop plays.

Live, Makin' Time were fairly energetic, the twin vocals giving them the duality that Brian Auger and Julie Driscoll had thrived upon. It gave them a commercial edge but it was something that the band never seemed to use to its utmost. Reviewers in fanzines were quite puzzled by Mark leaving the stage between vocals, giving the band a lop-sided feel.

But the live work was paying off, and by now the band were quite capable of selling out the 100 Club and grabbing a large and enthusiastic crowd in the capital.

The mod fanzines were giving the band a good back-up though. A letter to *Countdown*, which was a massive backer of Makin' Time from the start, spoke volumes about the state of play in the mod scene. A gig at Brady's in Liverpool was said to be in jeopardy because local mods, who were 1960s purists, refused to go and see a modern band; the letter also pointed out that Makin' Time were the first mod band to play in Liverpool for years and urged support between the warring modernist factions in the city. It was this sort of weight of history that was always playing against the mod scene, a dead weight that made it very difficult for it to break out of its cult shackles.

RHYTHM AND SOUL

With a title that set out their stall musically, Makin' Time were showing just where their loyalties lay. Typically of any new band's debut album recording, the 11 tracks were built around their stage set. It was laid down on 21 and 22 August at Pat Collier's Alaska studios in London, and showcased a young, tight band being recorded fast on a tiny budget.

The songs included: 'Honey', 'Take What You Can Get', 'The Rhythm Takes You', 'Feels Like It's Love', a cover of the Kinks' 'I Gotta Move' and the single 'Here Is My Number' (the 12-inch version of the single featured 'I Get A Love From You' as well as the 7-inch's B-side 'Nothing Else').

The tracks are big brassy slabs of melodic pop, powerful and bold – it's a great pop album which fell between the cracks in the pretty mundane mid 1980s pop scene. It's bizarre that no one has re-released this record in the light of the Charlatans' eventual success.

A review in *Shadows And Reflections* modzine picked a bone with the album title, feeling that the band were somewhat overstating their case, grabbing for a purity or credibility, with the name of the record, but that vocalist Mark Gouden could 'not be a better vocalist' even if he was 'vain'. But they dealt the critical knives to Fay Hallam, saying that they could take her and leave her presence, meaning, 'we could take her keyboards and leave her vocals', saying that you couldn't sing soul in a clinical soulless voice and only on 'Only Know What You're Thinking' did she show any spark of passion. Mark, meanwhile, showed her what soul is really about on the wonderful 'Girl That Touched My Soul', claimed the review.

This is bollocks as Fay's voice sounds great on the record; *both* sets of vocals are perfect for the powerful pop the band were playing.

It was a patchy review which signed off by saying 'it wasn't a bad album'; in the world of mod fanzines they seemed to be a lone anti voice.

Most of the other reviews were more upbeat, and the album was well received. It seemed like the band was set for success.

The run up to the album's release saw Makin' Time on tour round Britain, playing to varying sizes of audiences in places like Edinburgh, Derby, Manchester, Belfast, Dublin and Cork, and *Countdown* thanked the mod societies for their support in putting the shows on – the close-knit nature of the scene was paying off again by supporting this upcoming band.

They also played a near residency at their local Long Acres pub in Willenhall. On their home turf they were the biggest band in the area and quite certainly the only mod band.

Eddie Piller remembers taking up a posse of London media and music biz heads to check the band out here. 'We went up there and there was a massive fight! The local Brummie scooter boys tried to smash the pub to pieces, there was blood and glass everywhere and the journalists were covered in the stuff! It was back in the days when the youth would fight over anything like coming from a different town. It was the Brummie boys versus the London mods; it was quite a fight!'

Things were looking quite good for Makin' Time. They had started the year as outsiders in the backwaters of the Midlands and were now established as one of the inner-circle bands on an enthusiastic and tight scene. Writing great tunes and with a punchy and powerful sound they had what it takes to crossover from the underground; what they needed was a lucky break or a shift in fashion.

It was now just a question of hoping that the pop world would be turned on to their music and that they could hold the band together under the pressure of the no money, tough life of a musician in a cult pop group.

THE MISSING LINK FROM MAKIN' TIME, THROUGH THE GIFT HORSES TO THE CHARLATANS

In fact just as it seemed that Makin' Time were about to break through they fell apart. Things came to a head after a long European tour. The band had been making headway in Germany where there was a bigger mod scene for live bands than in the UK. These tours are long and strenuous and can put a strain on a band.

The strain would eventually prove too much and the band fell apart in 1986.

Terry Rawlings notes the band's demise, 'We just ran out of money and it became very difficult for the band to carry on. Eddie shut down Countdown and then re-emerged as Acid Jazz which is basically the same label.'

Countdown had played its role in documenting the mod scene, and it melted down with a series of mod compilations. Before re-emerging as Acid Jazz, they had a brief tenure as Re-elect The President, putting out a smattering of acts. Piller was helped out in this enterprise by James Taylor, the Prisoners' keyboard player who was now putting together his own outfit, the James Taylor Quartet.

Things were changing in the mod scene, people were moving on. Dingwalls on Sunday afternoons was becoming the focal point of a new mod. Giles Peterson was DJing, playing an eclectic host of stuff including hip hop and jazz; purists may have been appalled but there was no time any more for the sort of early 1960s R & B that had been the staple diet of the scene for years.

Inspired by this new energy Piller launched Acid Jazz, still dealing in some pure mod stuff; some of the old faces were recording more jazz-flavoured takes on the supa-style-soaked pop that they were in love with, James Taylor in particular popping up in several different incarnations creating new sounds. Acid Jazz signed the Brand New Heavies and a host of different acts, changing the emphasis on just what mod was expected to be.

But even this change was under threat from the new high-speed dance style that was creeping in over the horizon, the E-fuelled acid house explosion, which would tempt many mods to move on to the new street scene.

Things were changing fast.

In this sort of climate it was going to be even more difficult for a group like Makin' Time to survive and they became casualties of the new way.

Martin Blunt went back to the Midlands licking his wounds after they split and formed a new band, the Gift Horses with Graham Day from the Prisoners on guitar and Fay on vocals, their drummer was a certain Jonathan Brookes . . .

Jon's youth was spent in West Bromwich and, just like Reni from the Roses his parents ran a pub, the Fox And Dogs. The long quiet days when his parents were sleeping off their late nights saw Brookes bashing away on the pub's drum kit.

'I just went and sat at the drum kit every day,' he told a drumming magazine.

The pub's resident band had a drummer called Harvey who was happy to show Jon a few different styles.

Jon Brookes had also worked in a saw mill, 'half severing me fingers every day', and he spent any spare moments trying to make his own drum sticks. When he was 18 two mates scored a publishing deal and asked him to play drums for them, so he moved down to Crystal Palace to play on demos, believing that he had finally hit the big time. He took four pairs of sticks and two spare snare heads. The sessions were a disaster; the guitarist spent hours looking for the right drum sound and Brookes broke all his new sticks.

Whacking away on his ride cymbal, Brookes attracted the unwonted attention of the studio people. After a while, a bloke said, 'Son, people don't use ride cymbals any more. No one makes records like that now.'

'I never really understood their music, I knew it was crap but I didn't know why,' admitted Brookes, who moved back home and played the local circuit in a band covering everything from the Small Faces to ZZ Top.

He went then to Ibiza before returning home up north, where he cut his hair and dyed it yellow – it was this wild haircut that attracted Martin Blunt to him, asking him to join his new project, the Gift Horses.

The jigsaw was beginning to fall into place.

The Gift Horses gigged around the country playing a more abrasive version of the Makin' Time sound, and eventually they got to record a single, 'Rosemary', an upbeat pop song with Fay's vocal for a German record label

Pop-i, the A-side was a Fay Hallam song, whilst the similarly uptempo B-side, 'Learning To Bring Yourself Down', was a Graham Day number, also sung by Fay.

The band did sporadic dates in the UK and German tour, but if they expected to do as well as Makin' Time had done in Germany just because they had half the first line-up then they were mistaken, as promoter German promoter Henry Storch remembers, 'The Gift Horses were very small in Germany. Before, Makin' Time had been getting 500 people at their gigs but with the Gift Horses it was more like 50. But the band said that they weren't mod, they said that they were pop, which confused everybody. Makin' Time had been doing very well in Germany – they were as big as the Jesus & Mary Chain at the time.'

The Gift Horses were at the bottom of the pile but saw no reason why they shouldn't climb back up to the top again.

In Germany in the mid to late 1980s there flourished a scene that was hooked on to the garage/psyche/punk/mod crossover, paisley shirt aficionados who dug British beat groups with a vengeance, and many bands from the era went over to Germany to cut their teeth. Some, like the TV Personalities, were huge stars there and several of the Creation acts would be passing through as a package. The Pastels and the Mary Chain were big underground bands and likes of the Membranes and other noisier British bands passed through the same circuit, picking up sizable followings.

It was a great scene, and one that answered the rock & roll dreams of many of these groups, with endless hotels and free booze and food given to them, the sort of stuff that never existed in the UK, no matter how big your band ever got.

Not that the Gift Horses' tour went off without any wild times, as Henry recalls, 'I put them on at the Okey Dokey club in Düsseldorf and after the show we had a few drinks. Martin and Jon stayed in my flat and they made the mistake of drinking a lot of the very strong German spirits which can affect you somewhat, and Martin puked up all over the drinks cabinet!'

Despite these hi jinks when they returned to Britain there were more problems with the line-up.

Suddenly Graham Day left the group.

They needed a guitar player fast, and so Martin racked his mind and remembered a bassplayer from a local band called Blue Toys who might be cool for the part.

He picked up the phone and gave Baz Ketley a ring.

BAZ KETLEY GETS THE CALL UP

The great lost man in the story of the Charlatans, Baz Ketley was more than just a mere bit player in their history. In the pre-Tim Burgess era of the band

Ketley was a key figure, writing the bulk of the band's material, playing guitar and fronting the band.

Born in Malvern, the quaint hill town in the Midlands on the Welsh border, Ketley moved to Wolverhampton in 1978, the year after punk rocked the pop world. Punk gave Ketley the Clash, the first band to have a profound effect on his life, swiftly followed by Joy Division, the doom-laden Manchester band that affected a massive disaffected pop crowd with their bass-led downer rock. Joy Division took punk and twisted it into new shapes, helping to lay the foundations of the northern pop scene that was to dominate the creative efforts of musicians like Ketley in the years to come.

'I grew up with groups like Joy Division and Echo And The Bunnymen. I was like everyone else, just listening to records and dreaming of being rich and famous,' he sardonically intones now from his Wolverhampton home.

Except, instead of dreaming, Ketley started playing the bass, and joined up with the Midlands-based Andy Leek Band.

Andy Leek had been the original keyboard player in Dexy's Midnight Runners, forming his own band to gig round the Midlands circuit, and had played on the first sessions for the Dexy's classic 'Geno', but had left after he had found band leader Kevin Rowland's extraordinary vision too suffocating.

The Andy Leek Band managed a few gigs outside Brum, getting down to London for a few shows at places like Islington's tiny Hope And Anchor pub cellar, a sweaty, beer-stained room where bands from all over the country drive down with hopes in their hearts that some music biz person is going to stumble in half pissed and sign them on the spot. Legendary groups have worked the gaff alongside the thousand of failures who have headed back up the motorway to their small-town traps.

Eventually Leek, noting that his young bass player was turning up to rehearsals with a whole fistful of songs of his own, encouraged Baz to leave and form his own band to showcase his talent.

In 1983 Ketley formed the Blue Toys with himself playing bass and singing, and in one of those weird crossovers, the drummer of the band was Pete Barton who had recently left Martin Blunt's Makin' Time; it was the first point of contact between the two musicians.

With a set of Ketley-written tunes, the band got themselves off the ground by releasing the single 'A Good Day'/'This Is My Heaven' on the London-based Sedition label. The record generated interest in the band and they recorded a session for the then Saturday night Radio One show hosted by Dixie Peach, the band trooping down to the legendary Maida Vale studios that bands used for John Peel sessions.

Maida Vale reeks of the BBC, a huge studio complex that looks like it was built 100 years ago, housing a complex of recording facilities. In some rooms whole orchestras are working away, their minds on the pub and when they clock off, while other ragged musicians are shoving their amps through the back entrance hoping that their late-night radio patronage is going to be the break that saves their asses. The sessions are always recorded quickly, ten hours is the max and is basically a live set from the band. Ketley was treading where many had gone before, but it was still a proud break for any band trying to escape the clutches of failure.

The single was produced by the same Pat Collier who had produced the Makin' Time stuff and he gave the record that typically tight punchy sound that was his trademark, with the heavy-duty compression harnessed to good effect.

'It was a typically mid 1980s northern pop thing, just sort of contemporary pop of the times,' Ketley modestly intones.

From 1983 till 1986 the band toured the whole country from Nottingham to London. It was hard work, grinding it out on the toilet circuit in one of those periods of pop when the live circuit is grinding to a halt.

Despite some good reviews in the local press the Blue Toys began to fall apart in 1986. At first they fell out with their manager, 'because he was trying to turn the band into something it wasn't,' explains Ketley, and they ended up in court with him.

Then the final death knell was rung when their label, which had already changed its name to Activate, went bust, leaving the band high and dry with three years of hard work down the pan. But Ketley felt anyway that things were changing. 'I think the band had run its course. I was starting to change; musically you can't stay in the same place for ever. With the label gone I thought it's time for a change.'

Ketley knew he had put the time in and that he was a good songwriter who just needed a break; and then came the phone call from Martin Blunt. 'It was Mart that asked me in. I had known him for a long time since I had poached Peter Barton for drums to form the Blue Toys. Also we used to have some lights for the Blue Toys which we used to rent out to Makin' Time when they did all their gigs at the Long Acres pub in Willenhall.'

The bass-playing Ketley was asked in to play guitar for the Gift Horses to cover for the recently departed guitarist Graham Day.

'I'd never played guitar before on stage. Remember, I was a bass player, so I was totally shitting myself,' says Ketley.

Crap-stained pants or not, he was about to change bands again though.

LOOK THE GIFT HORSE IN THE MOUTH, KETLEY GETS BLUNT!

The group's short-lived career was already in disarray however. The single 'A Good Day' had come out but had hardly set the world on fire; their tougher, more garagy take on the sort of bold mod pop that Blunt had been dealing with since first picking up a bass was finding few supporters.

Graham Day quitting the band had left them in the lurch too. Losing a guitar player can leave one hell of a hole in a band and the hole was getting filled by a local musician who was really a bassplayer at heart, but people like Martin Blunt who know that they have got something to offer can be grimly determined at the worst of times; making it as any sort of artist is as much about drive as it is about talent, and the two combined will always out.

Blunt says Baz Ketley was a known musician, having fronted a band; he was no slouch as a player. Okay, he may have never played guitar on stage before but he had definitely played guitar before.

'I session guitared for the Gift Horses really,' says Ketley. 'I did it to see if I could play guitar. We played a couple of gigs together.'

The Ketley-Blunt line-up of the Gift Horses played about three shows in London (one of which was supporting an Irish folk band), and one of them was at the Cricketers.

'They were a good band,' points out Ketley. 'There is a single out on a German label, they were good but it wasn't what I was after, it was punky, garagy sort of stuff, a lot harder-sounding than Makin' Time.'

The band were playing a set of Fay and Graham's songs, leaving little space for the songwriting Ketley to find his own self-expression. Being a mere session player Ketley was always going to be at the mercy of whatever whims took the fancy of the original line-up. In any case, after the first few gigs, Day decided to rejoin the band, and Ketley was back out on his arse.

The band's German label had booked them for a tour of the lowlands of Holland and off they went for a Euro jaunt with all its added attractions of good money, big riders and well-organised gigs.

Despite this, a rare perk in the lives of a British touring band, on returning to Blighty everything promptly fell apart. Graham Day and Fay Hallam left to set up the Prime Movers with Simon Howard and Alan Crooks from the James Taylor Quartet. They plied the London pub circuit with a powerful full-on set of garage pop suplemented by their favourite cover version, Deep Purple's Hush.

Eventually Fay and Graham Day would get married.

Again Martin Blunt found himself bandless. A lesser mortal would have packed in all this music lark but he had other plans.

He put a call through to Baz Ketley.

Ignition

STARTING OVER

Back in their Midlands bolt-hole the new band started from scratch. Each member had played in several groups but nothing had quite gone as planned. They knew they had the ability: Blunt had put together a really good band in Makin' Time, Ketley had a songwriter's touch and Jon Brookes' drumming was coming on in leaps and bounds.

But first they needed a name. Ketley suggested the Charlatans but Martin preferred the Law Lords. It was settled on the toss of a coin.

Ketley remembers the final decision process, 'We had a toss of coins. I had heads for the Charlatans and Martin had tails, and it came up heads.'

So the Charlatans it was.

Blunt's vision of the group definitely saw a keyboard player in there too; he wanted that Prisoners sound, that garagy rush with a Hammond flooding the sound with its warmth and classic power – it just made the choruses surge. You couldn't get away from the fact that it was a classic instrument and one that gave the group a definite edge. Blunt had been impressed by some of his mod band contemporaries' keyboard sounds; Makin' Time's keyboards, not being whacked out on a Hammond, lacked the power of its molten valves.

Baz Ketley remembers those first rehearsals and the trio's search for a compatible keyboard player. 'We tried out quite a few keyboard players at those first rehearsals but we eventually found someone after a lot of searching.'

This keyboard player seemed to really fit well and the band was starting to cook but after several rehearsals it all went badly wrong, according to Ketley.

'We'd had about four or five rehearsals and then the keyboard player died. It was awful,' a still-shocked Ketley remembers.

No one is quite sure what happened due to the mist of time, but there was talk that the original Charlatans keyboard player died choking on his own vomit due to his drugs problem.

The next keyboard player they tried out was an unlikely looking candidate who arrived at rehearsal with his Hammond and a musical taste that was mainly hooked around Deep Purple and the prog rock side of keyboard playing. They had heard him down the rehearsal rooms and they knew that he was good even if his taste was a tad different from theirs.

Jon Brookes knew him the best having spent a brief amount of time playing in a group with him when he was about 16.

Rob Collins was playing in a rock band at the time, as he recalled to *Looking For The Orange One* fanzine. 'I was playing in this naff rock band when Martin, who knew the guitarist, came to see us, and after the gig I sat down and had a chat with him. I didn't know Jon was with them but I knew that Makin' Time had split up. I just said that I would come down to a rehearsal. When I turned up Johnny was drumming and Baz was there as well.'

'Rob was really into rock when we first met him,' Baz warmly remembers, 'he liked all that early 1970s sort of stuff, like Emerson, Lake & Palmer, and prog rock.'

Rob Collins was an unlikely candidate for a band formed by someone used to the super-sharp ethics of mod, but he was one hell of a keyboard player, and as soon as he set up and played the band felt that they had stumbled on to something quite special.

Even if he did have a moustache.

'Here's a really daft story,' laughs Baz, 'in some of our early band pictures taken by this girl, Rob was stood there – we had to etch out his droopy moustache!'

ROB COLLINS

Born on 23 February 1963 in Sedgley in the Black Country, Rob Collins was naturally gifted at the piano at school, and played in various bands before teaming up with the nascent Charlatans. Booker T ('Green Onions' and a host of other killer tunes) was one of his biggest influences.

Collins' mastery of the Hammond was the key factor in the band, especially in the early days where this magnificent beast of an instrument, played with the raw power of Collins, made the group stand out from the typically English jingle jangle of the indie competition. To many Rob was the soul of the band.

Martin Blunt told Q magazine, 'Rob really formed the group. He's had a Hammond for six or seven years now. He just likes the sound of it. Besides he got it cheap, he couldn't find a decent synthesiser.'

The Charlatans was born the moment Rob Collins pushed his knackered old keyboard into the rehearsal room, as Baz Ketley recalls, 'We met Rob and put together the Charlatans. Rob wanted to form a band built around his Hammond keyboard and get an early 1968 Jon Lord/Deep Purple sound going.'

It has to be remembered that Deep Purple weren't always the monsters of rock outfit; with their roots in soul, they played a heavy fuzzed-up freaked version of soul in the late 1960s. It was certainly clumsy enough to mutate very easily into heavy metal, but for tracks like 'Hush' they certainly had it well together.

Collins brought a different flavour to the group, his dark and malevolent presence gave the group a tuffer edge, and having spent five years working in a boring job, he was itching to get on to the road and into rock & roll. But his wildness and commitment to the rock & roll lifestyle would constantly land him in trouble.

The Charlatans were now complete.

FIRST REHEARSALS

Right from the start it was Ketley's songwriting and Collins' keyboards that dominated the band's sound.

'I was writing most of the songs at first,' says Baz. 'It was mainly in-your-face up-tempo sort of stuff.'

Baz's songs gradually weeded out the band's covers, which included Department S's 1981 number 22 hit 'Is Vic There?' With rehearsals going well and a few well-received local gigs under their belt the band went to record the first of three demos that marked the Ketley era.

The band's first demo was recorded at Phase Two Studios in Dudley and showcases a band playing stomping power pop with the white soul flavour that they were trying to capture. Three out of the four songs were written by Ketley, including 'Dadjida' which is about 'a hypothetical Indian bloke who makes his fortune and finds out that making all that money isn't quite what it seems. The group definitely sound like the Charlatans of the later period that was going to become famous; Blunt's powerful running bass is driving the tracks along and locks tight with Brookes' spot-on drumming. From the start the band had got the most vital cog in rock & roll – a razor-sharp rhythm section.

The Hammond is everywhere, it's wash gives the track a class that is rare to find on a group's first demo, and when Collins breaks out for a solo it's a brilliant release. Ketley's guitar is used to support clean chords and twangy gutter licks when required.

It's the vocals that are quite different from the later Charlatans. Ketley has a powerful voice, sort of like the geezer from Talk Talk but with enough of that nasal whine of someone like Kevin Rowland to land the tracks on to the right side of the pop barrier. Ketley is a 'proper singer' and, combined with the backing vocals, the tracks are punchy, tight and commercial; it's very difficult to see how the band couldn't get a deal with this guff.

The second track is the urgent 'Wave Goodbye', the one song not written by Ketley on the demo (it was provided by Blunt and Collins), and it has a magnificent keyboard break reminiscent of Alan Price's superb breaks in the Animals' 'House Of The Rising Sun', one of those watery notes everywhere attacks that grab the heart strings.

'Tropic Of Love' is driven along by staggering riff and witnesses a neat solo from Ketley, the chorus has a fab chanting backing vocal, the main vocal is pure Dexy's, one of those too many words hooking around a great vocal melody that Rowland specialised in; catchy as fuck, the song shows a band with a vast potential already proving themselves to be effortless songwriters.

The best tune is the northern-soul-riven stomp of Ketley's 'Summer By The Severn'; 'As the DJ plays the Isleys' sings Ketley over the sort of soul-infused pop that Ocean Colour Scene would go on to make their fortunes out of in the 1990s (what is it about Midlands and soul music?). The mid section has one of those stunning melodic interplays between the keyboards and the guitar that the Stranglers made their trademark in the punk days, dripping minor-key lament and pure melody. If there had been any money available this surely would have been the single.

Today, Ketley, like most musicians, apologises for the sound on the demo without realising that this collection of four songs kicks the fuck out of most demos that float around.

SHAPE UP OR SHIP OUT . . . THE BAND'S SOUND COMES TOGETHER

Already the band felt that they were working in some sort of tradition, the harder-edged mod end of the pop scene, inevitable really when you consider Blunt's pedigree in Makin' Time and Ketley's classic influences on his songwriting style. The band were touting themselves as being very much in the tradition of a West Midlands mod soul band with an intense belief in the power of music, like the Spencer Davis Group and the early Dexy's. (What a band! At this point I advise any readers to go out and buy the Dexy's first album and get ready to believe in the potent power of music played by people who truly believe; the Dexy's are one of the most important British bands ever and one of the most under-rated, Kevin Rowland is a genius . . . investigate or remain ignorant!)

Local press was, not surprisingly, very favourable to the Ketley era of the Charlatans.

The group's second demo, although not featuring as sharp a sound as the first, showed a band developing. The songs are more held back, and the group composition 'Nothing's Left' is the first time we get to hear the pure purr that Collins got out of his Hammond which would become his trademark. The tune would fit perfectly on the band's eventual debut album, possibly being a stand-out track. It's got a great sense of dynamic, building and releasing the tension and exploding into the chorus; this is spot-on songwriting.

This demo included their best song so far, 'Angelica', as well as a long organ-dominated track, the aforementioned 'Nothing's Left' and an extra song called 'Drowning In A River Of Tears'. The three songs recorded in Birmingham 24-track Different Disguises Studio showed that Ketley had a breadth of different song-writing styles and that the band, although not that distinctive as yet, had a definite talent. The nascent Charlatans were fusing soul and R & B with 1960s garage. The initial press release for the band described Ketley's songs as having a 'depth and character which deterred any talk of revisionism'.

Andy Woods, who after joining Charlatans' manager Steve Harrison's Omega record shop as an assistant when he was only 16 and was now Steve's managerial assistant, remembers 'Angelica' as being the best track on the demo. 'Baz may have not had those youthful good looks that Tim had but he compensated by being a great songwriter.'

The demo was reviewed in Birmingham institution *Brumbeat* in February 1989, who thought that the 'power and passion' of 'Angelica' was as good as Ketley's former outfit Blue Toys, but it was less impressed with the other two tracks, describing 'Nothing's Left' as an 'overlong organ work-out mood burner' and 'Drowning In A River Of Tears' as an uninspiring beater' (whatever a 'beater' is) – it suggested that some more band gelling would be well in order.

Excellent.

'DRIVEN BY THE ORGAN . . .' THAT HAMMOND SOUND IN FULL . . .

Perhaps one of the quintessential classic pop instruments, the Hammond's distinctive swelling organ (ha!) sound has been the angelic lick on many-a tune (list them and the classic players) clocking in tuff with the guitar and base – it's a slab of magic in the trad rock sound. An expressive instrument like the guitar, in the hands of a player like Collins, the moodiness and strength inherent in the man's character would always come tumbling through . . . check 'Weirdo', one of the best slashes of Hammond ever whacked down on a pop record – the single is one of the Charlatans' greatest musical moments . . .

'The organ is just one of the most beautiful instruments ever,' says Jon Brookes. 'It's like a whole orchestra on the big massive, brown box. You feel it in your chest, but you can't hear it. That's the sort of noise it makes; it's brilliant.'

Rob Collins used a C3 with a Leslie cab. The whole set-up is ridiculously heavy and for a band starting out on the trail of the toilet circuit is not the most practical instrument.

When asked why he just couldn't use a modern instrument to recreate the sound and so avoid carrying the massive keyboard around everywhere he would reply, 'It would be like trying to reinvent the wheel, it just wouldn't be the same.'

And anyone who had ever borne witness to the power of the Hammond will know exactly what he's talking about . . . not only does it sound brilliant, it's the sheer percussiveness of the instrument that makes it a key component of a band's sound, adding a heavy rhythm to the overall sound.

In conjunction with the Hammond which was the backbone of the early Charlatans sound he also used synths like a Yamaha or an Emax, but he was never the most technically minded of people. 'We've got this girl that comes in, this MIDI operator who does all that side of stuff for us, but it baffles me,' Rob once said.

Comparisons to contemporary keyboard players would irk him also. 'Clint Boon [the Inspiral Carpets], he's just crap isn't he? You may as well go and get a tune a day song book. He's on page two, isn't he?'

Collins was a quintessential Hammond player, perfectly understanding the innate power and beauty of the greatest of all keyboards. Not only was it a powerful brute of an instrument but in the right hands it also made songs sound classy and thicker by its sheer moody presence. It would be fair to say that without the crucial swelling Hammond dominating their sound the Charlatans would have been hard put to make it out of the pile of bands that were attempting to get their break in Manchester in 1989-90.

MANAGER

During this time Blunt was building up his record collection with frequent forays to a specialist record shop 40 miles up the road in Northwich called Omega Records, managed by an enthusiastic music fan he had met on scooter rallies called Steve Harrison, and wanted him for the band's manager.

Baz remembers Martin pulling in his old mate from the scooter days. It was a decision that made a lot of sense as this level-headed mate of Mart's had built up a chain of independent record shops in a bunch of small towns on the edge of Manchester; it showed that here was someone with a good business sense.

'Steve Harrison was a friend of Mart's from the mod days,' says Baz, 'and his name got mentioned when we were talking about getting a manager. Mart said, "I know this guy in Northwich and I've got him interested in coming to see us and put some money into the band. We knew that he was an experienced business man because of his shops.'

Ketley, like the others, was also impressed by Steve's knowledge of the music scene and the way he kept on harping about these bands. 'Fairplay to Steve, he kept on going on about these three Manchester bands who he thought were going to be totally massive, and remember this was way back at the beginning of 1987. He thought that the Roses, the Mondays and the Inspiral Carpets were going to be mega, when no one in this area knew anything about them.'

The Charlatans were about to make one of the wisest decisions of their career.

Enter Steve Harrison.

HURRY UP HARRY! . . . STEVE HARRISON

In the late 1980s Manchester pop boom, personality managers were all the rage. The Mondays had Nathan McGough, a fast-talking wide-boy who managed to captain the unsteadiest of ships with a deft hand and a rock & roll lifestyle as ferocious as that of his charges; Northside had Macca, a wild youth built like a boxer and a great Manc character who talked so much that he would virtually do his group's interviews for them; the Roses had Gareth Evans, a legend in his own and everybody else's lunchtime; and the Inspirals had Anthony Bogianno.

The Charlatans had Steve Harrison, who kept a much lower profile – which did the band a lot of favours. Unlike most of his contemporaries he had grafted his way to the frontline of the music business. He had started as a total fan and still has that wide-eyed appreciation of pop music that soaks through the whole of the band.

Steve Harrison may act dumb but he's one smart fucker. He may play the semi-surprised kinda-cute thing to the full, he may look like he doesn't really know what's happening – but this is one sharp businessman.

Harrison plays the small-town record dealer thing to the hilt, pretending to be out of his depth, when really he's got a complete handle on what's going on. Building up a chain of independent shops in an area not known for any serious underground activity and carefully managing a band from nowhere to the heart of the hottest scene in the UK takes some nous.

A devout Manchester City fan, Harrison knows what true suffering is too. In 1989 he told everyone within earshot that the only person he wanted the band to sign to was Howard Kendall, then the manager of Man City (one of the hundreds they seem to have had since the war).

In 1989 the 28-year-old Harrison was a self-made man and a pop fanatic. He could have happily built up his shops but distraction was lurching towards him.

Born in Northwich in 1961, Steve was smitten by pop music as a six-year-old, who by the time he was nine had fallen in love with Herman's Hermits' 'Lady Barbara' (number 13, November 1970) and the Beach Boys' 'I Can Hear Music' (number 10, February 1969). 'I remember going out to the shops to buy these, the Beach Boys one was on Capitol,' he recalls, his mind ticking meticulously like a man who owns a chain of record shops.

In the ragbag of musical styles that fell out of the tale end of the 1960s he was heavily influenced by the tastes of his relatives. 'My dad's cousin, who is a lot younger than him, had a lot of prog stuff round his house and from listening to that I got into Deep Purple, Genesis and Led Zeppelin. Remember I was only about 11 at the time, but it was all that I was hearing because we used to go over to his house a lot.'

Steve is one of the few people of his generation who will admit to being tainted by the evil hand of prog but this wasn't his first real true musical love. That came about the same time when, like some sort of pop knight galloping in to save the early 1970s from an ignoble and greasy-haired death, in charged Marc Bolan, one of the greatest pop stars this country has ever produced.

'I used to go round to another relative's house and we used to play Subbuteo and Scalectrix and all those kid things. In the back room his older brother was always playing music and there was one album that I really loved which was *T Rex* by T Rex; eventually he sold it to me and that was the first album that I ever bought. It was the one with the fold-out cover with a picture of Marc Bolan standing next to Mickey Finn with his orange Les Paul. "Ride A White Swan" was on the record – that was such a great song,' Harrison's eyes steam over at the memory of taking home this rock-solid pop classic.

T Rex, in the early 1970s were as big as the Beatles, with what seemed, at the time, a never-ending string of classic pop singles. The ace up their sleeve, though, was that they could also make great albums, something that so few pop bands at the time ever did.

Bolan was the king of pop, he invented glam rock. Bowie followed him, and then a whole crazy mob of impersonators followed. Eventually, by 1977, he had got fat and burned out, not that Harrison agrees with this version of events.

'I was privileged to see Bolan live at Hanley Victoria Hall in 1977,' Steve says, 'with the Damned supporting, and he was getting really good again. He seemed to have put all his bad times behind him.'

It was to be a short-lived revival in fortunes though, as later that year his car crashed into a tree in Barnes, South London, killing him. It is one of the biggest tragedies in the history of pop.

In many ways T Rex had occupied the same sort of space that the Charlatans do now, straddling the divide between pop and rock, between pretty-boy sex appeal and serious rock acceptance. Their lyrics seem like gobbledygook but hint at cool stuff just below the surface – it's a fine line but some bands pull it off.

The early 1970s saw as classic a pop stand-off of the times as Blur v. Oasis was in the 1990s. Slade and T Rex were considered opposites of the pop spectrum, so battlelines were drawn, and Harrison was no exception when it came to taking sides.

'I remember I always hated Slade, which is weird now as I see Noddy Holder around quite a lot and he's a great bloke. I remember we went on holiday to Blackpool to a caravan site and this kid that I knew hung his silk Slade scarf out of his window, so I hung my T Rex one out the window of our caravan! I remember when "Jeepster" made number 2 and Slade held it off number 1, I hated them so much for that!'

But what a combination: 'Coz I Luv You' by Slade as number 1 for eight weeks, and T Rex's 'Jeepster' at number 2 – a double whammy of pop brilliance!

Aaaaah! The glorious irrationality of the pop fan – only a proper manager can understand those feelings!

'I just thought the kid with the Slade scarf was a total twat; it's weird because now I know him really well, he works for a big record distributor,' says Steve.

The early 1970s Harrison was, by his own admission, 'a teenage oddball', digging T Rex on one hand but still checking out Genesis, Led Zeppelin ('who were my favourite rock group') and odder-than-odd Blue Oyster Cult. 'I went to see Blue Oyster Cult at the Free Trade Hall with Motörhead supporting, that must have been 1976 I guess; I got into them because of "(Don't Fear) The Reaper".'

The young Harrison was one of the few to actually get into the BOC further than that, though '(Don't Fear) The Reaper' is well worth checking out – a dark, black-hearted romp through almost-Byrds territory with a sinister soft-sung vocal line that adds to the spook of the song; it's one of those forgotten classics of pop.

'By then I was a long-haired grebo, I suppose you could call it, and that's the way things would have ended up until punk rock came along and saved my record collection.'

Cutting across the mish-mash of the mid 1970s, punk electrified about five kids in every town in Britain, and in Northwich the already fanatical about music Harrison was ripe for the new way. 'I remember we came back from the summer holidays [to Sir John Deans Grammar School] and a handful of us had got into punk rock quite independently from each other over the summer. We hadn't spoken to each other all summer and suddenly we are all into this new thing.'

Fired by records like Eddie And The Hot Rods' *Live At The Marquee* EP ('not strictly punk but exciting enough') and the Pistols, Clash and the Damned, Harrison and his chums were on a pop high.

'It was the most exciting thing ever, everyone had all the records. I remember they were really easy to get hold of, I had my hair all spiky and had all the clothes. It was really heavy walking around Northwich, the reactions we got off people . . . no one would talk to us at school any more. We were totally left out.'

Travelling up to Erics in Liverpool and the Electric Circus in Manchester, the 16-year-old Harrison and his mates took in all the front-line punk action. It was a thrilling pop time.

'I had a mohair jumper and safety pins. It was probably the best time of my life; there was a real sense of belonging between us all. I guess there was an element of exhibitionism. Everyone was trying to improve their punk CVs, pretending that they never liked groups like Genesis before, and we were all desperately trying to find out about the roots of punk, trying to get into groups like Iggy And The Stooges and the MC5.'

Only the year before the pre-punk Harrison had marvelled at 'the sixth formers who did technical drawing and had their school folders covered in Yes logos that seemed to be the coolest thing ever, and now it just looked stupid'.

Quickly punk became mainstream and within a year the people who had ostracised him were turning up at local punk gigs wearing 'their school uniform with tight ties and safety pins all over the place. It still wasn't that safe in Northwich to go out and about, although things were a lot easier in Winsford where I lived.'

Like most punk rockers Harrison chanced his hand at being in a band, playing guitar in a local pseudo punk band called the Nice Guys: 'It was never that serious.'

'I thought that the two guys who wrote the songs were incredible. They wrote all their songs taking the piss out of this bloke called "Hughie". I thought they were total geniuses, but then I never had the privilege of owning the *Live At The Roxy* album which contained Wire's song "Lowdown" which they totally ripped off for every song they ever wrote!'

Unlikely as it seems, Northwich had quite a punk scene. Steve explains, 'A lot of bands played here: Crass, the Fall and the UK Subs, but by then I had moved on from standard punk and was getting into Joy Division, who were the next band that really changed my life after T Rex and punk rock.'

Travelling up to Manchester all the time it was inevitable that Steve Harrison would eventually see Warsaw, the band that eventually flowered into Joy Division. They played a lot of the support shows at the Electric Circus. 'I think it was actually at Rafters that I saw them. They really turned my head, and the other band that I loved as much at the time but who never followed through their initial promise for me was the Gang Of Four.'

These two bands entered the post-punk fray promising a brave new world of rock. If punk had attempted to tear down rock & roll, bands like Joy Division and the Gang Of Four were putting the talk into practise. In the post-punk late 1970s the groups of the early 1980s were attempting to construct post-rock music, and brave new sounds were being thrown up in a desperate race to avoid conformity. It was an amazing time of weird and wonderful pop.

Joy Division, with their cranked, stripped-down mash of Iggy's prime-time Stooges and Birmingham's harbingers of doom-laden metal, Black Sabbath, were scoured with a restless soul and created some of the darkest rock & roll ever, whilst the Gang of Four playing an agit funk scarred by Andy Gill's brittle electric guitar.

'Andy Gill was one of the most innovative guitar players that I have ever seen – absolutely brilliant. They were superb live and their first single was stunning. They never seemed to reach those peaks again, though.'

This left Joy Division in Harrison's head as the sole standard-bearers of whatever was going to come out of punk. 'They were unbelievable, remarkable live, and with Barney's under-rated guitar and Hookey's bass they had two of the best, even if they were technical impaired, most innovative musicians on the scene. I followed them everywhere, I taped a lot of their shows.'

Also digging groups like Cabaret Voltaire, Harrison was totally into the experimental end of the punk thing. 'Punk had got awful with Sham 69 and the UK Subs. I was more into the experimental stuff like Cabaret Voltaire as well, that period from 1979 to 1981 was a remarkable period.'

Also getting heavily into reggae at the time, Steve bought up 'hundreds of reggae albums' digging the likes of Aswad, Misty, the Mighty Diamonds and the Gladiators. The reggae flavour was a relief after the heavy, heavy duty of punk but it was also committed to a certain level of excellence. 'The reggae bands could really play, they really made an effort. You'd see the mixed punk and reggae bills and the reggae bands would make the punk bands seem so awful.'

After a couple of jobs as a trainee manager at British Home Stores and a buyer for a clothing manufacturer, Harrison was planning the escape route. From the age of 15 he had wanted to own a record shop, a perfect job for a music fanatic who had no serious inclination to be in a band.

Still young enough to be looking for kicks though, he did what a majority of youths did at the time and bought a Lambretta. 'It wasn't a specifically mod thing in the north, it seemed like everyone had a scooter, Barney and Hookey from Joy Division had them, I met Ian Brown and John Squire [the Stone Roses] on scooter rallies, it seemed like everyone was into it.'

Riding with the Cheshire Midnight Runners, it was only inevitable that Steve would eventually bump into Martin Blunt. 'I knew him on nodding terms, I would see him on scooter rallies and I remember that he wasn't specifically just into mod music.'

Harrison's cousin had a scooter in the 1970s and he remembers being thrilled when as a kid on holiday in Penzance a scooter gang had whizzed through town; these things leave an impression on a young mind.

'The people in the club called me "UK Sub" because I still looked a bit punk at the time with my drainpipe jeans and sneakers on, but there was a total mix of people there; you'd even see people with massive flares on the rallies. It was here that I got heavily into northern soul, and I bought up a big collection of records.'

The interest in northern soul and the sheer, almost anal, collector's mentality that pervaded that scene gave Steve the chance to start buying and selling records.

'In 1982, I think it was, I set up a mail order list, at first dealing in northern soul and then American West Coast bands like R.E.M., Dream Syndicate, Rain Parade, Green On Red and that Australian band the Church. That was the massive scene that I was getting heavily into.'

Apart from R.E.M. none of the bands ever went on to become mainstream names, although their influence is tangible. Harrison remembers the likes of Ian McCulloch (Echo And The Bunnymen) and Terry Hall (the Specials) checking out the neo-psychedelic strokes of the bands whose melodic drone rock suggested myriad possibilities in the post-punk landscape stretching all the way from country rock to west coast psychedelia, but played with a punk edge that made sense in the mid 1980s.

In 1983, with the mail order doing really well, Harrison opened a 'tiny shop' called Omega (named after a 1970s scooter club) in Winsford, which ran for 18 months. 'I really opened the shop as a place to keep all my mail order records, and people started turning up from all over the place buying up the American West Coast stuff; like we would sell 12 copies of the Church's album on the day of release when they were selling virtually no albums anywhere else in the country.'

From this point Steve started stocking country rock and 1960s American psychedelic. 'I was expanding to groups that fitted in around the bands that I was heavily into.'

One day a small scruffy kid, barely a teenager, drifted into the shop and started chatting to the 21-year-old owner. Tim Burgess astounded Steve Harrison with his deep knowledge of music.

'Put it this way,' says Steve, 'he was the only 13-year-old I'd ever met who was massively into the Fall, let alone Joy Division; he was a massive music nut like I was, and the age difference made no difference at all.'

'I was just the pest at the end of the counter,' laughs Tim.

In some ways Burgess and Harrison are quite similar, massive music fans who dig fanatically a mass cross-section of music, sharp minds belied by an easy-going nature and a ribald enthusiasm, they are misfits because of their sheer passion for something in a society obsessed by nothing. It was obvious that they were going to be big mates, and Harrison started getting Tim into all sorts of other sounds.

Another friendship that was being struck up at the time was with Martin Blunt, who stayed over at Steve's a couple of times after visiting his shop. 'He was another massive musical nut and he had a band, Makin' Time, and I went to see them a couple of times. I liked them and I thought that they were pretty good.'

As the shop was doing well, another was opened in Northwich, and in his spare time Steve was playing guitar in the Joy-Division-influenced band News From Nowhere, a group named after the London anarchist book shop.

The Burgess kid was still there hanging about in the shop looking for a new musical fix. It was obvious to Steve that someone this into music should be in a band; he had a thing about him, a quirkiness and an obsessive knowledge.

'I almost took him to a couple of auditions. When Ian McCulloch left Echo And The Bunnymen there was talk of going for the singer job there,' says Steve.

'But Tim [then about 18] figured the Bunnymen were "too old". Then Stephen Holt left the Inspiral Carpets after one single and on the brink of cult success.'

Steve adds, 'I rang up about that one but I think the job was already taken.'

Future band publicist Alison Martin remembers this as well too. And another person on the scene recalls, 'I could swear that Tim went for an audition with the Inspiral Carpets . . .'

Someone who did go for that audition though was Noel Gallagher who, although he didn't get the job, got the Clint Boon mop top and a job as the Inspiral's roadie.

By now Tim was singing in the Electric Crayons, a band that didn't really impress Steve: 'I didn't like them that much, it was sort of sub Stooges thing if I remember.'

It was at this point that Martin Blunt, now having gone through Makin' Time and then the short-lived Gift Horses, was putting together the Charlatans with Rob Collins; they needed a manager and Steve got the job.

'Martin asked me to go and see them at a gig, I think it was the Walsall Overstrand. They were good enough to get me interested but they didn't totally knock me out. They weren't the greatest thing in the world, but the Hammond really stuck out and Martin is a really sussed person – you can trust his judgment.'

The Charlatans picked Steve to be their manager because of his dealings with the indie music scene. Running the chain of shops had built up a series of contacts and he knew the wheelings and dealings, and in contrast to some of the more extrovert figures on the Manchester band management scene he had actually got some sort of experience in the grass roots of day-to-day slog of how to run a band.

'We were cheeky, we had already got an attitude,' says Jon Brookes. 'We needed a good manager, not someone who got us slogging up and down the motorways. We needed a plan and we knew we had to do a certain amount of smallish gigs, which we enjoyed. But we made sure that those gigs were packed out as we didn't want to waste any time.'

This was one of the key moves the Charlatans made. Instead of bumbling along and hoping for the best, they had someone at their helm who was a tenacious bugger, someone who understood the retail side of breaking a band, someone who was a music fanatic who had toured the country following groups and understood the fan-band relationship, and someone who realised the road to the top was full of twists and turns.

Harrison agreed to manage the band although it wasn't something he had planned to do.

But what the hell.

1988
Who Wants To Know?

THE KETLEY-ERA CHARLATANS PAYS ITS DUES

Steve Harrison was on the case typing out his press releases, pumping up the band's then pretty limited accomplishments and trying to find a space for the group to breath in.

Accompanying the press at the time was a series of unflattering press shots. They were the usual local band snaps, all work clothes and hands in pockets, eyes screwed up in the sun. It's difficult to tell who is who, and only Baz Ketley seems to have any attitude. It was going to be some time before the band got the posing knack down to a T.

The November 1988 Harrison missive told the world about this Wolverhampton band that was formed in isolation from the town's current pop sensations.

Wolverhampton may not be a town dripping in pop glamour, even football glamour has been hard to come by (due to Wolverhampton Wanderers lengthy exclusion from the premier league), but it's had its moments.

The roots of the Charlatans lie deeper in the far less fashionable Midlands than they do in the hip as fuck Manchester. The Midlands have been maligned for years by the rest of the country; maybe it's because the people there are far less cocky and pushy than in other regions. Their self-effacing sense of humour and idiosyncratic accent has had them awarded low points by hipsters for years – pop hipsters who conveniently forget the area's crucial contribution to pop history: half of Led Zeppelin, Black Sabbath, the Specials, Roy Wood's Move then Wizzard and then Electric Light Orchestra, Traffic, Spencer Davis, Dexy's . . . and all the way to the kings, one of the greatest bands in pop history, the mighty Slade!

Slade hail from Wolverhampton and were one of the greatest bands that had ever blasted out the three-minute pop single in British pop history. Noddy Holder's shit-kicking vocals scorched through an amazing run of singles that saw the band as the most successful British pop act of the early 1970s. They were like the Beatles if the Beatles were a full-on working class band without the art school aspirations. Slade's thick Black Country accents could only add to their authenticity and charm, and they gave the town a hell of a legacy to live up to.

By the late 1980s the three main bands in Wolverhampton were the Sandkings, Wild Flowers and Mighty Lemon Drops, who all rehearsed in the same rehearsal rooms as the new-born Charlatans.

Whilst the Charlatans were hustling a keyboard-driven classic guitar pop rooted in the 1960s, the three just mentioned princes of the local scene were either playing grebo rock or post-Creation leather-pant guitar pop.

Further north in Manchester everyone was starting to lose the energy and the stylistic trappings of punk and were searching deeper into psychedelic pop of the 1960s for their inspiration. The Inspiral Carpets playing some of their debut shows in the city plying a keyboard-driven psychedelic pop, the Stone Roses were starting on their long strange trip with their newly established and now classic four-man line-up, and the Happy Mondays were making a very contemporary drugged-out hooligan funked-up freak beat that could hardly be mistaken for being a flowery or hippified version of drug rock.

1988 was the year that Manchester's rumbling anarchic music scene started to get noticed down south, as since the 1980s indie dominance by the Smiths and New Order, the rest of the city's bands had been pretty much ignored. The Happy Mondays had been mentioned in dispatches but no one was buying their records, and the Stone Roses were getting grudging recognition, their self-mouthed hyperbole hitting first gear, claiming that they were going to be bigger than the Beatles and the first band to play on the moon.

Weirdly enough, the band that seemed most likely to break out of the city next were the Inspiral Carpets, whose *Plane Crash* EP was released that June and seemed primed to send them on that sort of big indie band that brushed with the top 40 trajectory. Meanwhile James were huge locally but ignored elsewhere.

Acid house was the main buzz in the city with the Hacienda ruling the roost and countless smaller clubs popping up. Everyone seemed to be on E or else pretending to be – drugs were taken openly after being frowned upon for years – flares were on the streets and clothes were getting baggier, completely balking at the tight-assed indie styles of the past few years.

Bands were making the choice whether to go with the flow or ignore it, and in the autumn the Happy Mondays released *Bummed*, one of the greatest albums of the era and one that set the lifestyle codes for the times.

Liverpool looked on amazed as Manchester got all the credit for 'scally' culture. The scene was small but it was there and waiting to be ignited.

But the echoes of the soon to come Manchester scene were yet to be heard 60-odd miles down the road.

The Midlands had a very different flavour to its own music scene. Whilst the Wild Flowers were plying a post Echo And The Bunnymen moody pop, the Lemon Drops (who featured Dave Newton from the Wild Flowers) were a leather-kecked, skinny-geek poppier take on the Mary Chain caustic pop but were running out of time – they had grabbed a major deal on Blue Guitar and had had some hits (their lower-chart efforts 'The Other Side Of You', 'Out Of Hand' and 'Inside Out').

Nearby, in the Stourbridge scene, the so-called grebo thing was flourishing (grebos were long-haired poppy takes on biker metal crossover rock) that had seen lank yob pop in the tradition of Slade but updated to the 1980s with bands like the Wonder Stuff and Pop Will Eat Itself. Pop Will Eat Itself had been around for years playing under different names, plying a Jesus & Mary Chain-influenced fuzz pop with the Wonder Stuff's Miles Hunt on the drums; they had split up and reformed as the far more gothic Wild And Wondering before, almost as a joke, putting together Pop Will Eat Itself proper. In 1988 they had scored a bagful of indie hits but were on the verge of a big success, likewise the ebullient Miles Hunt's Wonder Stuff. Hunt, a man whose uncle had been in Wizzard, had taken his new outfit to the brink of big-time indiedom plying a cynical tuff pop. They were on the verge of a massive run of hits. The Sandkings were in similar mould but they were the band that missed out on the big time, until frontman Jas Mann went on to form Babylon Zoo who would have 1996's biggest smash single with 'Spaceman'.

The Charlatans were a long way apart from any sort of current Midlands scene, quoting the likes of the Spencer Davis Group and early Dexy's Midnight Runners as the sort of West Midlands band action that they liked to be confused with. These were intense pop bands racked with raw soul and were the sort of groups that they saw themselves in the same sort of tradition as.

The early Dexy's, built around the enigmatic Kevin Rowland, was a massively influential band – the Dexy's dug the purist soul and cranked it with the full-on intensity of prime-time punk. They pumped in the punk energy and attitude but they kept the sweet, sweet sound of the soul. Front man Rowland, wired and intense, wouldn't speak to the music press, preferring instead to place adverts of self-penned essays to his fans. They banned alcohol from their gigs and stared sullenly from a series of photographs. Their first album is a document of soul power and a statement of intent that far more groups should use as their starting block instead of the sodding Beatles.

Of course the Dexy's connection was more than just some cool name-dropping by the outfit, Baz Ketley having been in the Andy Leek Band, the group built around the former keyboard player from Dexy's.

Playing the usual bunch of local shows the Charlatans were beginning to pick up some local press attention. Reviews at the time of live shows described the band as Martin Blunt's, referring to his Makin' Time past, and were pretty upbeat about the band, talking about the strong driving vocals and Hammond sound. Whatever they were aiming at, it looked like they were definitely going in the right direction.

Brumbeat reviewed the second demo: 'The Charlatans put some of my reservations about them live to rest with their new demo which shows Baz

Ketley heading back to the form of his illustrious old outfit the Blue Toys.'

Baz, looking back at the demos, points to the gradual change in style that the band were developing. 'From the first demo to the third demo there is a big change. The first demo is pretty punky. On the second demo there is one track that is pretty laid back, and by the time we did the third one in Macclesfield, it was all getting pretty laid back. Also the sound was getting more of a balance. On the first demo my guitar isn't that prominent because I wasn't that confident as a guitar player and I kept on saying put the guitar down in the mix, but by the third one its in there as well.'

The third demo also included a track called 'Hey Teen' which became the band's first mini anthem.

The first national press review was in *Sounds* on 3 September 1988 when they were supporting the, frankly, pretty naff Broken English at the near-empty Manchester International (the venue run by Gareth Evans, the erstwhile Stone Roses manager, and the place where the Stone Roses used to rehearse). The review was by local stringer Stephen Kingston who panned the sub-Stones workout of the headliners and in a dismissive last paragraph turned on the Charlatans and lambasted their 'standard sound' that he saw sharing the same treadmill as the headliners, 'only this time it's keyboards-driven.' He added that 'not even a song dedicated to "Henry Miller [who wrote *Tropic Of Cancer*] fans" could help', but felt that 'old Henry's probably pretty chuffed'. This curt dismissal was the Charlatans' first national press mention, a full year before anyone else picked up on them, and it didn't bode too well.

Those first lines of print are always the most crucial in a band's career and are read over a million times as musicians try and glean some meaning, good or bad. The words, quite often spat out at random, set the heart racing – it's the tuffest step on a long and slippery ladder.

Meanwhile Steve Harrison was feeling bolshy as he signed off his first press release: 'They won't remain a secret for much longer . . .'

It would be a couple more years and several line-up shuffles before he was to be totally correct.

'EVERYBODY MUST GET STONED'

As any good manager does, Steve got the band out working, hustling Gareth Evans for supports with American guitar bands like the Thin White Rope. The Charlatans were also out on the Midlands circuit proper, piling up the gigs, touring hard, working up their sound.

They may have been feeling the isolation of being a full-on guitar pop band in the late 1980s, an era when playing guitar pop was hardly likely to score a band much success. Then, the idea of a band writing perfect pop tunes and shackling them to classic guitar strokes seemed quaintly uncommercial, almost like a museum culture, and for any band trying to make headway against the current cul de sac of electronic pop it seemed more like a hopeless cause.

There was talk, though at that moment maybe mere whispers, that there was something stirring up north in Manchester. 'The Stone Roses,' said the grapevine, 'were massive in Manc and were plying the sort of 6-string pop that we Brits are the kings of.' And there was a connection, a connection that Harrison can't have missed – the Roses' manager Gareth Evans used to visit Omega Records. It was a connection that was too valuable to miss.

Steve Harrison picks up on how he blagged those crucial Roses supports. 'Gareth Evans used to come into the shop and drop off tickets and pick up the money from tickets sold for his International venues in Manchester. I knew he was managing the Stone Roses, whom I had already seen and I knew were brilliant, and I got some supports off him at places like Walsall Junction 10, the LSE in London, Trent Poly and the International in Manchester.'

Baz remembers Steve getting the gigs with the Roses. 'Steve kept going on about how massive this band would be and how they were going to take over the world, so we were well up for it. The first show that we played together was at the LSE in London and there was only about 20 or 30 people there in a massive auditorium. We were surprised after all the hyping up that Steve had done with them!'

The Ketley-era Charlatans would play with the Stone Roses five times. After the surprise of how few people there was at the London gig, the next show they were booked to play with the band was at the Manchester International 2, two weeks later. 'Of course we were totally shocked this time by how big the crowd was, it was totally chocker,' says Baz.

The other shows, at Walsall Junction 10 and Trent Poly, were back to the smaller crowds. The Roses as a phenomenon hadn't caught on outside Manchester as yet, but the International 2 show had been enough to show that something was stirring and that all Steve's maniacal raving about the band wasn't the talk of a deluded madman.

'The Roses were cool, we talked to them. In a band everyone is usually huddled together in their own groups but, in Walsall, I think it was, John Squire borrowed my guitar amp; they seemed like decent guys,' points out Baz, adding, 'unlike when we played with Broken English, they wouldn't even let us share their dressing room!'

Blagging Evans for supports with incoming Yank guitar bands was easy, the American bands may have been inconsequential gigs but the Roses supports was something that would change the Charlatans for ever.

STILL GETTING STONED!

While the Charlatans were sweating away on the arse circuit the Stone Roses started on the gradual ascendancy to the top, and as 1988 turned into 1989 it was becoming obvious that the Roses would be grabbing some sort of major success. For the astute pop observe the future was happening right now.

The Roses was a connection that Harrison, no fool, was going to play on, and in the band's initial press releases he touted the Charlatans as the Roses' favourite support band. Harrison saw a gap, a space that his band could move into. The choice was stark: forever be a worthwhile guitar band slugging around the circuit, or hook up with the Roses and the whole new pop era that was unfolding breathtakingly in front of their eyes. This wasn't a case of Harrison pushing his charges on to the bandwagon; it was plain bloody common sense and an opportunity that only a fool would pass by.

From watching Reni's amazing drumming Jon Brookes copped a few licks. 'I learnt a lot from Reni on how to loosen the drums up. They seemed so loose, they would fall apart. It was good, we really got to watch the Stone Roses develop. They were confident all the way – I got the Roses' drum feel out of a packet: just add water and the white of an egg . . . The Roses really inspired us; watching Ian Brown we knew we needed a bloke as confident as that to front us.'

And it had already crossed their minds where this frontman could be found as, checking a local Northwich rock & roll band, the Electric Crayons, they felt the band's skinny-assed punk singer could be the man they were looking for. 'When we saw the Electric Crayons we knew that Tim was right for us and he was so into what we were doing that it seemed perfect,' the others claimed.

Poor old Baz Ketley's days were numbered. The rest of the band had seen their future and decided that he had no part in it. The Stone Roses were changing the whole blueprint for what rock & roll was all about in the UK and the Charlatans were the first of many bands who were inspired by this.

A reviewer was bemused by the Charlatans. Like just who the hell were they? They felt that Baz Ketley's band was brand new and were shocked that this was their third appearance in the Midlands, before deciding, '1960s psychedelic fringed with a 1980s feel, Dr And The Medics they are not'.

The reviewer dug the intro song – 'it brings back memories of Brian Auger and Spencer Davis' – a well-spotted slew of references plugging at two of the key influences on the band. The reviewer also noted that the band went down really well and set the stage for the 'mighty Stone Roses, the best band in the world since The Smiths'.

Although the Stone Roses supports may have been a great break for the band the Charlatans didn't really blow the crowds away. Steve grimaces, 'They weren't that brilliant at the time. When Baz eventually left they didn't keep a single song from that old set. They hardly set the place on fire at those gigs but it was handy in that it got them known outside a couple of small towns.'

'BYE BYE BARRY'

The Stone Roses supports hadn't gone as well as hoped and this caused tension within the band. The Charlatans had glimpsed the future, they could see which way that pop was turning and they also saw that there was a place for them in the new way.

Baz Ketley knew that there was something amiss with the current line-up, according to Steve Harrison, 'Baz left because he didn't feel that the band was getting anywhere. There was also a directional division. Baz was a really good songwriter, he wrote all the songs, but shall we put it like this, he was more into the content than the style, good songs over presentation and with Manchester looming on the horizon there was a whole scene where style was as important as content.'

And for the ex mods in the band and the management, style was crucial. In British pop, style is all, and a band made up of some ex mods and managed by a youth culture and pop obsessed manager wasn't going to miss out on what was just over the horizon. After all, what Manchester was offering was a whole scene of bands committed to playing the sort of music that the Charlatans were already grasping at.

'This was a music scene that was tailor-made for them,' pointed out someone who watched some of their Midlands gigs in the early days, 'they would be fools to miss it.'

All this talk makes it seem like Baz just did the 'right thing' and quit to improve the band's chances. But for Ketley it was a quite different situation as he was enjoying his time with the Charlatans after a long time struggling in the music business and it seemed like he was finally in a band that was on its way up. Some good gigs, a well organised band and a powerful distinctive style – it all felt right.

'Good things were happening, it was all going the right way,' he says. 'We started to get influenced by the Manchester thing soundwise, we were getting more laid back, we could see where things were going and it definitely suited where we were going as well. We were starting to get a bit of a following, we were getting, like 200-300 people at each gig. Things were happening for the band.'

So what made him leave?

'It was a personal thing. It was nothing to do with music or the band. It was a daft situation. My girlfriend left me and went to live in Germany. It was a bad time in my life. I just couldn't face being in the band as well so I left.'

The personal crises pushed Baz over the edge and he quit the band right at the crossroads of their career.

After the Roses shows the Charlatans knew that they were going to have to change but no one had really thought that it was going to be this drastic.

The Stone Roses supports had set their minds thinking. The intense charisma of the Roses and their fanatical following at their shows affected everyone at the time. How many groups formed from the clusters of kids at those gigs picking up on the brilliant tunes and the almost evangelistic belief in the power of pop would be immeasurable.

The Roses were a total catalyst for a band like the Charlatans who were feeling their way towards something – they were like a blinding revelation as Jon Brookes is honest enough to admit. 'Baz Ketley was very much into the punk sort of thing. We were a very intense band, smashing our gear up, Baz was really into the Clash. But after playing with the Roses we really saw that we wanted to do something much more up to date, different.'

Steve's assistant Andy Woods could see that line-up alteration coming. 'Baz left knowing that something had to change.'

Steve Harrison noted the musical differences and watched the band make some tough decisions. 'We parted company with Baz when he started going in a different musical direction from the rest of the band. We started looking for a singer and a guitarist early in June and after auditions in the West Midlands and in Manchester we thought we had found a singer. Then Tim came along. He was amazing, ideal.'

And all along he had been right under Steve's nose, hanging around in his shop.

Ketley had left 'on good terms in the summer of 1989' and was last spotted in a band called the Hedonics in Wolverhampton.

Steve told Q magazine, 'He just phoned up one day and said he was packing it in. It wasn't altogether a surprise because of the band's general development. Originally Barry had put in a lot of songwriting content, but Rob and Martin were getting more involved in songwriting. They were pulling in different directions. But it did come as a blow at the time.'

Within a month of leaving Baz got the bug again, as it's almost impossible for a musician to lose interest in playing – once you're in it's very difficult to get out again.

'I remember it was only a month later and I started trying to get this band together again,' says Baz. 'I didn't want to sing, I just wanted to concentrate on the guitar. I didn't want the double responsibility. I got in touch with Glenn Dodd who used to be in the Sandkings and talked him back into being in a band. He was pretty disillusioned with everything after the Sandkings, very cynical about the music business like I was.'

Ketley was still coming to terms with quitting the Charlatans as he was putting his new outfit together. 'I thought what the fuck have I done this for, but I got on with starting the Hedonics. I knew a bass player and then got Pete out of Blue Toys and Makin' Time on drums and a keyboard player who was always crap. The band's music was more guitar-based. We couldn't use a Hammond for obvious reasons, so I got a Fender Rhodes in.'

Ketley shows little remorse at the Charlatans swiftly gathering ranks and then going on to being really successful. 'Tim was perfect for them because they wanted that Manchester connection. Tim fitted the role, he was prime for the part – I never had any grudges.'

The Hedonics got off to a good start, they were playing regularly and getting some good supports, with the Verve at Buckley Tivolis and playing around the country. In 1993 the line-up changed with the drummer and keyboards quitting. They recruited replacements and have kept the same line-up to this day, opting out of the toilet circuit treadmill. Now Ketley is playing his understated and psychedelic pop at the most unlikely of settings. Raves.

'A mate of mine got into all the rave stuff and got us some gigs at raves and it really worked. We're friends with these people called Aura Orange who run the Astro cafe in London. It's a pretty big scene and they put on illegal raves around the country and we get to play quite a few of them. Their base is the old Pumphouse cafe in London, they put on great nights there. It's really brilliant. I can't take playing the old pub scene any more. This is a much better life; we played a festival in France, we're on the outside now. I refuse to ring a record company, I prefer an illegal party in the middle of nowhere.'

By the late 1990s Ketley was seeing much less of the rest of the Charlatans. 'I don't see them that often. I'm still in touch. Rob was the one I got on with best out of anyone, I think in many ways we were kindred spirits, a little bit wild, I got busted for drugs and arrested for criminal damage, Rob sort of things!'

KEEP ON KEEPING ON

For your main songwriter and singer to leave a fledgling group was potentially disastrous, the sort of body blow that could blow a group apart. But Harrison felt that this was an opportunity to clear the air. He had had some misgivings about the way the band was going and felt there were some all round improvements to be made, and now would be a good time.

'They just didn't need a vocalist,' he points out. 'They needed to get their act together really. They were a bit directionless at the time, to tell the truth.'

The Charlatans were left with a problem now that their singer/ songwriter and guitarist had upped sticks and gone. All that was left in the band was the basic trio, and they needed a singer and a guitar player. They advertised for a guitar player and scratched their heads for a singer, not realising that the solution was staring right at them in the shape of the eccentric scruffy kid from Northwich with a head full of crazy pop love and a pair of massive flares that did all the talking that was needed in terms of fashion.

Tim Burgess's band the Electric Crayons had already played with the Charlatans, and in retrospect it must seem odd for Baz to have shared the same stage with his replacement. 'Oh no, no way. The Electric Crayons were a great band, Tim especially. I got on with Tim. He came to our gigs from time to time, he was a mate of Steve's, I mean I only saw him at gigs and we'd talk about music stuff, y'know, band talk. On stage he was wild, he did the Iggy Pop thing. He was a lot wilder than he is now!'

As one front man bowed out another wandered gamely into view.

Step up to the mic Timothy Burgess.

SO YOU WANNA BE A ROCK & ROLL STAR?

Just what the hell is a pop star?

It's that combination of sex and charisma, that extra edge – an indefinable X factor that can be faked and can be exaggerated; the machine will always make sure of that, making things seem greater than they are. But then there are other people who goofily bumble into the role, scuffed-shoed naturals, who have that innate star thing down off pat. They are the ones that don't fit in at school, the outsiders, the cranks, the too-smart kids that won't fit into the system.

Over the years we've seen every possible shade of person being applauded as a pop star – every chancer, every blagger on the block has had a crack at the pot of gold. For some it required a lot of effort and for some it required a lot of bullshit.

But there are those people who seem to have no choice in the matter.

In pop you are dealing with your assets, it may be a cheap gimmick, some whacky day-wear of a goony-looking singer. It may be a knack of writing great choruses or connecting with the people. Of course the Charlatans were champs at all of these, but it was Burgess's lips that were breaking them into previously untapped areas. Sure, Ian Brown had classic features but that was more of a guy thing, baggy football males getting a non-sexual crush on the Brown man was the closest they were going to get to the hallowed teen gurl crowd, the crowd that can make your band into millionaires if you press all the right buttons. And none of the Manchester bands were really capable of that. Primetime Shaun Ryder was considered sexy by some, and the Inspiral Carpets? Well, they weren't first in the queue when the good lord was handing out cute looks, were they? Nope, the early 1990s rock bands were, in general, not really dealing out the sex card. And this was where Tim unwittingly stumbled in rubbing his sleepy eyes. Although in reality an all-out teen delinquent, by the time the Charlatans hit first gear he could easily be mistaken as cuddly pop pin-up, armed with the sort of lascivious lips that would get you bullied at school and lusted at for your pop star pin-up life.

Of course it was Jagger that was the first in pop to use flappy lips as an asset. In every picture he would slap them out, drooling, looking like they had just been pulled out of hot sex action. This was how to use big lips and the Charlatans' frontman wasted no time in his promo shots pumping up the facial love muscles.

The reluctant indie pin-up was walking that thin line between cred and teen sex symbol, and walking it well. 'I guess most girls don't really like the Chippendales type of guy. They like normal-looking boyish people like me. So I guess I'm just lucky really . . .' he once told the press, still bemused by his new found 'love god' status.

Born on 30 May 1967 at Hope Hospital in Salford, Tim Burgess is one of those people who seems to have arrived a star. It's difficult to imagine someone like this doing anything else, and his pop star sparkle was perfect to lift the Charlatans from being a tight and talented band into pop star material. The band may have had the whole music thing nailed down tight but they were hardly going to be pinned up on anyone's walls, and if you want to escape the underground ghetto you've got to have that glint of sex.

Remember kids, in pop sex sells, and Tim came to the band stuffed with the sort of sex that was going to get the band noticed. He also came armed with a naive cool and a total passion for music that would mean that the boys weren't going to get turned off by a lightweight pop pin-up that was only there for the gurls! It was the sort of pop star appeal that worked for Marc Bolan and Jim Morrison, and as Jim Morrison himself once sang, 'but the little girls understand'.

Tim Burgess is a bit of an enigma, i-D magazine once summed him up as 'a lovely, sensible young man and, alternatively, a barely on the ground, tightrope-walking wild child'.

Down to earth, he's got the 1990s pop star thing right down – from the Manc swagger, baggy gear and cool attitude. On the other hand he isn't as macho as many of his contemporaries and is far smarter than he often lets on. His conversation is peppered with an almost childlike glee and goofball observations, with occasional flashes of wisdom and huge dollops of eccentricity. He makes up words that a three-year-old would use, is fun, insecure, shy, and yet at the same time, confident, boisterous and plain daft.

Music is his religion and there is hardly a group you could mention that he hasn't got an opinion on.

He inhabits one of those weird pop star bodies with the skinny frame and large head and, armed with those large lips, he couldn't be anyone else but the singer in a band. The Jagger mannerisms are easy for him to master, and not surprisingly Jagger was always a key influence on him. 'I bought a Rolling Stones book and he looked brilliant. He's ace. They obviously took a lot of time on how they were looking and everything. They don't look so good now though, do they! It's an offence that they are still going. Kick 'em off and give someone else a chance!'

His initial aping (ha!) of king monkey Ian Brown hasn't done his stage presence any harm either. That sloping pimp-roll shuffle and out-of-it half stare have become key components of many nineties frontmen. You either react against it or go with the flow; Tim went with it and eventually carved his own idiosyncratic presence. He might lack the menace of Ian Brown but he makes up for this with a cute persona that sees him regularly voted as one of the few pin-ups in what was frankly a pretty ugly scene.

A hyperactive man-child, Burgess is a constant fidget, and his non-stop fiddly energy is the key component to his personality. 'Why am I so hyperactive? It's just the way that I am. When I gave up smoking I had these nicotine patches and I was running round like a madman. Crazy.

Combined with this is a full-on positive attitude that seems to be unquenchable. Tim Burgess is a bit of a one-off, a five foot seven, buzzing, vibed-up explosion of enthusiasm, still – damnit – untainted by the cynicism and pessimism of the modern world. He talks in child speak and yet sometimes sounds quite smart. In an almost inspirational way Burgess is spreading the good vibes to the people, his theory being, you feel good about yourself and then everyone else will feel good about themselves. 'I fucking love being in the Charlatans. I fucking loved being me even when I was ten years old. I was a bit of a narcissist. I think that's healthy; if you can't love yourself, no one else will.'

The contradictions in his personality started early. He had every girl in his school (Leftwich High) digging his cute trip and yet was a ten-year-old glue-sniffing punk rocker; he is quite shy and yet a total extrovert; a bundle of contradictions . . . perfect frontman material.

Tim had moved to Northwich from Salford when he was seven years old. As he once told the *Melody Maker* he had a happy childhood. 'I had a great childhood, Christmas was always the highlight of the year. Even more than birthdays. I had some great toys. You know the helicopter you used to get when you were a kid that would always pick stuff up, fly away and then drop it again? What was it called? Well, that was great. I never got stuff like Ataris and that. I had Subbuteo though. My teams were Brazil and Uruguay because they had the flair players.'

Despite this background he was a delinquent yoof and trouble was always nearby, something that could be bumbled into almost by accident as he once told the pop press. 'At the age of 13 I was going around with people who were 18 and 19. There were about seven of these older friends who went to a pub one night. I didn't go because I was too young. I woke up the next morning and my mam and dad told me that they'd all been arrested for stabbing this lad. It was pretty lucky that I wasn't there. They all got about 12 months in prison!'

Naturally drugs were lurking in the Burgess canon, and he was caught smoking at 11 and then sniffing glue when he was 13. 'Being addicted to glue was the worst thing that happened to me. It happened when I was about 14. I went from building model aeroplanes to sniffing glue! Everyone does really mad things and it's your curiosity that gets you into really mad stuff like that. I was lucky, I got attention. They got the social workers around and things like that.'

Like a lot of teenagers Burgess experimented with drugs. It was once reported in *i-D* that when he was a teenager he used to take speed and run up to the top of the highest hill that he could find. It was this kind of deviant nuttiness mixed with the totally innocent (whoever ran to the top of a hill on speed!) that makes the man.

'I never had any reason to get into a lot of violence or crime. I was probably spaced out on magic mushrooms. They're alright when you're 16 to 20. It's all part of growing up – a bit of glue, a few mushrooms, a bit of draw, stomach pumps here and there, waking up in hospital, over-indulging in alcohol, Southern Comfort,' he told *Q* magazine.

Back in those long-lost days of pre-acid house, drugs were by no means the lowest common denominator to youth culture that they are now. Few kids were experimenting with the altered states. It was the school freaks that had the dark rings round their eyes and muttered strange gibberish to each other. For the small-town weirdo there wasn't even that much you could get your hands on. E may as well have been non existent for the amount of it that was actually available (in those days hardly anyone had even heard of it). Draw (marijuana) was available but a hippie drug and smack was an inner-city thing. Acid was there but magic mushrooms were the real currency; all you had to do was go to a field and pick them, attempt to swallow them – trying to ignore their vile taste and the maggots wriggling around in them – before tripping for hours. You could never tell exactly how much hallucinogenic you were putting into your system with a fistful of mushrooms – for many it was a bit of a laugh but for some it was the fast route to mental hospital.

For the teenager in a small town there isn't much going on. City kids may live in shitholes but small-town kids have very little space to get any sort of life going. At least in the city you can dream of escape and go up town and hustle, but in Northwich and the hundreds of other backwater Brit towns there is absolutely nowhere else to go. All there is are nights on the piss, lager louts rampaging up mediaeval streets shooting the shit, bearing grudges against each other that can last decades.

'Pretty decent isn't it, Northwich,' Tim once joked to the *NME*, adding, 'a bit like Sweden really.'

Looking back at his hometown he commented, 'It's getting a bit posh now but the whole place was custom-built for the ICI factory.'

It can be hell for someone who dreams of getting out, especially if they dream of escaping into rock & roll. There are very few bands that make it from small towns and beyond; there is no infrastructure, no way of hooking into the music business. There, the rock & roll dreamer has to look towards the big city to escape. Many drift down to London and link up with the countless misshapen bands that eke out a meagre existence in the capital.

And you can't get any more typically small-town than Northwich; too close to Manchester to have its own identity, it feels almost like one of the suburbs that spin out of the city on its southside. A paved-over high street with the typically nondescript shopping precincts and supermarkets mixes with the Tudor black and white beams of ye olde Cheshire high street. The town's station is a good mile from the centre and the trains never seem to turn up in that typically crap British Rail way.

At school Tim wasn't noted for being that bright. He was heading down the plughole like countless other kids that just don't fit in, spat out by a system that's geared towards sloggers and squares, and certainly not glue-sniffing dreamers digging weird and wonderful records.

'My school treated me as though I was backwards and stupid! Put me in a lower group instead of trying to understand the cause of everything.'

Not that school was a total disaster for Tim, as the *NME* later reported that he was good at sport, being captain of both the school's football and rugby teams – the article stated that he had no interest in the academic side of things, just doing woodwork and metalwork and games. It was hardly a grounding in rock & roll, but instead a sure sign of someone who was just drifting through the school day dreaming their way through life.

'My teachers laughed at me, saying, "Burgess, you've got no chance". It wasn't a put down, it was the truth,' he remembers.

Leaving school with only one O level and an already burgeoning misfit mind he drifted towards employment.

For the boy dreamer, Tim Burgess, there was only one thing for it, roll up yer sleeves and go to work. 'I decided to prove them wrong right away, getting a job.'

He worked in an office as mail boy and a stamp-licker at the local ICI factory. His father was a foreman there but he didn't get Tim the job.

'Everyone thought that it was my dad that got me the job but it wasn't. I just said it was a brilliant job, said I'd be top and I could do it better than anyone else, so put your faith in me.'

The factory's huge hideous sprawl somewhat dwarfs the rather quaint environs of Northwich. It's weird configuration of heavy-duty industrial pipes and twinkling lights seems so at odds with the mock-Tudor old-world charms of the Cheshire belt that surrounds it.

Burgess's debut in the world of work was hardly going to challenge his admittedly lazy mind, as he told the *NME*, 'Yeah, I did work for five years in the end after leaving school. I started at the ICI when I was 16. First of all I did the mail, just like in *Quadrophenia*. I had this bicycle with a sack on the front and I'd ride around the factory doling out all the letters to everybody. It was a real laugh, but after two years of that you had to change and I had to clean out all the toilets and all the lockers and stuff.'

Not that he had been in any rush to start his new career. 'I went to Austria with mates from school when I left. We just messed around in the snow all over Europe, when I went back home I went to work in the factory – got involved with chemicals and things like that.'

Even though the jobs were crap Tim took great pride in them. 'I've always wanted to do every job I've ever had properly. Whether it's in the mail in the ICI or working in an office pressing computers – that's the scary thing, I must be a jobsworth! Just pressing things into a computer.'

He also worked as a cycle messenger. 'We just used to ride around on bikes and smash them up. It was dead good. We used to have competitions of who could wreck their bike first, and I always used to win. We used to start at about 20 to seven in the morning and by quarter to I'd smashed all the bikes up! I got involved in a few dodgy deals, I can't tell you what, ask someone else. I tried forming a few groups, spent my money on going out in the evenings and finding ways of existing on as little money as possible.'

After his work as cycle messenger and a toilet cleaner at the works, he moved on to contract work, bricklaying, carpentry, and scrubbing asbestos-coated ceilings and the crabby insides of chemical tanks.

'I had to sign a contract saying that if I died of asbestosis me mam and dad or me sister can have a four-year legal battle for a load of dosh.'

No wonder he dreamed of being a rock & roll star.

From the age of 11 he had been a massive music nut, and when he saw the savagely primal post-punk band Killing Joke (an awesome group; at their peak around their first album *Killing Joke* they were putting together a brutal raw record that was hooked around massive beats and a red-blooded punk rock intensity married to a powerful funk, sounding like a punked-up Chemical Brothers about 15 years too early), young Tim was at the gig in his school uniform.

'At school I would be running around with a Vibrators badge on, I remember seeing Crass play and being stunned by the sheer power of anger of their sound.'

He often referred to his punk past in interviews, talking fondly about long forgotten bands like Zounds and their great single 'Demystifaction', and the inspiration he got from the main band on the anarcho scene, Crass, and shocking interviewers with his articulate breakdown of the differences between 'pre-Spanish revolution bands like Crass' and what he considered to be the less meritious bands like 'the 1960s anarchy bands like Conflict that was well past its sell-by date even when they latched on to it'.

Burgess had even seen Crass when they had played in Northwich in one of the band's few outings round the country, with their intense music that worked by its pure articulation of anger and fierce political intelligence, and had inspired countless unlikely kids like Brett Anderson from Suede; for many at the time they were the only punk band that never really sold out.

Crass were one of the oddest anomalies in the history of pop, hardline anarchists who lived in a commune and made records that were attacks on the state. They were the punk political dream made pure – they sold their records at cost price, were fiercely intelligent, brooked no bullshit, and they mattered. At one time it was impossible to pass a bus shelter anywhere in the UK without their name or logo stencilled on it.

Their big line-up and vigorous attack of different vocalists, and love of politically inspired pranks, had inspired a whole sub genre of bands, one of whom, Chumbawumba would take the template and eventually end up selling millions of albums in the late 1990s.

Tim's other choice bands as he grew up were the Clash, Iggy and then New Order. He was still enamoured enough with this spiky period in pop to be name-checking Wire and the Slits as his favourite bands, and the Gang of Four's 'At Home He's A Tourist', the Ramones' 'Pinhead' and the long-forgotten anarcho Zounds' classic 'Subvert' as some of his pet singles . . . the kid had been listening intently at the time, there was no way the young Burgess had been just a punk rock tourist.

For most British kids deeply passionate about their rock & roll punk rock served as a standard to rally round. The trendies in the big cities may have been announcing its death when the Clash signed to CBS but for the kids in the small towns and the true believers it really did mean something. Kids as young as ten or 11 picked up the standard when the hip crowd got bored. It was just how they were going to redefine its energy that was important in terms of UK pop culture.

Instead of directly aping its form, the energy of punk was diversified in many styles. The Roses may once have been Clash obsessives, the Mondays may have dug the Pistols bad-ass attitude, even punks, like the eventual singer of Northside, Dermo, were reared suckling on the power of the form through outfits like the massively popular and yet written out of rock history Dead Kennedys.

The weird and wonderful bands that came pouring out of the fallout of punk have never fitted in tidily with rock's neat lineage; you know, the Beatles, Stones, Beach Boys, the classics, the narrow selection of records that most bands cop their riffs from. But there is far more to music than these bands, and Steve Harrison knew this as he hitched round the country checking out the Gang of Four and Joy Division, whilst Martin Blunt picked up the bass, partly influenced by the Stranglers massively influential bassman JJ Burnel. But it was Tim who was the one most besotted with the primal rush of punk rock.

Interviews and conversations with the singer are pitted with references to the UK Subs ('he can remember all their album titles!' one interviewer gasped) and other old-time punk bands.

The first record that Tim bought when he was ten years old was 'Automatic Lover' by the Vibrators. It was the band's finest moment and their closest brush with the top 30, but it wasn't really real punk, more like supercharged pub rock.

'I don't know why I bought that,' he claimed. 'It could have just as easily been any other record.'

Being ten when punk exploded, Tim was far too young to be caught up in the initial raw rush but as he told the *NME* this was the music that really sparked him off on his music quest.

'I used to like Discharge and Crass – I missed out on original punk. When I was 13, 14 and 15 I tried to be scruffy and as much of a disgrace as possible, just so people would notice me,' Tim once told the *NME*. 'The way that people would do it at that age was having no bottoms on your trousers, having your ass hanging out your pants, your hair many different colours, and as many zips as possible. But my parents, they're pretty decent minded – sussed – they're young, so it's easier.'

At the time he also got a tattoo done. 'I had it done when I was 15. I got a homemade one, I just got one of me mates to do it for us. It's just like a blob. It's really faded now so you can't tell. It was just like a T. Yeah, it's on my arm. I don't like 'em at all really. But each to his own.'

Eventually Burgess would tire of the bitter nihilism of punk as really it didn't sit easily with his more optimistic idealistic nature.

'Well, you fight sour times with beauty, don't you? In the punk thing they all fought violence with violence and I think that's pretty stupid. If things aren't great around you, you've got to create something that's a lot better.'

He spent nights at home like most music freaks hooked on to John Peel, listening to those dulcet tones warmly greeting the new freaks from the boundaries of pop. It was here that he picked up on Primal Scream, rushing out to buy 'It Happens', and then getting hooked on the Fall and New Order, putting together imaginary set-lists for the two classic Manc bands.

'New Order have always been my favourite band. Each record they have put out has been better than the last,' he told the *NME*.

'My favourite Fall album is *Slates*,' he once said, marking out the quintessential Fall 10-inch 6-track – neither album or EP – release from the early 1980s which was the band at their best. A set of tight, mean songs riding on the melodic buzz of great basslines, forming a rock-tight foundation for razor-sharp angry vitriolic lyrics. It's a great record that sounds as vital today as it did on its release. Now and then you can grab a whiff of Fall frontman Mark E. Smith's idiosyncratic wordplay in Tim's lyrics. Burgess was a confirmed fan. 'I've got everything by the Fall. What I love about his lyrics is the way that he puts things that don't go together together. Like, it always reminds me of when you meet a girl and you want to impress her and you're talking, blurting stuff out. You know what you're trying to say, like, what you mean, but you're not making any sense, you just keep saying what comes into your head.'

The Fall, through a whole stack of records, have been northern pop's narky old uncle. Mark E. Smith, the idiosyncratic lyricist from the most belligerently anti-pop pop band of the past 20 years, curmudgeonly sneering at the whole music circus cruising past him.

Tim's two key bands both approached pop from totally different angles – the Fall have retained a loyal following with their bass-driven, often catchy as hell, and always witty and abrasive near-pop shots; New Order, of course, were the shiny pop beast that dominated the 1980s. One of the first bands to see the creative power in marrying electro to post punk, they also brought along a minor-key pop sensibility to their crafted pop singles that sounds like smooth machines contrasting neatly with vocalist Bernard Sumner's almost frail human voice.

Inspired by Barney's idiosyncratic guitar playing Burgess attempted to learn how to play like his hero, asking a bass-playing uncle if he would give him lessons, but typically his impatient mind got the better of him and he fucked the guitar off. It was only natural for an ebullient, music-loving fast kid like him to become a singer; it was the easiest way that he could be in a band.

For Burgess the music fanatic there was still heaps of other records to get into. 'I used to go to record fairs and buy records. Stuff like Small Faces mainly because of the sleeves! And then I got hooked on to the music. I loved the Jam and the Clash because of the energy. There's been Marvin Gaye,' he told the *Melody Maker*, adding, 'and Isaac Hayes and the Who. I always really liked the Fall, then Steve got me into Primal Scream, Joy Division and the Byrds – all brilliant, and then the late Beatles, it was great seeing where the Jam were influenced after reading about them in books.'

He fed his vinyl addiction at the local record shop Omega Records, hanging around the counter for hours on end checking out the new sounds; unwittingly it was the best career move that he ever made.

Andy Woods recalls the kid sticking around the shop that he used to work in. 'Tim used to come in on Saturdays and hang around the counter. I knew Tim's name from being around town and stuff, he was always about.'

Burgess was giving himself a massive musical education. 'I was into loads of stuff, just finding out about guitar bands . . . and then I got into the house thing.'

Acid house was the first big generational shift in the music scene for the whole of the 1980s. For kids like Tim it was the chance to get into a scene that was for them. 'House music is the greatest thing that's happened in my lifetime, musicwise. It opened people's eyes to feeling cool, feeling incredible, feeling great about going to discos again.'

This was a great musical education.

But there was still some rocking and rolling to be done. Some Iggy shapes to be thrown onstage by Burgess as he hooked up with local rockers, the Electric Crayons.

GIMME, GIMME, SHOCK TREATMENT!

Some mates were putting a covers' band together called the Electric Crayons; it was a bit of a laugh and they need a singer. Tim had that weird thing about him, that look, that goofy likeability, and he was also the sort of person who didn't mind making a fool of himself, perfect singer material. The band did Iggy Pop songs like 'Cold Metal' (a rollicking late-period Iggy solo track from his 1988 *Instinct*) and a bunch of Zeppelin tunes, and Tim would shout them out, giving it the full-on Iggy thing on stage, all strutting, stomping and energetic frontman bit, the opposite of the de-energised 1990s Britpop style.

Northwich is 40 miles south of Manchester and is typical of the small-town England that harbours most rock & roll fantasies until the town's prime movers make the big city break. But festering in these environments sometimes are the coolest and most active pop scenes. A couple of determined shakers can electrify the local teens into some severe pop action. Northwich was such a place and as the years rolled by Manchester's influence was getting stronger and stronger.

The indie scene there fitted firmly into the northern indie feel of no bullshit outsiders' rock; most of the hip kids in the town were checking out the leading edge of pop and rock and forming their own bands.

In the mid to late 1980s there was a strong alterative scene. Joolz Mclarnon had her own band Candy Darling and played a couple of gigs with the Electric Crayons. 'We did two shows with them. We were like the Velvet Underground of Northwich whilst they were like the Stooges of the scene. Their singer would go mad on the stage throwing himself around everywhere, just like Iggy Pop really.'

The young singer was, of course, none other than Tim Burgess copping his stage act from one of the best rock & roll performers of all time, Iggy Pop. Iggy, who had fronted the seminal late 1960s outfit, the Stooges, was the proto punk; with the Stooges he virtually invented three-chord fuzzed-up nihilistic rock & roll. Their three albums still sound as vital today as when they were released – primal rock & roll has never sounded so good, and they have been the touchstone and the key influence on generations of bands, even quiet, shy kids from small markettowns in Cheshire.

Iggy also pioneered the totally wigged-out stage persona, taking Jagger and Morrison and cranking them to infinity. Rolling round on the stage smeared in peanut butter and cutting himself with glass was just another day out for the Ig, and even though his act has been toned down over the years he remains a consummate performer.

This sort of crazed behaviour terrified rock critics in the 1960s who were too stoned or too smug or too full of hippie shit to dig it, but it has touched the nerve of generations of desperadoes since then.

Truth to tell Tim was always maybe too nice to be one of the real rock & roll madmen that he dug. It takes a particular sort of desperation to become Iggy Pop, a special sort of insanity. Tim was too English, too small-town, and anyway he had his own curious charisma to work on.

'Tim was very quiet offstage,' remembers Joolz, 'but onstage he was really manic, running around, ripping his shirt off.'

This impression of Tim the wildman on stage is borne out by everyone who saw the band. Andy Woods checked out the Crayons, 'I saw the Electric Crayons at the Northwich Vics club and Tim was into doing a lot of jumping around.'

Burgess also had a sex appeal thing going. 'There were always loads of girls following him around. At his school he was considered a really big sex symbol although I can't see why!' Joolz laughs. She remembers him hanging around in Northwich. 'He was funny and he'd hang around with the morbid, cardigan-wearing indie alternative crowd!'

In the makeshift, do-it-yourself scene, most of the gigs were at the Northwich Vics club, the club that was part of the Alliance Premier club's ground and one of the two non-league football clubs in the town, the other being Witton Albion, the club that Burgess claimed to have gone and watched and which also had a social club where the bands went and played.

The other band on the scene was the Mystic Deckchairs, formed by Nick Hewitt, whose brother now plays drums in Placebo. It was a tight-knit scene, a get up and go, make something out of living in a small-town scenario.

So tight-knit was it that the drummer with Candy Darling, Alex went on to join the Electric Crayons when Joolz's band split up. Joolz was, as ever, one of the main instigators in the local scene. 'We would put our own shows on at the football clubs or go to the Hanging Gate pub. The two shows we did with the Electric Crayons we headlined, mainly because we booked them and designed the posters. No one was really that big, we were both playing to a load of mates,' recalls Joolz, who went on to front Peel faves, the Thrush Puppies.

Tim was big mates with Steve Harrison and Steve was managing the Charlatans. When they went to see them Tim was blown away. He noted the powerful Hammond governing the music; it made them sound different, it gave them an edge, and it made them stick out from the heaps of also-ran bands.

The one thing that they did lack, Burgess noted, was a frontman. 'I thought the singer was poor,' he told the music press years later.

The Electric Crayon's only single, 'Hip Shake Junkie', was released by Oxford label Emergency Records. The record has come in for a bit of a bashing in certain circles but is in fact a pretty cool shot of rock & roll.

Maybe the production is a tad flat. The record was recorded at Amazon Studios in Liverpool when it was out in Kirby, and Swallow Studios. The band can play pretty well, and they churn out a garagy rush of excitement. The A-side, 'Hip Shake Junkie', is driven by a frenetic splintering guitar shape, that squeals small-town Stooges. The flipside, 'Happy To Be Hated', with its 'happy to be hated, happy to be backdated' chorus is Burgess the town outsider cocking a snoot at the then crummy modern times and singing in that nasally whiny voice he makes work really well. The song hooks on a riff that hints at the track 'Slates' by the Fall, and builds and falls on a driving garage band dynamic. The vocals are strong and, especially on 'Hip Shake Junkie', it's great to hear Burgess almost snarl with a hint of snotty, just out of teen anger whilst detailing some junkie business.

He sounds very assured and confident, and this is a cool record, a record that if it wasn't for Tim's future fame would be lost in the mist of time like so many great underground records.

The Electric Crayons eventually notched up some posthumous notoriety when the band's mugshot was featured in a pisstake in the *NME*. It showed the group pouting at the camera, two longhairs and two quiffheads, one with a short sharp quiff and one with a luxuriant mop of hair quiffed up, ferocious diggers and a spotty billowing shirt. The latter was Tim Burgess, looking more like a Stray Cat than a nouveau mop top.

Burgess, though, was already casting his net wider. Maybe he hadn't gone for the Inspiral Carpets audition but Harrison was now coercing him into the Charlatans. It was a move that would have dynamic effects on all involved.

1989
'Come Together'
The Classic Line-up At Last!

THE TIMES THEY ARE A CHANGING

Whilst the formative Charlatans were struggling with their line-up, a pop war was raging all around them. 1988 going into 1989 was a time when pop was thrilling, wrestled from the hands of the music business and placed firmly at the feet of the punters.

This was the high-water mark of the Madchester baggy scene and as the months thundered on great records seemed to fly out – the Roses, Mondays, Inspirals and 808 State were buzzing. The local home-coming gig in Manchester was suddenly the massive GMex, number 1 albums were becoming what was expected, and the new flash pop millionaires were all over town. The goalposts had been more than moved – they had been stolen.

You could feel the horror of the music biz as this out of control beast of northern boys (and it was a boy's scene) seemed to have mastered the rudiments of three-minute pop.

Finally the fear of being labelled copyist was chucked out the window. If you liked Hendrix you copped the riff and then sniggered about it, there was none of the old skool way of nicking tunes and passing it off as your own genius. The new bands were cut-and-paste guides to great pop. It was a formula that would eventually serve Noel Gallagher very well when the curator of British pop got Oasis off the ground.

RIGHT PACE AT THE RIGHT TIME

The 1989 Roses small club tour has now taken its place as one of *the* legendary pop tours, and people mutter darkly about how they were there. In half-empty halls across the UK a legend was looming, the supa-cool Mancs were on the crest of a wave. One night in Manchester they would play to 1,000 people at the International 1 and the next they would be staring out at 20 hardy souls at Brighton's Richmond pub. It didn't seem like the whole of the UK was getting this thing, although it was catching on fast; word of mouth was powering this phenomenon along.

House had totally affected the music scene, and bands either reacted against or went with the dance craze. Groups associated with the Manchester music scene seemed far easier with the form. Some, like the Stone Roses, talked the talk, walked the walk, and loosened up their look.

Musically the band that came closest to incorporating a house flavour were the Happy Mondays whose wonky weirdness and interest in chemicals was perfect fodder for the new style; that, and the 4 beats to the bar bass drum copped from house records and the sequencing which crept into their work were the closest that anyone came to being a full-on Manc house band.

Bands like the Charlatans, meanwhile, mentioned house music in passing, some members of the band danced to it and there was a mutual interest in the associated rock & roll lifestyle of hedonism that the dance scene waved the flag for. But the group's music was firmly traditional with, perhaps, only Jon Brookes' drumming – a loose approximation of the Reni shuffle, which in turn is a loose approximation of the genius drumming of James Brown's Clyde Stubblefield, the man who invented the 'Funky Drummer' beat and is, arguably, the best and most influential drummer of all time – being the closest they got to the nu indie dance swing.

Mind you, with the bassman rooted deep into mod music there was already a natural nod to the dancefloor in their sound. The Charlatans always scored heavily there by just playing what they had set out to do in the first place.

Those who were about to join the Charlatans were more aware of the culture wars raging around them. The core three members certainly were nodding towards the action but it was Tim Burgess, being younger than his band members, who made the deepest lunge into the new music, and his knowledge of contemporary street styles was crucial. It stopped the Charlatans from being just another band and allowed them to slot perfectly into the moment.

And in pop, the moment is all.

AND THEN THERE WAS FIVE

The Charlatans wanted another guitar player. They had decided on their new hip young Stone Roses style communicator for vocalist but decided to get their guitar player sorted out first; the singer was going to have to carry the whole thing and didn't need to be hampered by a guitar.

They didn't have to look far. Yet again, it was a case of searching through the ranks of the local bands and asking around in the bars and clubs of the Black Country – someone was bound to turn up. One night in Walsall Martin Blunt bumped into a face he vaguely knew and asked him if he wanted to join. Initially the guitar player pointed out another player to him but it was only a matter of weeks later in that July of 1989 that Jon Baker would be asked into the group and accept.

Jon Baker had been playing guitar for a few years in garage bands around the Midlands. His roots, though, stretch a lot further back into the late 1970s when he was first totally fired by music, becoming a pre-teen second-wave punk in his home town of Chuckery in Walsall. 'Next door there was this guy whose elder brother was four years older and he was really into punk rock in the late 1970s and from that I got into punk when I was about 11, listening to his records.'

A couple of years later and Baker was one of those little ragbag punks hanging outside the Virgin Records shop in Birmingham City centre, a hangout for the multi-coloured fallout from the last wave of punk action. 'I had bondage trousers, crazy hair the lot . . . my mother went mad!' he laughs.

Buying up records like X-Ray Spex and all the whole heap of multi-coloured vinyl punk singles that seemed to shoot out every week he was caught up in the carefree abandon of the energised music form.

'I was really into stuff like Slaughter And The Dogs, especially their single "Where Have All The Bootboys Gone",' he reminisces, remembering the Manchester band that was one of the prime influences on the Stone Roses and their classic raw ultra violence record that should have made them far better known . . . but didn't.

Baker got to know a lot of people on the Brummie punk scene and hung out in all the places where the city centre punks would idle away time in the early 1980s. Places like the Indoor Market and the Oasis shopping centre, the loose abandon of mad clothes shops, secondhand gear stores, used-record shops, beat-up old cafes . . . every freak in town was there. The hardcore punks with their mohawks and battered gear, and the sharp and viscous skins, all hanging out with nothing better to do.

It was great fun.

'The indoor market was a great place, there were all these record shops downstairs and weird rubber shops and sex shops upstairs where the punks bought their plastic trousers,' he says.

The punk scene in the Midlands, though, wasn't as strict on its rules and regulations as in other places and, like the north of England, there was plenty of cross-pollination going on, and different musics were getting mixed in with the thrash guitar form.

'In the Midlands there was a big two-tone and northern soul scene, punks, skins and rude boys. It was a weird mixture, the punks would go to northern soul discos and check all that stuff out. It wasn't a narrow-minded scene,' Baker recalls.

Punk affected the whole country in different ways. In London it was a super hip art-school driven scene, cranked with pure speed and with a beady eye fixed tight on fashion. In Manchester it was, of course, deliberately the opposite, being low-key and dressed in secondhand gear, the music was experimental, non flash and curmudgeonly, and it threw up defiantly individualistic bands like the Fall, Joy Division and the Buzzcocks – the foundation bands of the eventual baggy scene. In Liverpool it was lively, colourful and freaky, reacting against the conservative vibe of the city. But in Birmingham it was a multi-racial, multi-ethnic mix, a melting pot of different styles and different musics. The Midlands polyglot resulted in the 2-Tone scene, Dexy's Midnight Runners, UB40 and the Beat – bands that were fusing punk with soul, ska, dub, reggae, soca and a whole heap of styles bought up in cheap secondhand shops. It gave the area a musical mix that has been ignored as more fashionable cities have placed themselves higher up the fashion rollcall for the last 20 years.

Attempting to articulate his new musical love, Baker started playing guitar when he was 13; his mother had given him a cheap battered instrument with a dreadful action that was barely playable. Not surprisingly he packed it in pretty fast even though he had been keen enough to take some lessons. When he was 17 he started again, and this time taught himself to play.

When he had mastered the instrument he formed a band called the Violet Slides, and having expanded his music base from punk, was bringing in a whole host of new influences. The Violet Slides were a garage-influenced band that got most of their riffs off the classic series of *Pebbles* albums, a series of releases culling the great lost 1960s garage bands from the US who all wrote one brilliant song each in their quest to copy the Stones or the Beatles.

This garage scene was big enough to fill pub venues in the mid 1980s, pubs that it still fills now; one of those great unsung scenes that the mainstream media will always ignore but provides a great grounding place for many musicians.

'We played quite a few gigs,' says Baker. 'We even got banned from quite a few places. I remember this guy used to organise one of those battle of the bands competitions and all the bands that entered were always these really poncy sort of groups, and it was always rigged. There was no way that we could win, they always looked on us as this horrible rough sort of scally band!'

The band was in existence for a year and a half, the classic teen garage band, an excuse for a doss, a bit of action before real life got in the way and fucked everything up.

'We were a serious band but we used to have a laugh. We would play, get pissed and cop off. I ended up booking gigs at the Overstrand in Walsall where the Charlatans line-up with me in it eventually played its first-ever gig. I booked the Violet Slides in there and then just carried on booking other bands in there. I became the venue booker.'

By 1986-1987 the Violet Slides had fallen apart. But Baker, although still booking the bands at the Overstrand, wanted to go on playing so he got a new band together, the fantastically named Liquid Egg Box. 'We were still playing garage sort of stuff. I still had the keyboard player from the Violet Slides and some new members. The drummer played stand-up drums, just a tom and a snare. We played a few gigs around Birmingham and we even played a couple of supports up in Manchester supporting the Poison Girls.'

Liquid Egg Box even went as far as making a demo. One of the tracks they recorded was a cover of 'Ain't No Friend Of Mine' and Baker got it played over the Thursday indie night at the Overstrand, a bit of self publicity that would have a profound effect on his life.

Over the weeks he had got to 'vaguely know' Martin Blunt who used to hang out at the club as well.

'One night he asked me who was doing the cover of the song because he liked it. The conversation just went from there and he said, "We're after a guitarist, would you be interested?" I told him that I wasn't interested as I was doing all right with Liquid Egg Box but I gave him the phone number of this other guitarist that I knew who was available, and they rang him up and he went and had two or three rehearsals with them.'

In one of those quirks of fate it turned out that the bloke who Baker had sent down to rehearse with the Charlatans didn't really have much of a clue how to play and not surprisingly it didn't work out.

'So they rang me again and I went down and filled in for him. Tim wasn't in the band at the time, there was just the four of us. Tim had been approached but he hadn't come down for his audition yet. After that first meeting, I went down again a couple of weeks later and we started jamming, that's how we really wrote stuff. There was always a lot of jamming, or Rob or Martin would come in with something that was the verse of the chorus and we would jam it out or groove along from there.'

With Baker now in the group all they had to do was slot in the new young vocalist and then they would be ready to take on the world!

TIM BURGESS JOINS

In late 1988 the Baz Ketley Charlatans and the Electric Crayons had played together at a gig in Northwich which would have catalytic results for the frontmen of both bands.

The Charlatans had told the local press that there were several labels interested in signing them and plugged a local show at Northwich Vics club on Friday 30 September; tickets were a quid in advance and two on the door, cheap local entertainment for a town with a surplus of teenagers that always made sure the venues were packed.

By now the band was building a bit of a following in the Cheshire town. There had been a time when only ten people had turned up to see them at the memorial hall but Harrison's relentless plugging of the group had built up a good local fanbase, including Tim Burgess, who even went as far as joining the band on backing vocals for the encore, in a step across the line that can hardly have harmed his future prospects with the band.

Tim couldn't have missed the Charlatans playing around his hometown, a music nut he hardly missed anything. 'I used to go and watch them play gigs. One day I said to the manager that they were good, but I thought that I could do better. Not singing wise but as a frontperson, if you know what I mean. I thought they were lacking in something, and not blowing my own trumpet, that something was like, me!'

The band at the time were a bit nonplussed. 'They thought I was a bit of an idiot,' he guffaws.

He told the *NME* that he walked up to them in a pub and said, 'You're in that shit band called the Chaplins, aren't you?'

The Charlatan he accosted hit back with, 'Yeah, you're that dickhead that comes to see us.'

'And so we gave the dickhead a chance,' they laughed.

'To be honest I always thought that Tim would be good singing for the Charlatans,' confides Steve Harrison. 'No disrespect to Baz, but I thought that Tim was a great frontman and just needed a strong unit behind him. He couldn't do it on his own, just like the Charlatans couldn't do it without him.'

Four weeks after the Electric Crayons had split up Tim Burgess was at a loose end hanging around at the end of Steve's shop counter, and he was asked into the Charlatans. Harrison remembers, 'Tim was always interested in what Martin was up to. He had seen Makin' Time a couple of times and he had seen the Charlatans. I reckon he thought that he would have been good fronting them. He definitely knew that he should be a singer by then.'

The band had been auditioning other people and thought that they had found a replacement but after Tim's first try out with the band it was pretty damn obvious that their future was there right under their noses.

Tim went down to the rehearsal room in Walsall. Imagine what it must have been like for the younger Burgess to walk into the room with this fully formed band who had been on the road proper; these guys hadn't just played a handful of youth club gigs, they were like pro musicians. One of them, the moody bassplayer, had made two appraised albums and nearly made it, the surly keyboard player could obviously play a bit, and they had played gigs with the Roses. They had been there and done it, and they were older than Burgess. It must have been intimidating, but instead of being overawed, Tim went the other way and started off with his Iggy thing, throwing himself around the room like a maniac, posing like a rock & roll demon and totally forgetting his singing, which didn't sound right at all.

Jon Baker, himself fresh to the band, remembers Tim's first time in the rehearsal room with the group. 'Tim came down and he was like this hyperactive skinhead. Steve Harrison walked in and said, "This is Tim from Northwich," and he went off running around all over the place. We thought,

"Who's this mad fucker from up north?!" But he soon calmed down and fitted in.'

The Charlatans, used to more sedate things, were a bit taken aback. They had seen Tim do his thing with Electric Crayons but they didn't realise he was going to do it here as well. They stopped playing and Martin, being the band's closest thing to a leader, explained to Tim that if he calmed down and got on with just singing then it just might suit the band better. The new standing around Tim grooved with the band; it clicked and he was in.

Not that it was ever going to be any other way, the guy was a natural.

The first rehearsal was obviously a bit flaky but Harrison knew that this was going to work.

'I remember we went to Rob's wedding and talked about it there. I had the idea in my head. It seemed so obvious to get him in the band. Tim couldn't do it on his own. He needed a great band. Tim expressed a desire to sing for them and the group was aware of him.'

The addition of Tim to the band was a master stroke. The chassis of the band was a solid powerful group, intense in their love for the music, but they were hardly the most outgoing of people. Burgess was the spark that put the life into the band. Outgoing and extroverted, he was the perfect frontman and added a flash of colour to the pallid Midlander's outfit.

They rehearsed in the heat of August 1989, a month when pop was changing fast, a month when the Roses were rocking Blackpool's Empress Ballroom in a gig that marked the shift towards the sort of pop that the Charlatans had been in love with since they picked up their instruments. After initial worries the rehearsals clicked pretty well.

Still on good terms with the band, Baz Ketley came down to help the band through some of his parts of the songs. Jon Baker initially felt a tad uncomfortable about this, 'After a couple of rehearsals we had most of the stuff worked out and some new songs but there were some of the old guitar parts that I couldn't work out, so Baz came down to show me how to play them. At first I wasn't sure how I felt about that, it must have been really weird for him, but he seemed quite nice really, but I never really got to know him.'

Baz remembers helping the band through some of the old tunes. 'I was still in touch with them. We didn't split up on bad terms. When Tim joined I went to some of their practises to talk them through the songs.'

At first, obviously, they were short of material and were still playing through some of their old tunes, as Baz recalls, 'There were some crossover songs . . . They were still using some of my old songs. I taught the guitar parts to Jon Baker and Tim, the vocals.'

Some of the Ketley songs that they kept on were 'Hey Teen', which was on the original line-up's third demo and was one of the first songs that the band started to get attention for, even getting it played in the Manchester City centre indie club Legends and mentioned in the club's top 10 local tracks (number 4 in DJ Russ's Legends nightclub playlist; Legends was a long-running indie night in Manchester and was absolutely stuffed full of Manchester music).

There was even mention of a 'Hey Teen' t-shirt, which was placed number 8 in a local record shop t-shirt chart; mind you, it was Steve's shop in Northwich!

'My Shell' was another old tune that survived the initial cull, along with the one song that Ketley didn't write but had jammed out with the rest of the band, and it eventually made it on to the band's debut album, '109'. But apart from that the band were working on new material fast and furiously.

The first song they wrote together was 'Flower', and it was really clicking, the old hands and the new members knowing that they were on to something really good. Once the feeling is there a band takes flight, and the new Charlatans felt that they were away.

Steve Harrison could feel the good vibes coming from the Northwich rehearsal rooms. 'They were rehearsing every night and writing a lot of songs. When they had written "Indian Rope", which was one of the first things they came up with, I knew that they were on their way and when they came up with "Sproston Green" I knew that they were definitely going to be a classic band; that song was the turning point for me.'

Jon Baker could feel the band coming together in that first month. 'After a few weeks I thought, "This is sounding all right". It definitely had a direction and a focus. I remember Steve Harrison listening to the tunes with a big smile on his face, and thinking that we must be getting this right now. One of the first things we wrote was "Flower" which I think is a good song to this day.'

The band was churning out songs, and wrote as many as four in one day. They worked hard because they could see that there was an opportunity to make this thing work, that there was a space for their band; even Martin hunched over his instrument, carving out the backbone basslines, was beginning to feel optimistic.

They were hot and inspired, and summer passed away into autumn and the whole of the northwest basked in a euphoric pop glow. The right audience was there, and it was time that the band started to move towards them. It wasn't something that they were going to avoid – Harrison was guiding them towards a crowd that by right could easily be theirs; they had the connections and now they had tunes. After all, they had been playing this sort of stuff for years and now they had a hip young singer who was totally in tune with the times to go with it. This was the main chance and Harrison wasn't going to miss it.

'There was an element of association there, of course,' admits Steve, 'with their supports with the Roses they already had a toehold on the scene and being based here in Northwich, there definitely was a feeling that we were involved.'

Revved up and with a complete set of new songs, it was time to go back out on the circuit, no fancy big-time supports here, just back out on the bog circuit dipping a toe in, testing out the waters.

EARLY RUMBLINGS

In August *Hit The Bar* fanzine from Blackpool were the first-ever magazine to put the band into print, pretending that they had seen the band play a gig in Manchester that they called 'the private liggers event in Manchester', describing them as 'a modern-day Chocolate Watch Band' (a great US lost garage freak band from the late 1960s); the zine review also claimed that Tim was 'very very arrogant' as the singer declared, 'The Charlatans are necessary and necessary is something that you can't do without' – Burgess was already a champ at turning out quotes that both made total sense and no sense at all.

Tim was also asked how big he thought the Charlatans would become. 'We'll probably be the third-biggest band in the world,' he oddly claimed. The zine asked who the other two must be. 'I don't fuckin' know but they must be good!' he replied.

And as a concession to the then pop mode of t-shirts being more important than the songs, he elaborated, 'We were the sort of group that had our own t-shirts way before we had our own records.'

It was the sort of baffling talk that would make the young singer a press staple.

There was an uncertainty to where the band's sound was going. Harrison told a local paper, 'The new Charlatans will still have a swirling organ sound, but there will be more of a groove to it. We want people to dance to the Charlatans, not just bounce.'

It was an off the cuff comment but 'not just bounce' would become one of the band's catchphrases on their press releases for the next few months.

The first gig they played fronted by Tim and with Jon was a headliner at Walsall Overstrand on Tuesday 29 August 1989. It was hardly the most glamorous of beginnings – the entrance fee was a massive £1.50, but it gave them some breathing space to get things together. They were back on Baker's stomping ground at the venue that he had been the booker for.

The accompanying flyer showed a picture of the band lurking down a back alley in true garage band style. Brookes with that floppy curtain haircut combed to perfection and Burgess looking like a snotty-nosed kid, and the rest of the band hunched down glaring at the camera, looking a moody bunch of fuckers like some sort of Italian mod street gangsters from *Mean Streets*, all scowls and leather quarter-coats (no longer uncomfortably stood there in crap clothes), hair bristling in mop-top confusion, arms folded like a bunch of layabouts caught unawares by the camera. The band were at last looking cool in their shots – like a group that believed in itself.

In Walsall they told the local press that they were big in Manchester, the sort of white lie that would do them no harm, tying them in as it did with pop's hottest scene.

The gig clicked and the band were now in gear. That crucial first gig over, they were bursting with confidence. Steve Harrison videoed it but has since lost the videotape; well, that's what he claims anyway!

'There was hardly anyone there but it gave them the chance to get things together,' he says.

What few people did turn up had mainly come to check out Jon Baker and his hot new band from the north. Baker was on his home turf in Walsall and quite a large segment of the crowd came to the show because they knew him and the bands that he had played around the town in before.

'It was weird,' he says, 'because people had been used to seeing me in previous bands freaking out onstage. Before the Charlatans I used to leap around a lot more. It wasn't a conscious decision as much as that was the style of the music I was then playing. Now it was more just grooving along and standing there, more of a studied way of playing, I suppose. It was the same with Tim, who would wobble around when he wasn't singing.'

They then played Winnington Rec on Friday 1 September, a gig put on by the Transworld Consortium, the drinking and bowls club of the local ICI Factory. The Rec looms large in the town's small rock & roll history. 'Every local band plays there and there is always an enthusiastic crowd of kids who really want to go for it,' explains fan Wayne, who went to quite a few gigs in the area at the time.

On Tuesday 5 September the Charlatans played at Dudley JB's, promoted as 'contemporary psychedelics'. The legendary JB's was a venue that nearly every band that has ever played more than ten gigs around the UK has played at. Support was from Hollow Sunday, a vaguely-tipped Manchester band.

The local rag instructed anyone interested in finding out any more information about what the band were up to to contact Tim if they saw him wandering around town.

'He won't be hard to find in his 24-inch flares and Kickers,' they cackled, noting that the singer was now wont to dress to the hilt in the full new Manc baggy regalia.

During October the band recorded a demo at the Lanes End Studio, including 'Indian Rope', 'You Can Talk To Me' and 'White Shirt'. The same month they put together their first demo tape culling tracks from their studio forays . . . the photocopied sleeve was a smudged shot of the band from the Ancoats (an area in Manchester) back-alley session with a big 'October '89' slapped underneath. Inside there were three songs, the recently recorded 'Indian Rope' and 'White Shirt' as well as 'Chose Time', and they were typical demo fare. You can definitely hear the band's patented keyboard swell in full force on the songs but there is an uncertainty to the sound; the songs sound slower and the production is too clean, with that sort of shimmering guitar, tinny sound that groups like the Teardrop Explodes were peddling at the back end of the 1970s Mersey thing. But despite this the songs are strong enough and the melodies are well in place, pointing to a band that's got more than just a mere chance of getting out of the local band circuit.

This was the demo that was going to be the band's calling card to the local music business, and Harrison readied himself to pushing the tape.

In January 1990 they would record another demo, as Jon Baker recounts, '"Polar Bear" is one of the original songs, "Sonic" and "Only One I Know". I'm not sure which demo these are all on, but I remember we recorded the first demo at Lanes End Studio in Shropshire at this farm in the middle of nowhere. The guy who ran the studio was the farmer who owned the land and he produced the demo as well. It was his hobby. I'd completely forgotten about this demo and then one day years later I was playing in my band after the Charlatans in Gravesend and this bloke appeared out of the blue and asked me to autograph the tape, I don't know where the fuck he got it from!'

There was also another demo recorded at Cottage Studios in Macclesfield, but no one seems to be able to remember exactly what went on there!

On Saturday 21 October, for £2.50, the Charlatans played live at the Oakley Centre in Crewe, again put on by the Transworld Consortium. Punters were promised that it would be more than just a show, 'a happening', this meant support bands would be dispensed with and DJs would be used instead, playing 'rave music and 1960s music'. The band were claiming to fuse their Hammond pop with contemporary dance styles, everywhere you looked bands were taking a bit of acid house for themselves. The rave scene had blown the rock scene apart and everyone was trying to react to it. Pop kids wanted to dance now; tired of being earnest about their pop, they wanted to move around and react at the gigs. Bands were having to sink or swim, and although few ever actually sounded very acid house at all (still being far too traditionally rooted to make that jump); they adopted a sort of shuffle beat borrowed from Reni from the Stone Roses who was borrowing from the master himself, James Brown's aforementioned drummer Clyde Stubblefield. It would be the beat that dominated most of the period's guitar pop releases and one that Jon Brookes had no qualms about using.

Typically of the times, with a psychedelic hue across the music scene, the band announced a series of gigs with a full-on trippy light show and a DJ playing house records between the different groups' sets of the night. During the 1980s most small-time gigs had been defined by crap PAs and a shit cassette of Queen's greatest hits slapped on by the grumpy soundman. There was no effort at making a show and the bands just didn't seem to care; the very idea of a show was total anathema to the generation of bands still sulking about the failure of the punk revolution.

But acid house's near demolition of the live circuit had caused a rethink and for a nation of teens and 20-year-olds like the bands new singer gigs were going to have to be vibed up again to make them work.

If just months earlier the band had maybe felt that they were at the end of a scene and were busy describing themselves as a 'modern-day Chocolate Watch Band' and were planning on some sort of cult status plying ancient freak beat grooves, now they suddenly found themselves in a bright new world full of fellow revellers. If there wasn't going to be a revival of guitar psychedelia then acid house was going to have to do.

Ironically enough acid house kick-started the psychedelic revival that the band had been dreaming of. Far from killing rock & roll, it gave it the impulse to explode and survive throughout the 1990s.

In the meantime the Charlatans were still on the local circuit, gigging out the tailend of 1989, keeping a sharp eye on the massively expanding music scene and tightening the group up on the small-town circuit, biding their time, waiting for the breakthrough.

A following was building up, much of it down to their manager's non-stop verbal promotion of the band. Steve Harrison had been plugging the band heavily from his Northwich shop, and the manager's great enthusiasm and hard work for the band impressed Jon Baker. 'He was ramming the band down people's necks. He created a vibe and would sell loads of tickets for all the local gigs. I remember the gig in Crewe. It was a really hot night and really packed. There were loads of people there from Northwich who had started to follow the band around, people who would come into the record shop and Steve would bore them shitless with talk about the Charlatans! He would also be on to the record companies and loads of them came to see us but none of them was really biting the cherry.'

The Harrison build-up, coupled with great gigs and a buzzing word-of-mouth hotline, was taking effect. The band was now riding high on the latest twist in pop's tale – the coachloads of fans phenomenon. For years any band that brought a coach of fans with it was guaranteed to be a crap local act in the big city with a pubload of boorish mates laughing at their crap beer-stained onstage jokes, but now bands like the Charlatans were pulling in the baggied-up new generation in packed buses, delirious good-time kids who just wanted to dance.

People were supporting groups like football teams, and terrace lads were coming over to pop, bringing their lifestyle with them. Where, in the 1980s, indie pop had been a student preserve the Roses and the Mondays had opened it up for the council estates, and the bands were now attracting a mixture of football fans and indie waifs to their shows and these fans brought their own culture with them. Indie music shifted from being a middle-class preserve to being across the board and the 1990s would see the two cultures become further assimilated with football-style merchandise for groups, and musicians looking like football players and sports stars looking like rock & rollers.

The Charlatans had learned their lessons from the new leaders. They were affected by acid house like all Manchester bands although they didn't play music that was remotely house at all; the drummer copped a few funky beats and glued it to their 1960s-fused pop. It made perfect sense. Their trademark sound was that fat Hammond played with a vicious twist by the excellently moody Rob Collins, and their trump card was Tim Burgess, the first singer of all the new bands who was almost the same age as his audience.

Mid November saw the release of the Happy Mondays *Rave On* EP and the Stone Roses single 'Fool's Gold' (perhaps the greatest release from the whole pop period and the pinnacle of the so-called 'baggy' scene, defining the sounds emanating from Britain's rehearsal room's for the next couple of years as bands tried to emulate Reni's superb drumming mashed into that hypnotic breakbeat, John Squire's wah guitar and Ian Brown's stoned drawl). The two releases represented the peak of the Manchester music boom and that night in late November when they both played on *Top Of The Pops* was as good as it ever got; it was a piece of classic pop TV. The Roses moved their operation up a gear with a show at London's Alexandra Palace, drawing in 7000 people, a feat unheard of for a band in the 1980s that was connected to the so-called 'indie scene'.

On 2 December the *NME* was almost virtually dedicated to the northern scene with its 'Manchester, So Much To Answer For' edition, paraphrasing Morrissey and celebrating the nu skool. The Charlatans, though, didn't get a mention; they were just another struggling local band outside London at the time – the clock was ticking away, there was no time to be wasted.

For the Hammond-pumping band fronted by the scruffy kid in flares all this big-time hussle seemed a long long way off. But there was some local press looming on the horizon. One of the first reviews that they got was on 8 November in Manchester's *City Life*, a snooty put-down of the demo: 'What a dreary derivative effort this. Sub Inspirals, nearly the Stone Roses, reminiscent of everyone around, and no one in particular. They even throw in bits of Pink Floyd and the Doors, with that oh so fashionable organ sound and petulant vocal. Stop rifling your record collections, make your mind up and do it.'

Despite this initial Mancunian snub, the band was slowly moving away from its Midlands origins and was gradually becoming more Manc-based. It was inevitable as they were already playing the same sort of music from the same sort of roots and now with their hip singer they could easily be passed off as a band connected with the scene that was beginning to totally dominate the British pop scene.

'It wasn't a conscious decision,' remembers Jon Baker, 'the band was gradually becoming more based in Northwich with Tim and Steve, and Tim had the flares! When any scene appears it kicks open the doors and loads of groups appear afterwards.'

On 9 December they played their first gig in the pop mecca of Manchester, the city that they were going to have to really break if this whole thing was going to make any sense. At the legendary Boardwalk, supporting Cactus World News, armed with their coachloads of local fans, they succeeded in humbling the headliners by rocking the place and then leaving the venue virtually empty when the coaches took their fans back to the Midlands.

By now the band was cooking. 'Indian Rope' was the highlight of the gig and had hit single stamped all over it. The band were already shaping up to be something special.

Was it Tim and his hip connection to the modern pulse and the fan who understood just what makes great rock & roll through his massive record connection; was it Jon Brookes' shit-tight drumming which had just enough of a roll on it to make the band eminently danceable; was it Rob Collins and his great Hammond playing, coating the songs in the special magic of that instrument; was it Jon Baker's garage guitar, or was it Martin Blunt's powerful intensity hunched over his bass, like he was going to explode, one part pure rubberband finger-snapping basslines and one part exuding the same sort of caged animal power with which JJ Burnel had propelled the Stranglers with in their heyday that was giving the Charlatans their edge?

Or was it these disparate characters, a collision between introvert and extrovert, just combusting? One thing for sure was that this band was more than just lightweight pop, and bands like Cactus World News were waking up to the new truth.

'There were about ten people left in there for Cactus World News,' remembers fan Sue, who was at the show.

Steve Harrison vaguely recalls the gig: 'We played Manchester Boardwalk supporting someone but I can't for the life of me remember who that was. It might have been someone like Cactus World News. All I remember is that most of the crowd left after we played!'

The gig was also attended by Chris Nagle, one of the main local producers with a fistful of credits to his name. Nagle had started off doing sound with 10CC and had been a key player behind the legendary Martin Hannett sound, and he had been the engineer on some of the key Manchester releases post punk (his stamp can be heard on stuff like Joy Division), and to get him to work with the band would be quite a coup.

Chris Nagle spoke to the urgent young manager at the tail end of 1989. 'Steve phoned up with a tape and brought it over, it was a live gig with stuff like "Sproston Green" and "Indian Rope" on it. I thought it was reet poppy! I then went down to a rehearsal to check them out and then to the gig. I really liked the songs and we decided to get down to the studio to record the first single.'

The Manchester Boardwalk gig also saw them get their first-ever national press from Mike Noon in the *Melody Maker*, who was actually pretty favourable, which was unusual, as you would expect him to be at the band's throat like the irascible terrier that he was in his writing days. He claimed that the Charlatans were 'typical of the scally bands in that they were the revenge of the C86 crew so roundly reviled in the recent past', and went on to say that they 'were so enthusiastic and happy that bands of their ilk were becoming a positive tonic to the thousands of miserable bastard bands we've had to endure in the past few years'.

He caught the feeling that indie music was so into a whingy doldrum that something had to break. Right now the bigger Manchester bands were taking so-called indie into the mainstream, and for good or bad there was to be no more glorying in the underground. This was the time when the culture was to become everyone's, guitar music was back and the dullard bands who had been holding the torch in their clammy guilty hands like Simple Minds and Big Country were going to have to move over as the new generation set out its stall.

The crowd at the Boardwalk, mainly bussed in on the cut-price transport arranged by Steve Harrison, went down the front, an event unusual enough at local band nights to warrant a mention in Mike Noon's review. Local band supports are usually a lonely hell, a smattering of mates makes a drunk noise as the band struggles through the gloomy evening. It's a buzz getting to play a bigger club but it can also be a strangely empty experience. The Charlatans, though, had come with an agenda: they were determined to be part of the Manchester explosion, a music scene that they felt a strong affinity for, and this Boardwalk gig was the scouting mission. Next time they would return and they would really go out hell for leather to capture the hearts of the big city scene.

The band was now getting serious and it was becoming more and more plain that this was something that could go full time, so obvious in fact that band members were getting marching orders from their day jobs.

Jon Baker was one of the first to get his papers. 'Initially I was allowed a lot of time off, but in the end it was like I was having months off and eventually I got sacked from my job working for the council; it was about the same time as Jon Brookes got the sack as well.'

On 15 December the Charlatans played a second show at Winnington Rec, a gig which quickly sold out.

The 'Indian Rope' single that they were recording with Chris Nagle was nearly ready now and the machinery was falling into place to put the band into the A stream. An international t-shirt deal was signed with Mobile T Shirts, and a 20-date nationwide tour was booked. Piccadilly Records in Manchester compiled their top 10 buzz chart for the *Manchester Evening News* and mentioned 'Indian Rope'.

Bizarrely enough the next piece of proper national press the band got was in the *Sun* on 28 December, which had a 'five bands to watch from Manchester' list, and featured the Charlatans, along with the Inspiral Carpets (already doing pretty well, thank you very much), Stop Laughing (never heard of them), Social Kaos and Hollow Sunday. The *NME* was yet to mention the band and here they were in the sodding *Sun*!

With things moving fast on the national scene, it hadn't taken long for a manager as astute as Steve Harrison to realise that it was time to capitalise on the band's potentially very hip situation by getting some vinyl out. Hence the phonecall to Chris Nagle and the band recording their debut single after only a handful of months.

The demos had proved that the band certainly had the studio thing together, they had a producer in Nagle and they could feel the time slipping by almost daily, so it was time to get things together.

It was decided to get a 12-inch out on Harrison's newly christened Dead Dead Good Records before Christmas, but the band weren't interested in being a purely indie band.

'We've got no faith in the indie scene; they didn't want to know when we started. We had to put our own records out,' explained Tim Burgess.

Steve Harrison packaged up the band's second demo with a swiftly copied local press kit and a sharp shot of the band looking skinny and mean. This time it was for real; the plan was to return to the Boardwalk in the New Year and ride the buzz created in Manchester, hit all the scenemakers, journalists, and crazed animals that hung around on the new northern rock & roll party scene, pack the venue out with their fans and these music biz hustlers, and then just light the fuse. Now Steve just needed someone on the inside to help him out with the necessary contacts.

THE DEMO HITS HOME

After years in the wilderness, the Charlatans began at last to make the right connections: the demo was hitting targets.

Harrison mailed one off to the pop page of the big local mass-circulation *Manchester Evening News*, whose pop writer Sarah Champion was a then 18-year-old writer who had already written a book on the Manchester scene and certainly knew her shit. If the band could get on this page, the hallowed Friday evening pop column, then maybe the ball would start rolling.

Sarah liked the tape and passed it on to her friend Alison Martin, with whom she had started a press promotion company called Scam (the name Scam fortuitously came about from the pair's initials). This was exactly the important connection that Harrison was looking for.

A hard-working face locally, Alison Martin had been on the fringes of the Manchester music scene for years. At one point she had been the host of the local BBC show that played all that sort of late-night stuff that usually gets bagged as John Peel music in local radiospeak. The show ran for a few years before it was dropped. By then Alison was running her own radio promotion company, dealing specifically in regional radio and taking on the accounts of several London-based labels. She liked the Charlatans' tape and set up a meeting with Steve Harrison at her office at 23 New Mount Street.

That address means a lot in Manc music folklore. It's a converted mill that has housed the offices of most of the local entrepreneurs over the years – the Inspiral Carpets' mini empire was based there, with Noel Gallagher always lurking around the strange-smelling corridors avoiding any heavy work. Simon Moran, the biggest concert promoter in the UK is in there still, and Brian Cannon, the Oasis and Verve artwork man, was based there for years. It was a complex of home studios, rave promoters, DJs, bands, magazines, etc. in a rabbit warren of offices. It was into this hive of activity in the heart of the booming Manchester music scene that Steve Harrison walked.

It was an important and yet informal meeting.

Alison was asked to do the radio for the band, and then their press as well, even though that wasn't really her department, although after a few years in the music business you have contacts everywhere. She took 120 copies of 'Indian Rope' and mailed them off to the usual suspects, like Radio One, Key 103 (the local Manchester radio people), James Brown at the *NME* (who later found fame as the editor of *loaded*) and Bob Stanley at the *Melody Maker*, as well as *City Life* and Sarah Champion at the *Manchester Evening News*.

Whilst the records were in the post, Steve went back to see Alison, this time with Tim.

'I remember the first time I met Tim, he had the biggest pair of flares on that I have ever seen in my life,' laughs Alison, adding, 'I thought, "Oh my god, those trousers are amazing."'

By now, Tim was the genuine Manchester popster. He had the bowl cut, the flares, the beads, the bagginess – as a youth culture vulture he knew exactly the look and the walk, but he didn't come with the overbearing arrogance of his big-city contemporaries.

'He was really quiet and seemed really shy at the time,' remembers someone from Alison's office.

This was the way that young Tim was too when *Sounds* interviewed him: 'Steve Harrison told me that he wanted to be in on the interview and look after Tim in case he dried up or said the wrong thing but despite being quite shy he was pretty cool,' says the journalist.

The second time that Tim visited New Mount Street, he had just been involved in a terrible car crash and had vowed to never drive again.

By then the music had hit its targets and the buzz on the band was building. John Peel loved the stuff and had booked the band for a session.

'We were surprised that John liked the stuff,' explains Alison, who knows John Peel and has actually helped him to catalogue his legendary huge record collection. 'He didn't seem to like most of the Manchester stuff. I guess it was a bit too mainstream for the sort of thing that he played on his show.'

The session was surprising indeed when you consider that Peel has never played the Stone Roses; but maybe that's because of the rumour that someone working for the Roses had stuffed a £50 note into the record that he got sent in a clumsy attempt at bribing the least bribable DJ in the world; if so, it was something that rubbed Peel up the wrong way, and the most influential band of the generation missed out on his cult radio play.

INDIAN ROPE

'Indian Rope' was a typical first single, recorded low-budget, in a rush. It was a case of pulling in favours from Chris Nagle, the Stockport-based producer blagging downtime at his local Strawberry Studios.

The track was recorded in an all-night session and mixed in another hectic coffee-fuelled all-nighter. Not satisfied with the mix, Nagle managed to squeeze another night session out of Harrison's tight budget, 'just to get the mixing done right'.

The red-eye night sessions are dreaded by most people but are the perfect climate for the likes of Chris Nagle, who seems to have super-human powers when it comes to sleep and how to avoid it.

'Indian Rope' was a fine debut for a band that had been together for only a few months. It played to the band's main strengths: that oozing Hammond, pumping bassline and insidious vocal melody.

The record was pressed up for three grand, an impressive outlay for a new band in an always uncertain pop scene. But even if Harrison was nervous he had an inkling that his belief in the band was about to be matched, as after all he hadn't managed a record shop for nothing and he hadn't been a long-term music head without understanding just what made a good group.

Single recorded and pressed, and money doshed out, the risk had been taken, hopefully now the groundswell of support was going to kick off big enough to carry the band through. It didn't take the shrewdest pundit to work out that here was a band that the Manchester thing was begging for; the big bands had gone supa nova and there was a definite space for some new action. Was there anyone out there who dared to take the challenge and follow the lead of the most important street rock & roll bands since punk?

Geographically almost there, musically great in their own right and cool enough to fit in with the pop zeitgeist, 'Indian Rope' was going to put the Charlatans on the map. The only thing now was to get the damned thing released at the right time.

With the recording done and dusted in November and the usual six-week turnaround in getting the thing pressed up and ready for release pushing the release date into late December, it was decided to wait instead for the first few weeks of the new decade. The Christmas rush buries bands and the New Year is traditionally the time when the music business starts looking for new acts.

And now it wasn't only a new year but a new decade, a new dawning. The 1980s music scene had been buried sonically, and now that the 1990s were dawning, a new pantheon of pop heroes were called for. The question was whether the Charlatans had the talent to pull off this most audacious of moves.

1990
Teenshag Supastar . . .
The Explosive Rise

HOLD YOUR BREAATH, HERE COMES THE LANDSLIDE!

'What we are into basically is non-league football and left-wing anarchism,' memorably quipped Tim Burgess in early 1990, buzzing on the band's growing success.

It must be great making it in a band. After all that arsing about and rampant uncertainty, those touch and go gigs, penniless years, freezing cold vans and nonplussed audiences. Suddenly fashion comes right your way and with a few minor adjustments you're there.

Pop's a dirty game and there are plenty of broken hearts.

Talent can have little to do with success – timing is all. The Charlatans are a great band but there are other as great pop bands that struggled through the mean shit-haul of the 1980s to mass indifference before splintering apart before attention came their way. Pop's a bastard and fashion is the whip-master. A few months one way or the other and you're dead meat; you've got to seize the opportunity and get through, and any band that escapes the pigswill of the struggle has a combination of utter luck and talent.

The Charlatans could effortlessly write pop songs, we know that. But a lot of their success has to be laid down at the determination of Martin Blunt to survive all the way through the 1980s; it takes a tough bastard to survive on the shit circuit . . . take it from one who knows.

In late 1989 with a charismatic singer grafted on to the band, they could see the window of opportunity getting cranked wider and wider open, so they took their chance and jumped right in. So fucking what if they weren't exactly from Manchester – who cares? By 1990 Manchester stretched all the way down to the Midlands anyway!

As the new decade rolled into gear the world was a different place. The arse end of 1989 had seen the grey, quite definitely not rock & roll fake Communists of Eastern Europe thrown out by people power, and the pop equivalent was kicking off in the UK.

The Charlatans entered the new decade sitting pretty. They had a great single under raps, a readymade crowd of fans who had their own surrogate Manchester band to cheer and a large audience just a release date away.

January was spent hustling the big city. They had the hinterlands under their control, that sweep of towns that falls away from Manchester: Crewe, Northwich, and on into the tops of the Black Country, towns that were now well and truly under the cultural swing of Manchester.

The Charlatans must have needed some nerves here as one fuck-up at this point could have seen the whole project fall flat on its face. They knew they were good, but then so did countless naff local bands who were talking it like the Roses but walking it like a bunch of flabby-arsed morons allowed out of the rock & roll playpen to molest the frankly naive public of the time.

Steve Harrison targeted the local media with a mailshot. It hit the letterboxes across the city, a bolshy handout plugging the upcoming Boardwalk gig, the moment when the band would be launched properly.

The city's pop phonelines were buzzing. Unbeknown to those outside the so called 'scene' most people in Manchester were pretty keen for anyone to come in and 'cash in' there; the more bands the merrier, the more great pop music to wallow in.

First, though, the Charlatans had their debut national headlining tour to go out on, playing a series of dates through January and early February in the small backroom 'toilet' venues of the UK.

On 10 January they started with the Wheatsheaf in Stoke. Stoke is one weird town, in fact it is more like six weird towns pretending to be a big city. Stoke itself isn't even the main centre of the conglomeration. Hanley is the real centre. The Wheatsheaf is in Stoke proper, which is a two-road town where the streets seem to be totally deserted when night comes down. With the University round the corner all is not lost though with a few daring students making the dash across town to the venue. The fact that the Wheatsheaf had managed to survive says something about the tenacity of the owners.

The Charlatans arrived as a local band from just up the road, representatives of this new-fangled flared-pant scene that was stretching the fabric of the pants of the yoof. They were promoted again as the Stone Roses favourite support band; it was getting pretty obvious which horse they were riding into town.

Support came from, fashionably, a couple of DJs, the Introspective DJs Buck and Daz Willet, 'to complement the band's deep house sound' the publicity blurbed, although there was very little evidence of this deep house sound on the stage when the Charlatans got up there, just streamlined shit-tight northern pop that was surfed with keen tunes and a knowing knack for squeezing some excitement out of a trad form.

The gig was sold out and when you started selling out the likes of Stoke then there is definitely something going on.

If the rest of the country was baggied up and dancing, in Sheffield things were a tad more sullen. At the city's Take Two club the crowd (who formed the biggest queue outside the venue that the club's management had ever seen) sat on the floor looking bored and waited for quirky locals Blammo to finish their set (rooted deeper into the weirder Bogshed end of C86; Blammo were never going to make it in the middle of the baggy scene).

When the Charlatans came on, though, the place went mad – it was the same old story across the whole country. This was getting too damned easy.

There was some excitement in the camp as a few days before the *NME* had given them a tiny mention on their On page, claiming that the band that had supported the Roses had a debut single soon, 'Indian Rope', a mix of Stone Roses/Inspirals with a great looping organ sound and dreamy moods; hot on the heels of a mention in a *Sounds* playlist it seemed like the press were starting to take notice of the band. The question now was how to puff this up.

A few days after the Sheffield gig on 13 January *Melody Maker*'s Bob Stanley did the first national press review of the Charlatans, published in an umbrella feature on the Manchester scene looking at the second wave bands tipped to follow through in the footsteps of the big two. Bob was the paper's main champion of the pop cause and had been hip to the Manchester thing from the start, popping up at all the key moments. He was even in Wolverhampton for the Stone Roses' trial; he seemed to be everywhere, and eventually he put his own band together – Saint Etienne.

His piece buzzed excitedly about the band and was accompanied by a shot of the band taken near Manchester's Piccadilly station.

Burgess told Bob that the first scally band were the Beatles and that he was into a lot of Creation bands like Primal Scream and the Bodines. He was also quoted at the time as being into Ashley And Jackson, the smooth Hull-based dance team, Public Image's superb mental breakdown of a tune 'Annalisa', and the ever present Fall's mental 'And There In' – it was impeccable taste but as weird as ever! Tim spoke to Bob Stanley about other press-hyped musical movements. 'But C86 was just a combined nightmare, wasn't it? Is this scallydelic thing going to get like that?' he muttered, wondering whether the current rising bands getting lumped together could prove to be their downfall, as in past media-fuelled pop movements.

C86 itself was the fabricated movement created up by the media in, er, 1986, grouping together an unlikely bunch of independent groups and trying to make a scene from them. John Peel affectionately labelled the whole scene 'shambling' and stymied a whole bunch of bands in the process. Bands as diverse as the angular thrusting A Witness, the underrated mental scuzz pop of Bogshed, the neo love psychedelic pop of Primal Scream and the fuzzbox crunched pop of the Shop Assistants were lumped together, and then destroyed. None of the bands really had an opportunity to flower.

Tim's fear now was that the whole so called 'scallydelic' thing (a term made up as a joke by a spiky northern music journalist) was going to go the same way, with unrelated bands claiming to be a movement and shot down by a bored music press waiting for the next thing to happen.

Tim wasn't that comfortable with the term scally anyway. 'If you go to Warrington you get called a scally for not having a wash. It's such a nonentity word isn't it? No one really knows what it means.'

Bob Stanley thought that 'Indian Rope' barely 'caught the energy of their live performance, but let's be fair, it is their first single', whilst Tim believed that it 'creates a bit of a swirl, doesn't it?'

It was now official – the Charlatans were no longer a small-town band looking for an escape route; they were part of the second wave!

On 19 January James Brown from the *NME* reviewed 'Indian Rope' on the singles page, digging the track. 'It's as refreshingly long as it is laid back,' he snarled, adding, 'an excellent first single.' He claimed in his typical way that 'Indian Rope' has lashings of eerie organ, trippy vocals and a charisma that'll have the James Taylor Quartet cowering behind their Hammond and Shaun Ryder trembling in his purple moccasins – 'the ones he'll only wear inside his flat'.

That same week the effortlessly cool Cathi Unsworth, usually a lover of darker and weirder stuff, gave them a really good review in *Sounds*, writing that 'anything that starts with a fully overblown hammy organ riposte then glides swan-like into sweetly vacuous vocals can only be another contender in the bands of the 1990s takes; they do it with such gauche, high-spirited humour they have to be commended.'

With across the board reviews like this the Charlatans were striking on all bases. There was definitely something going on here and a crossover appeal was discernible.

At the same time there was a small piece in *Sounds*, when yours truly went down to Northwich and interviewed a child-like waif with a big gob stuffed full of quotes and a nervous manager who sat there hoping his charge wouldn't put his foot in his mouth and say something daft. Meeting them upstairs in the old Omega shop it was a great interview; Burgess wouldn't stop talking, shyness masked with an affable confidence.

'To be honest I'd rather dance than sing, or just play tambourine solos. Sometimes I can't be arsed to sing,' spoke Tim, giving good copy from the start.

When I asked if he was going to lose some of his live Ian Brownisms he replied, 'No point wasting yer time dues playing. It was nerves . . . I didn't dare sing any louder.'

At about this juncture Penny Anderson gave the band their first interview in the *NME*. In that piece they claimed, 'People use the 1960s sound because it's so rich. We can't remember it, we can't remember punk, so we aren't harking back . . . it isn't a retro thing with us.' They asserted, putting their finger on what is a phenomenon of the times, the fact that pop is now so old means that retro was no longer a valid term. For a 16-year-old kid getting into rock & roll in the late 1980s the Doors, Hendrix and the Beatles were as new as what was going on at the time. They were no longer judged on being something from the tangible past; the drawback of this was that in the 1990s certain groups have been given 'classic' status, and the bands that are mercilessly copied and ripped off has been narrowed down to this holy list.

Armed to the teeth with some neat press and a packed tour weaving round the country the band were now ready for their assault on Manchester.

UNDER THE BOARDWALK

Perhaps the gig of the period and the one that was the point where the band went from small to big time was their second Boardwalk gig on 25 January. This was the band's chance to really break Manchester, their adopted pop city. If they could pull this one off they would no longer be the outsiders looking in but central to a scene that was already running away at an incredible speed.

The Boardwalk was legendary. Not that the band thought so, as for some reason they had a downer on the venue and refused to let Granada TV film them outside!

The Boardwalk, though, already had its place assured in the legend of Manchester. This was where the Happy Mondays and a whole host of other key players in the Manc thing had rehearsed, and the venue upstairs was the launching pad of many a career. For the Charlatans this was an important night when they were going to get right to the heart of the Manchester experience and they weren't taking any chances.

The concert saw a rave review in *Sounds*, claiming that 'all the hallmarks of the acid casual scene hang heavily on the band but that they have their own twist'. Acid casual was another phrase launched by northern pop journalists taking the piss, it would eventually end up being the title of a critically acclaimed late 1990s novel by Nicholas Blincoe. The piece was accompanied by a picture of Tim in full flow, spazz dancing on the stage, flapping his trousers and staring vacantly in the air. Tim had obviously been studying the Manchester thing and was decked in massive flares, a neatly chiselled pudding-bowl haircut and baggy top, but he carried it off, looking like a fresh-faced kid with the future in his youthfully arrogant swagger. He looked the part, the Madchester boy come home, and the band had the tunes. They looked like they were heading for the breakthrough.

The Charlatans were champs even before they hit the stage that night but they kept their cool and the experience of years of playing shitty venues to two-bob audiences paid off as they kept it tight and hard. They came on the stage to a tape of the Peddlars' 1965 number 50 song 'Let The Sunshine In'.

Steve Harrison, by now sporting flares and rarely spotted without his Man city top, looks back on the gig with a smile. 'It was totally horrendous weather that night and it was still packed. I remember that most of the A & R people that were going to come up and check the band out couldn't make it because of the weather. About the only one who managed to come was Martin Mills of Beggars Banquet who would eventually sign the band up.'

The A & R were up to their usual tricks, as Steve laughs, 'We had to cancel one gig in Aylesbury, the venue had been smashed up in a fight the night before, and one A & R man rang up and said that he saw us there and didn't like the gig that much, apparently he thought that we were a "bit average"!'

The Boardwalk show was packed, the marauding fans that had served the Charlatans well in the small towns were bussed in and made the venerable old venue a sweltering hot-house. Local bands were giving them the once-over – the unlikely figure of Mark E. Smith from Tim's idols the Fall skulked in the back corner, and naturally he hated it.

The heaving venue went wild when the band hit the stage, the Hammond filling the venue. It took a few songs for them to hit their stride, as their nerves were wired taut for this show, the most important of their career so far. Half expecting to be chased from the stage for beating most of the Mancs at their own game, they were warmly surprised to see the city embrace them as their own.

This time they had returned to Manchester and taken the city. It was the important moment that the Charlatans were recognised as prime contenders, the next in line for the baggy conveyor belt. With the single due in days, everything was falling into place.

The band's first national headlining tour continued snaking around the country. The next night they were at Warrington's Legends (supported by the Honey Turtles, a Midlands-based outfit originally called the Mock Turtles who had to change their name so that they wouldn't be confused with the Manchester band), and the story here was typical of the tour: a packed venue with fans queuing round the block. The buzz was increasing, a few rave press reviews had stoked the fire, and the ready-made audience was coming out to check the band.

'Indian Rope' singles were mailed out to all local music scene personalities and pundits. Terry Christian picked up on them in the *Manchester Evening News'* The Word pop column, a column named after the chaotic pop show that he presented on Channel 4. He was lukewarm: 'They've got all the latest Joe Bloggs gear. A few offensive fringes and debut 12-inch on the streets from Monday.'

Manchester was buzzing about the Charlatans but what about London?

When they hit the capital and played what's looked on by their fans as one of their greatest ever gigs at the now defunct Powerhaus with DJ support from Alex from the Orb, Ian McGregor, recently employed by *Melody Maker* as their teen baggy writer, reviewed the gig, noting that the crowd was 'seriously baggy – baggy hair, baggy clothes, baggy dancing. Lots of hooded sweatshirts and voluminous jeans in Kickers/Wallabees and those hats.'

Where most bands have to spend a long time toiling the fleapit venues in London for bog-all money (just like Martin Blunt had already done c/o Makin' Time) the Charlatans had fortunately bypassed all this palava.

The Powerhaus was packed; the coachloads from the North and the Midlands had seen to that. London was still stunned by the extent of the northern fans' commitment to their bands; the groups were commanding football-style followings, wearing their own baggied-up approximation of acid house gear. The Charlatans' fans were kids who wanted a Stone Roses of their own; years younger than the Manchester uber lords fanbase, the baggy generation had already split into two.

The single had been grabbing the Charlatans plenty of local media interest. They appeared on the Granada TV arts guide *The New* and on a local radio station KFM on 25 February where the DJ, Jon Slater, played 'Sonic' and 'Polar Bear', the tracks' first airings from the freshly recorded demo. The music business was already pricking its ears, and the Powerhaus gig was packed with A & R media, and the Charlatans delivered brilliantly, although some people were already a tad sceptical about the band, feeling that they were too perfect and that their name was maybe a little too apt.

Chris Hunt, reviewing in *Record Mirror*, pointed out, 'This may be the great rock & roll rave swindle but good luck to him, Kickers 'n all!'

The London crowd chanted 'Manchester La La La' and knew all the new moves. The *Melody Maker* noted that the band 'ooze arrogance but with a smile'.

James Brown from the *NME* was now totally on the band's case, sensing that of all the second-wave bands the Charlatans were going to be the champs. He raved, 'This is clear drug music minus the narcissism or drudgery, powered by an energy, adoration and mutual excitement.'

The Charlatans weren't messing around, this band was shit tight – the rhythm section with its bounce derived from listening to classic soul records and that hard-assed driving bass. Baker had the licks that gave the band its trippy flavour and Collins' cornerstone Hammond gave the band its total flavour; the Hammond makes the Charlatans stand out from their contemporaries, giving them power, melody and funkiness.

But Collins wasn't only involved in the organ as he also supplied the band's backing vocals, and his gliding, soft voice makes a classic backing vocal, packing in the ache and the melody that is crucial to the harmony.

All Burgess had to be was the star, a job he was born for.

The tape of Fifth Dimension's 'Age Of Aquarius' that the band were using as their intro tape faded out and a young Tim Burgess oozing confidence walked on to the Powerhaus stage.

'We're the Charlatans, probably the best band you'll ever see,' he quipped. In 1990 if you weren't armed with this sort of ridiculous self belief then no one was going to take any notice of you!

Not that anyone had told the DJ that this bunch of scruffs in their streetwear, who didn't look like your traditional indie band (at this time dreary indie bands were dressing in a disastrous combination of long shorts and shitty backward baseball caps), was a band.

'The venue told the bouncers to get the idiots off the stage,' chuckled Jon Baker, 'it turned out that the idiots were us.'

After the set the Orb DJed, much to the delight of the band. But although it was a great night not everything about the big smoke was to the taste of the band, as Tim moaned, 'The thing about London is I always come back with a headache and a blocked-up nose!'

Country boy!

On 9 February they played Stafford Polytechnic back in the heartland of their support. 'Indian Rope', now out, was at number 4 in the local charts provided by Lotus records in Stoke. At the same time it was number 2 in the national indie charts, tucked in behind Ride whose 'Chelsea Girl' EP was number 1.

Working hard at building up the local following, the next day the band played the Citadel in St Helens, one of the key local hinterland gigs. This is the sort of venue where legends are made, a meat and potatoes gig in a backwater rugby league town. Neither Liverpool or Manchester, St Helens is a surprisingly big place just up the road from Northwich. The Citadel was a venue that treated its bands well, supported by Out Of England and the Overground, the gig was £2.50 to get in. The local paper had the Charlatans tagged as a 'wildly original scally bunch' and made a meal out of their status as the Stone Roses' favourite support band. The Citadel's own promotional blurb had the band down as 'deep house with psychedelic undertones'; this deep house thing was begging to stick.

Bizarre.

On the night the gig was packed. The word was spreading, the new pop generation were looking for new heroes to add to the new baggy pantheon, and the Charlatans were making all the right moves. Many were locked out but members of the band let fans in through the window round the back – shades of punk super heroes the Clash and their innate understanding of the loyal fan!

The near hysteria of the gig saw fans climbing fire escapes in a desperate attempt to check out the new hot action.

A couple of weeks later the Charlatans played at the Crown and Cushion in Bolton, another venue that has been sporadically booking cool bands for years. It seemed like no town near Manchester was going to be safe from the band who, buoyant from their Boardwalk victory, were setting about consolidating on their success. A 100 tickets were sold in advance and a full house expected. It was another victory for the band buoyed up by some rave reviews of their showcase Manchester show.

Cramming out the packed shows on the toilet circuit the Charlatans were proving that they weren't just a press hype but a band that was prepared to prove that they could cut it on the frontline. The packed gigs were tantamount to their rapport with the audience, and the word was already out that this was more than just a late unexpected arrival on the Manchester scene – this was a seriously cool band of its own making.

At the Duchess Of York show in Leeds James Brown from the *NME* caught the band, and particularly its frontman, in gloriously upbeat form. In the upstairs dressing room caked with posters from gigs past and the windows where you can watch the crowd pour in, Tim was holding court.

'We're too young to be looking backwards,' he sneered at his detractors.

Whilst Tim was being wild and daft, smart and dumb, as a frontman, it was natural that it should be bassman Martin Blunt who was banging things back down to earth Black Country style. 'Big deal, everyone's been talking about the 1960s since 1970!'

This criticism has been hung on to every guitar band since 1970. Bands can't win, and anyway guitar, bass and drums is a classic songwriting format that wasn't invented in the 1960s; I think you'll find groups in the 1950s and way back beyond fooling around with that mode of expression. The 1960s get too much damned credit as it is.

Groups like the Charlatans may have roots in 1960s culture but there are heaps of sounds from the 1970s and 1980s who have influenced them as well, and in any case they were writing from a modern perspective, their songs sounded contemporary, and that's all that ever mattered anyway. Tim, of course, had a brilliantly dippy answer to that one. 'We are obsessed with going forward,' he grinned, 'if this is February's sound then we're looking forward to March's sound!'

The Charlatans, though, were a band that never were exactly avant garde, their forte was the power of pop, writing 3-minute inspirational rabble rousers, pop that gave you a huge rush. They may have roots in the 1960s ethic, one that has dominated 1990s pop, the beat band style that has become the hallmark of British pop; many argue that the Beatles' *Revolver* is the high-water mark of British pop, and for many bands this sad fact is true.

To the Charlatans' credit they have never sounded dated. They have always sounded of the now and they were always aware of where music was going and any contemporary styles that escaped the shackles, so 1960s pop has been allowed to flavour their basic beat group framework.

In an attempt to bring a shade of contemporary light to the proceedings Tim claimed that he was listening to De La Soul and he saw their upbeat daisy-age hip hop as an anecdote to the misery indie that occasionally dominated the scene. 'It's all right being full of teenage angst but at the moment everyone wants to have a good time, they're sick of pulling their hair out.'

He was favourable too about the so-called 'baggy' scene. 'This is the best movement and its all come out of the house scene. For the younger people something new has started. There's a lot of new bands doing well now. They've got their own space. The audience excite us. When they're responsive you respond back.'

For that tour when the band went onstage they entered to the Beatles wistful 'Across The Universe' ('they were like the first scally band, ha ha ha!' joked Burgess) and the Fifth Dimension's 'Age Of Aquarius', a bubbling piece of jolly cod psychedelia that heralded the new millennium age. It seemed a startlingly hopeful piece of music but one that caught the E-fuelled optimistic flavour of the times; the drugs were making everyone feel good and people really did believe that the 1990s was going to be a new era.

'Ecstasy's great, innit, it's a love drug,' explained Tim, 'but to be honest we're pretty drug free. We're fuelled by our own adrenalin. Macho? Nah, there's not much weightlifting goes on in our band, nothing athletical [sic].'

Despite the rush of success and the euphoric rise that they were enjoying hard practicalities were still having to be dealt with. Steve Harrison could see that the band were facing some difficulties. 'It's hard at the moment because the band are getting sacked from their jobs and when you do that you only get 12 quid a week. When you read the *NME* and everyone says nice things about you or you're getting offered nice meals by everyone it's hard to come to terms with the fact that you only earn £12 a week.'

Looking back on these dates a couple of years later the band was wont to romanticise this period of their lives.

'We played all the little attic gigs,' said Jon Brookes. 'Brilliant gigs – really shitty sound, but loads of people coming. That was the best time, that's when I enjoyed it the most. We were all on the dole, and at work and stuff, just gigging at night, getting in at four in the morning, always having the flu, cos you're never going to get any decent food, or getting warm. It's funny, you miss that part of it. I miss legging it from work half an hour early to jump in the van to go to Manchester to play a gig, now it's all organised – it takes a lot of the fun away.'

And it's true that this is the period that will always burn the brightest hole in any band's collective consciousness, the tight camaraderie and good times, as the pressure hasn't arrived and there's this monumental buzz as people just connect with what you're doing. You're still in control of your life and every day brings in some more excitement. It's an unbeatable buzz.

Already the band were feeling the pinch of being on a small label. The initial 1000-copy pressing was flying out, but they were finding it difficult to get more pressed up.

'With Dead Dead Good we don't really have the clout to kick the pressing plant into action when the shops are running out of copies,' explained Steve. 'So as the band do continue to get bigger they will have to sign to a better equipped label.'

By 1990 it was pretty clear that even while indie kids were buying into the music and the music was going mainstream there was absolutely no way that the record business could match the demand. It was one of the biggest ironies of the time, that finally after ten years of struggle the indie scene was going to be destroyed by its own success. Never again would purely indie labels seem like a real threat to the fat cat status quo.

1989 might have been the year that Manchester broke through, but 1990 introduced the second wave of bands to the scene. It was also the year it all started to get a bit silly. *i-D* magazine ran a big feature labelled the 'Scallydelic' (that word again – top tip, readers, when the going gets going, just make words up as you go along, and watch them catch on!) special: Northside, identity clothing, Joe Bloggs clothing (who along with the promoter Simon Moran were the real winner of this particular yoof quake, both of them going on to make a heap of moolah), even Leeds band the Bridewell Taxis (who packed a punch with a great horn section but also brought along a following more concerned with scrapping than love vibes, a following that effectively crushed their pretty good chance of making it); some people referred to it as the 'daisy age' after the De La Soul track – everyone was stoned and E was the vibe.

Strange daze indeed!

INDIAN ROPE

How many debut singles arrive sounding this fully formed, this ready?

The track, whose title could well have been making a reference to Martin Blunt's faves Brian Auger and Julie Driscoll's 'Indian Rope Man', a song that was massive on the scene, was a great opening shot. Coupled with 'You Can Talk To Me' and 'Who Wants To Know' this was a great first record.

The first of the so-called second wave of Manchester bands to get a single out, the Charlatans were leaving the likes of Northside and the Paris Angels at the starting block, as whilst both these bands were still finalising their deals, the Charlatans and their workaholic manager were getting their material out.

The single itself was nearly never released. In a premonition of the sort of ridiculous disasters that would come back to haunt the band the master tape was recorded at the wrong speed which fucked up the cut, then the cutting machine blew up, and finally the back-up DAT tape that had been sent down by a panicking management by Red Star from Stockport Station had a drop-out in the middle of 'Indian Rope'. But eventually the problems were solved and the single was ready.

They had to release it on their own label though as no one had been biting at their demos. The general opinion was that all the cream of the northern bands had been signed, sealed and delivered, that it was now down to only the runts of the litter. Experts felt that this was one bunch of chancers too many, and also that this group was too aptly named as well!

Jon Baker remembers the band being full of buoyant optimism nevertheless. 'We recorded "Indian Rope" by ourselves and I remember thinking that if no one signs us then there is something terribly wrong. But no one wanted to sign us; we could see that we had a chance of being massive but there was no one interested as yet . . .'

Of course everyone was nailing this as a Roses' rip off but comparisons like this always say more about the accuser than the accused. Thing only get compared to what the reviewer has heard of. And it was a lazy comparison – sure the band were operating in the huge space that the Roses had created, but Ian Brown's mob had never used a Hammond played with a deft and funky touch, and they were deep into a pop career where they just didn't deal with songs this simple and innocent any more. If there are similarities it was in dealing out highly melodic blasts of street pop with fey vocal lines, but apart from that, the Charlatans were already carving out their own musical space of which this record was a signpost.

Martin Blunt's bass typically sounded mean, and drove the song along with a huge hunger; Tim's breathless voice was the only acknowledgement to the scene overlords, but it was a melodic hushed whine perfect for the times. The vocal suited the song superbly. It's a northern thing – in a part of the country where men are men and a macho bravado is a way of life, it's odd how camply soft many of the era's pop singers sound. Maybe it's a chance to get in touch with a feminine side or just an opportunity to drop the tuff guard that makes a lot of this pop really work – walk it tuff and sing it soft – not that anyone ever accused Tim of being a macho figure!

It's a great vocal. Burgess sounds almost breathless with excitement as he charges through the track. It's always a rush making your first record and for someone like Burgess, imbued with optimism and lust for life, cutting the track must have been a blast. It wasn't the first time he had been in the studio singing but it was the most important. In *Melody Maker* Burgess scratched his head and wondered just what had made him want to become a singer in the first place, 'Well, I started off on the guitar and I wasn't very good at that. Then I went on to the bass guitar and I wasn't very good at that. Then I sang with a band and I wasn't very good at that either, but that was more aggressive and shouty. I didn't realise I could sing properly until I was told to. On "Indian Rope" I had 30 minutes to sing it. It was a last-minute state of panic thing. I have to concentrate . . . it's hard. But I get the feeling from everybody else and it comes through from that.'

The B side was the Strawberry Alarm Clock (fantastically named US

1960s acid-fused garage band) -influenced 'Who Wants To Know'. It was a hint of things to come, of a band that had captured the flavour of the times. In that return to traditional songwriting values, pop music was paying homage to the glory days of the 1960s but adding its own 1990s post-house swing to the mix. What was vital now was that you could dance to the 3-minute guitar rushes.

The record came in a sleeve which had a great shot of Brookes whacking his kit, it was a hair-flailing live shot that had a hint of the superb series of action shots that adorned all the US grunge label Subpop's covers. It gave the band a garage band feel, a certain classic rock & roll twist to their muse. The photos were taken by the band's road manager Dek.

The single itself cost three grand to make, money well spent and money that the band only just had.

'We had no backing,' remembers Jon Brookes, 'we just got all the money from gigs and sold the van. But we thought that we had got a certain following, and we thought that they would buy it – and they did. That was the best thing, cos we really did it on our own, and it went straight to number 1 in the indie charts. We prove that you don't need a massive record company, you just need someone to distribute your record.'

The Steve Harrison factor also played strong here as well.

'We were lucky – our manager was in the trade. That was probably a key point. He never put any pressure on people when he was dealing with distributors or his shops, but he'd say, "This is a record by a group I'm managing, check it out,"' says Brookes.

In the music biz contacts are worth a weight of gold, that's all any group ever gets by on. A manager is someone who either knows the right people or gets on the phone to them. The key to success is endless hustling; it's the only way to escape the ghetto.

Initially they pressed 1000 – for all their bluff northern confidence and Tim's boasting talk of them being the best band in the world, this was still the era when indie records would be doing well to sell out of that first pressing. The 1980s had dented pop confidence, and if you were hustling classic guitar pop then you had to be underground, as Martin discovered in his days with Makin' Time. Purists just didn't sell records; it was something between you and your fans. Sure the Roses and the Mondays were spiralling into the big league but they were way ahead of the pack. The Charlatans had a believe that in the future after a slow build-up their records may be big sellers, but for now it was a case of let's be sensible.

So it was some sort of shock when the record took off . . . almost instantly it was single of the week on Simon Mayo's Radio One *Breakfast Show*. The record moved so quickly that when the band were featured on *The Chart Show* they hadn't even got a video to give them! The programme had to use photos instead.

The single crashed into *The Chart Show*'s indie charts at number 1. Jon Brookes told *Select* of the total buzz he got the first time the band were on TV, 'I knew we had done well, but when they said it was number 1 I went fucking mad. I did a lap of honour around the front room.'

It's probably the greatest moment in any band's career, that split second when their first recognised record gets the break; the adrenaline rush is incredible.

Some reactions weren't quite as favourable. Terry Christian, finally reviewing the single after mentioning the band in recent columns, writing in the *Manchester Evening News*, felt that it wasn't the 'most exciting piece of vinyl' – but he went on to point out that the Roses' debut 'So Young' wasn't that exciting either and was now selling on the streets for up to 70 quid. Christian was supportive of the band but he was just worried that the single would set the band up for a kicking from the 'jealous' southern press. This was typical of the time when everyone was expecting some sort of mean backlash, Manchester had had it too good too long, and a year of ruling the pop roost meant that some asses were going to get kicked. And even if the Charlatans were really from the Midlands they were now perceived as a Manchester band.

The second wave of bands from any scene are the ones that usually cop the full blast of the backlash; thought of as bandwagon jumpers, they are ripe for a slagging. The Charlatans, themselves, at first were likely prime contenders for this. They could easily be seen as being too-generic bandwagon jumpers, but the band's innate strength, live power and pop talent was already too good to be that easily brushed aside.

Meantime Tim Burgess was shooting his mouth off in the press, claiming that the band's influences included 1960s psychedelic bands, and especially Pink Floyd with Syd Barrett and *The Piper At The Gates Of Dawn* album, mentioned in reverential tones. Tim also claimed that the Charlatans are 'the most danceable band in the planet – even a sheep can dance to us'.

And in 1990 there were plenty of sheep around to buy into this new pop phenomenon!

GIVE 'EM ENOUGH ROPE

The single was an instant indie and student disco floor-filler, nights like the Wednesday night at the Ritz in Manchester reacted cautiously, playing it early the first week, but the demand was so instant that the following week they were playing it as one of their main tunes. It was classy, catchy and dancy as hell, the perfect guitar pop single hitting on all requirements.

Brother Keith Curtis who ran the nights remembers how quickly the track took off. 'We played it a couple of weeks before it came out and everyone was asking what it was, and when it came out everyone was going for it. It quickly moved from being one of the early tracks on the night to one of the main anthems.'

It was that rush of pop success, it's the beauty of the form, that every now and then someone comes along and grabs the moment.

The Charlatans filmed the video for the single in a warehouse in Sandbach near Northwich. The shoot sparked more interest than they bargained for, as Martin remembers, 'The police turned up! They were just being nosy. It was getting filmed quite near a housing estate in Sandbach and there were a couple of massive searchlights, you know. It was all getting a bit loud. At about 11.30 three carloads of police turned up . . . I think they were a bit disappointed that there was nothing going on.'

The single entered the grown-up charts on 10 February 1990 at number 90 and the indie charts at number 11, behind the likes of the soon-forgotten Fatima Mansions, Birdland, Telescopes and Edsel Auctioneer, all about to be obliterated by the baggy pop revolution.

It was number 1 in the indie charts the following week, beating future compadres Ride's *Ride* EP into number 2 spot and the long-forgotten underrated Birdland to number 3.

If the music business was feeling a tad sceptical about the band, then the kids were entertaining no such thoughts.

The tour was packed. Where two months before they had been relying on coachloads of core fans to fill out venues, now they were a proper full-on pop success.

'I remember Steve ringing up all the time going on about the queues round the block at each venue,' remembers a colleague, 'He was excited. Totally excited.'

People were locked outside, the toilet venues that bog so many bands down in their ascendancy seemed to be getting by-passed fast by the band. It was a mental time, as Tim describes, 'We played a gig once when we had to get out the back door, but there were people waiting outside who got shut out of the gig and they just grabbed hold of us. There were around 35 people around each of us wanting autographs. The people inside were waiting for an encore but we couldn't get back through the door. They were pulling like mad at us. I got my sleeves ripped off. At the time it was a bit of an ordeal, but afterwards we thought it was great!'

This was a band that was genuinely enjoying the sometimes uncomfortable fruits of stardom.

At the gigs they were tailed by A & R. The music business, slow to take up on the 1989 Manchester phenomenon wasn't going to miss out this time.

When those Manchester bands first broke everyone was looking the other way. The Happy Mondays had always managed to grab some press action and had some very vocal champions but the Stone Roses had been virtually ignored. 1989 was when everything changed; acid house had happened without anyone's permission and the biggest pop culture explosion in the country had, apart from sensationalist tabloid headlines, been totally ignored by the music media and bizness. Nirvana were about to change the rock & roll landscape for ever, yet were sneered at for being too heavy metal by most journalists.

People had really missed out then and were now determined to make sure that whatever came next they were going to get a full slice of. This situation could only benefit the Charlatans, the best new band to come through.

In Manchester itself the venues were getting accustomed to the odd sight of droves of A & R men working the city looking for new bands to sign, Manchester *A-Zs* stuffed in their pockets, pissed up and looking lost.

Some A & R people were much hipper than others to what was going on. Perhaps the coolest person on the trail of the band was a young woman working at Warner Chappell Publishing called Sam Durant. Sam already had a cool reputation after signing Hole and others. She signed the bands' publishing.

No one to do with the band had expected success this quick. It's the toughest part of a band's career, getting off the ground and selling the first 5,000 singles, and in some ways getting up to 50,000 sales is far easier.

The Charlatans were now very much in demand. There were interviews for Manchester's biggest radio station Piccadilly/Key 103 to squeeze into hectic touring schedules, and Granada TV came over to the Warrington show to film the gig.

Talk was also turning, on the road, to what the next single was going to be. The band favoured 'Polar Bear', but people following them had other ideas. 'I was going to nearly all the northern shows then,' remembers Alison Martin, 'and although I really liked "Polar Bear" as a song, the one that made the crowd go mad was "The Only One I Know". We kept telling them that should be the single. Everyone loved that song and kept telling them to release it.'

Another sign that the band were turning into more than just a mere indie success was the launch of the first of many dedicated zines that have been built up around the group over the years.

'Me and my brother put together *Looking For The Orange One*,' remembers Andy Woods. 'We put an advert in the *NME*. The fanzine was 40p and we got sent loads of orders with two 20-pence pieces stuck together with Sellotape! The fanzine was mostly about the Charlatans but we'd have bits of other related stuff in as well. The first issue had 150 copies and then we went up to about 500 copies.'

They ran the fanzine for a couple of years until *109* took over. The fanzines were crucial to the band; all bands have them but the Charlatans have a whole plethora of informed zines around them, and they are quite unique in that they are given plenty of access to the band. Steve Harrison is always on the case, helping out with titbits of information and good tickets for the band's shows. The group, being music fanatics themselves, understand the relationship between the fans and the band; they know about being a fan.

MANCHESTER, THE SECOND WAVE

Following the A & R chequebook rush, the groups came thick and fast and many of them had legitimate claims to some sort of success. There was the High, the band formed by Andy Couzens, the ex guitar player from the Stone Roses, and managed by Howard Jones, the Roses' first manager. They plied a hooky guitar pop, a crash collision between the Monkees and Joy Division with a touch of the Flamin' Groovies, and went off to a great head start with a major label deal with London Records where they seemed to fade away into nothing.

The Paris Angels signed to Virgin and were always an underrated band, their single 'Perfume' was a great post-New Order slice of techno pop, and their album, although flawed, showed promise, but the backlash would crush them as it did the likes of Northside.

Northside seemed to appear from nowhere with a ready-made following of council estate kids. They sold out the Boardwalk and then signed to Factory. Within months they had scored a rash of hit singles (1990s 'Shall We Take A Trip', number 50; 'My Rising Star', number 32; and 1991's 'Take 5', number 40), and they released one album, *Chicken Rhythms*, before being made the scene scapegoats. They struggled on for years, lost souls abandoned by the great baggy crash of 1992.

The Mock Turtles scored a lightweight pop hit (1991's 'Can You Dig It', number 19) whilst the likes of Rig and M.V.I.T.A never got the chance to get going. The best bet for many pundits were World Of Twist and Intastella, who both came so close. Those two bands offered a glam pop escape route from the decidedly unglamorous baggy scenario. The former gave up after being dropped by their label after going so close ('The Storm', a classic lost record scraping the bottom end of the top 40 in 1990, whilst 'Sons Of The Stage', 'Sweets' and 'She's A Rainbow' were lesser hits in the following 18 months). World Of Twist were fronted by Tony Ogden whose charismatic showbiz stage persona and love of glammy pop must have been a direct influence on Pulp.

Fronted by Stella, Intastella were about the only band on the scene without a male monkey on the mic. They cut a series of fine records but are still looking for that elusive breakthrough hit (although 'Dream Some Paradise' and 'People' were minor hits in 1991).

When you look at this cool and varied bunch of bands charging out of the city and getting stopped in their tracks, it makes the Charlatans' success seem even more remarkable. Because success in pop is so damned difficult to achieve, the Charlatans may have been accused of being bandwagon jumpers, but all these bands proved that being on a happening scene was not enough – you needed more, so much more, to make a real go of it.

GIVE 'EM ENOUGH (INDIAN) ROPE

In May, with 'Indian Rope' still doing the business, the band played a special gig for Piccadilly Records at the International 1, the scene of many a Manchester act's breakout from the underground and on to the fringes of the mainstream.

The Charlatans that night were sheer pop stars, with Tim as the bragging pop idol incarnate. Tim Peacock, reviewing in *Sounds*, stated that even if the band didn't have a totally original sound they were still skilled enough to withstand any upcoming backlash.

Prophetic words, Peacock!

Penny Anderson noted in the *NME* the large number of girls down checking out the 'cute' singer, and the genuine surprise of the band at their sudden jump in popularity.

Piccadilly Records is the key indie record shop in Manchester. For years they have been the best cutting-edge shop in town. Combining sharp taste with a staff that aren't only friendly but seem to be knowledgeable and into the music with which they are dealing, this combination has guaranteed the success of the almost homely shop and seen off plenty of competitors over the years. They have also been a key support for many of the breaking Manchester acts, spreading the word to the Saturday kids who come into the store from all over the northwest.

The Charlatans returned the favour by playing a gig for the shop.

Again Bob Stanley was there, he was like a one-man campaign for the outfit at *Melody Maker*! He commented that Manchester's 'foxiest boys and girls were there' and dug the pre-show DJ action which played the likes of Soho, Jimi Hendrix and Augustus Pablo. (Such taste in those days!) When the gig kicked off, his attention turned to the Charlatans, noting that the bassline from 'White Shirt' was 'remarkably close to the Stone Roses' "She Bangs The Drums"' and getting all excited about the new single 'The Only One I Know'. With his pop antenna finely tuned, Bob reckoned that the chorus to the next release was very similar to the Byrds' 'Everybody's Been Burned'; he too liked an instrumental and the 'almost rockabilly' chug of 'Sonic'.

He finished by reckoning that the band had little in the way of innovation to offer but that their set was remarkably packed with hit singles, and being a believer in the power of pop, he was backing them to the hilt.

The show itself was further consolidation of the Charlatans' position in Manchester, packing out the now defunct International 1.

In a couple of weeks, at the 1400 capacity Ritz, the big old ex-music-hall on Whitworth Street, arguably the best venue in Manchester and a place where you really had to be getting the big-time vibe before you could seriously consider playing, the Charlatans' gig was filmed for Granada TV.

The next day they were off to play in Belfast where a wild crowd made up for them cancelling a *Top Of The Pops* appearance to be there.

Whilst the Roses willingly withdrew from the white heat of public pop service and seemed to be getting drawn into a free-fall, the Charlatans were everywhere, accessible and for the people. They had learned the 1990s pop way from the Roses but they had a workrate of their own. They had the same sort of rapport with their audience as the Roses plus the pop muscle to back it up.

All around, the style wars were raging as Manchester's infrastructure was getting rearranged. Joe Bloggs, the Manchester-based clothing house which was responsible for turning the whole dressing phenomenon into a dull mess, accurately announced that the were 'to fashion what McDonald's is to food', while Manchester police chief James Anderton, the so-called 'God's cop', who presided over the city with a fistful of arcane Victorian values, was on the Hacienda's case after drug-related deaths hit the headlines.

It was during Manchester's most rampantly hedonistic era that Anderton attempted to rule the city with an iron glove. Seemingly a law to himself he made his mark by raiding bars in the gay village and made his famous announcement about Aids victims 'drowning in a cesspit of their own making'. Already yesterday's man, his increasingly banal pandering to the press with his renta quote stupidity would eventually be his undoing, and his heavy-handed running of the police did little or nothing to stem the city's cultural flow.

Across the nation the new pop bagginess was having an effect. The Farm were *NME* single of the week with 'Stepping Stone', marrying a cover of the Monkees classic to an infectious breakbeat filched from Snap's huge number 1 'The Power'. London's Flowered Up were getting talked about, while Blur were turning themselves from a struggling indie outfit Seymour to a baggy pop outfit before finding their own feet.

The Happy Mondays were photographed for the *NME* clambering over a giant letter E on the roof of a hotel whilst making their 'Step On' video. They looked cool, young, confident and cocky – the years of wear and tear had hardly kicked in yet and there was even an air of innocence about the whole party.

It was into this national pop feeding-time frenzy that the Charlatans were entering. Everyone seemed to have gone baggy in a few months, the pop weathervane had spun right round and you were either on the bus or off it.

The Charlatans were quite definitely on the bus. This was the biggest explosion in street pop in Britain since the punk era and bands were getting back to what they did the best, banging out slices of great life-affirming three-minute pop.

It was, indeed, a golden period of UK pop.

ON THE ROAD . . . THE SECOND UK TOUR

From all the flurry of A & R action, Beggars Banquet was the eventual winner. Steve Harrison had been impressed by the Beggars bossman Martin Miller arriving at the Boardwalk in the mid-winter blizzard to check the band out, being the only A & R man who had managed to make it in the typically shite Manchester weather. This, and the fact that Beggars was a label big enough to get the band into the charts but small enough to give the band the much coveted artistic control meant that they were dead certs for the job.

Recently there had been plenty of labels in the hunt as from the moment the band started to break through, the news was out – here was a bona fide success. This was the last piece in the new northern pop jigsaw, a full-on pop phenomenon.

There was a chase on, the perfect position to be in for a hip pop band with the smart manager. You've connected totally with the audience, you're young, hot and fresh, and those labels that would normally trash your efforts are on their knees trying to get you to sign to them.

Jon Brookes wryly looks back on this time. 'They really started to lay the bullshit on. They wanted to pay for hotels and things, so we'd run up fucking massive bar bills.'

A & R seemed to be everywhere desperately trying to pick the band up. 'You'd be introduced to people at gigs and you'd be in a bit of a daze, cos you'd still be in a bit of a high from playing,' says Brookes. 'And they'd be bullshitting you, cos they always do, you know – how much they liked this song and that song. I don't like 'em. People think they've got to have a record contract, but that's a fallacy. If you've got a good enough song and you believe in it, put it out yourself.'

With all the haggling and persuading the Charlatans eventually went for Beggars Banquet, and got the deal on their own terms, terms that your average band would mostly dream about, with total artistic control, something that people had talked about since the heady days of the punk revolution – the art in the hands of the artists.

But this was something that would cause them problems, as Tim pointed out later on, 'We have that much control, that we sometimes almost shoot ourselves in the foot. We always have the last say on things. So all of a sudden you've got a million things that you've got to say yes or no to. It does your head in.'

This was something that the concerned artists hadn't thought about. There were a lot of details to be rubberstamped. It may be tough but it's something that a band should take care of. You can always tell when a group is getting watered down by the music industry – first their sleeves go, then their videos, and then the music – little details start to go sloppy. The bastards will fleece you at every given opportunity, their weak taste stomping all over the group's initial vision. As a weary Tim eventually described, 'We spend a lot of time saying no to t-shirts, but this time we just said, "Fuck it, do what you think, I can't be arsed," and this video, we just said to them, "You come up with something," just to get summat. This was because we end up with nothing half the time, we try to direct the video ourselves and it's just a pile of shit.'

But the band weren't about to let go though. 'Everything we've ever done, sleeves, producers, posters, t-shirts and support bands, we've had control of and it does get a bit much, but it's always been our decision.'

The deal with Beggars Banquet saw their releases going through Beggars' subsidiary Situation Two label, with the band still retaining their Dead Dead Good imprint. It meant that the group now had the financial backing to get things done right and there would be no more red-eye studio sessions, no more small pressings of singles and the might of a proper promotional team behind them.

This meant casualties, and Alison Martin, who had done so much for the band, was taken off the case as the new label took complete control. The band sheepishly agreed to this, with only Rob putting up an argument against it.

To get to the top, though, requires big-money cash and Beggars were going to make sure that the band's initial inertia was going to be followed through.

That March the band played their second London show. An increase in size saw them jumping up to the Boston Arms in Tufnell Park. The Boston Arms was a big upstairs room of a pub and at the time it put on a whole bunch of indie breakthrough shows. I remember this show, joshing with Bobby Gillespie's mad ragtag Primal Screamers on the steps of the Boston Arms, shouting, 'ballads are for saps' at them after reviewing 'I'm Losing More Than I'll Ever Have' (the song that would be sampled into their definitive 'Loaded'). It seemed like everyone was checking out the Charlatans at this show.

This show was the Charlatans' first big London show and they pulled it off in style. Tim had the star thing down, shining like a star in a white polo neck and too perfect hair. The band were shit-tight – there was no way they were going to blow this one – the music was cool as fuck, and they looked great. It was their final hour of being an indie band as from now on in they were going to be a big deal, and their sheer class made them seem like proper pop contenders.

The venue was packed with adoring fans. The Charlatans had now obviously been adopted by the new pop generation. The years of preparation and wallowing in the doldrums were over. This was a band that was ready to take advantage of the situation. The band ended the set with a spiralling 'Sproston Green', which had turned into a huge monster complete with helicopter blades whirring their way through the climactic end section. The group were learning how to put on a big-time rock & roll show, utilising tricks that were going to prove damned useful as the band mushroomed in size.

The reviews were hot as well. They had captured the hearts of the pop press as well as the rapidly expanding fanbase. The one lone dissenting voice came from the *Daily Telegraph* of all places, who had decided that the band were a bit too obvious and were suspicious of them being bandwagon jumpers. It was a criticism that would constantly crop up in their early days, and there were some people who thought that they had had things just a little too easy.

But the Charlatans had to move fast as all around them people were scoring hits. The Inspiral Carpets had just picked up a big deal with Mute Records and were scoring their biggest hit with 'This Is How It Feels' (number 14, March 1990), whilst the Stone Roses were getting the *NME* front cover, stumbling out of court in Wolverhampton after throwing paint around their old record label offices. Major Manc bands were making immense moves; the Charlatans' fast rise was only just fast enough to keep them on the edge of the limelight. UK pop was going through a massive sea change and every week it seemed like a new band was popping up ready to grab the crown – one slip-up could spell the end of a band's rush.

During the tour Bob Stanley, in a measure of the group's quick rise, grabbed the band for his second interview with them in a month for the *Melody Maker*, and found them excited by the tour's success. The packed gigs and the mayhem were giving the band the thrill that can only come when a band is in its initial ascendancy.

As Tim buzzed, when talking about the craziness that would surround certain members on the stage, 'Rob's keyboard cuts out three or four times at every gig now. It can't take the strain. Everyone keeps pulling the leads out at gigs, the lead that goes into the cabinet thing, the, err, the amplifier thing.'

Said Burgess, proving once and for all, that he wasn't the group's technical wizard!

Martin Blunt raved about the 'communication' between the band and its fans. It was a vital connection that would stand the band in good stead for their future career. Few bands have such an understanding with their fanbase, the sort of unwitting electricity that bonds them with their fans.

The band told tales of mad crowds and small venues incapable of holding in the hysteria. Stanley found a manager seething that the records weren't getting pressed fast enough to get into the charts, and a band on the brink of promotion away from the also-rans to the major league.

The next single, though still undecided, was going to be crucial.

The Manchester University show in the Uni's Mandela Hall was a homecoming of sorts. The gig was packed and the back of the hall was full of local scenesters and celebs nodding to the band's Hammond beat.

Local listings magazine, *City Life*, described the Charlatans as a 'laconic bubbly Hammond-driven thing' and also called Burgess a 'teenshag superstar', a tag that would sit rather comfortably on the singer's narrow shoulders as the band crossed over into the teen appeal market without the slightest dent to their cred over the next couple of years.

The band kicked off with 'Intro' segueing into 'The Only One I Know', and they watched the hall erupt. After that they were coasting, it was hot and it was wild, and it was pretty damned obvious that the Charlatans were arriving very fast indeed.

By now the vexed question of the next single was raging with even more intensity, with 'Flower' getting talked up as the next release (despite everyone yelling into the band's ears that 'The Only One I Know' was the dead cert).

Sounds loved the gig and pointed out that the band were in the right place at the right time: 'Years ago they would have been rotting on the toilet circuit alongside great lost bands like the June Brides,' said the spiky journalist.

'Indian Rope' was getting a favourable thumbs-up all over the country, with many local pundits claiming it was a cross between the Inspiral Carpets' keyboard-driven pop with the Stone Roses' vocal style on top.

Not that the Charlatans were resting on their laurels. The single may have been fanning the flames but they were already back in the studio recording a new demo of material, and when they played it to Bob Stanley he was blown away with the new songs. One song that Stanley dug particularly was 'Polar Bear' which was again being talked about as being the next single, picking up on the line 'looking for the orange one . . .' a line that could either be sweetly innocent or about drugs, an orange one sounding like some sort of hip slang for Ecstasy.

'It's not about Revels, that song. That was just an, erm . . . the simplest description of what I was trying to say,' said Tim.

Bob wondered what the hell the Charlatans were doing, singing about polar bears.

'I think polar bears are really nice . . .' Tim bluffed. 'That's about it, really. I told a mate what a song of ours was about the other day. He was really disappointed when I told him what it was about . . . windmills! My lyrics come from things that amuse me, to a fucking massive degree. I can't see the point in writing about something that makes me unhappy.'

But as 'The Only One I Know' was blowing the crowd apart at every gig, it had hit stamped all over it, and the decision was made at last to record it. The Charlatans were about to release their first classic tune.

'THE ONLY ONE I KNOW'

In 1990 there was one of those pop booms that explodes across the UK every now and then. When the Charlatans released their second single it was in company of the Stone Roses' 'One Love', the Chad Jackson classic monster groove 'Hear The Drummer', the James *Gold Mother* album, New Order's 'World In Motion', MC Tunes' 'The Only Rhyme That Bites' and Ruthless Rap Assassins classic, way ahead of the game slice of Manc rap, 'Just Mellow'. Every week there was a great record – it seemed like a seamless and constant flow.

The band were going to have to be well on the case to not get drowned out by the competition. But they delivered, and how!

Borrowing generously from Deep Purple's 'Hush', 'The Only One I Know' is a classic piece of shimmering pop, driven by Blunt's urgent soul-fused bassline, a propelling, bouncing rush that drives the song along; it became the signal for mayhem at the band's gigs for years to come. A brilliant summer anthem, it captured the mood of the times perfectly and ushered the band into the pop mainstream. Flipped with 'Imperial 109', 'Everything Changed', and on the CD with 'You Can Talk To Me', the single was the band's calling card.

It was recorded at the Wyndings Studio in North Wales, and was again produced by Chris Nagle. 'I remember it was a 3-day session. I think we might even have managed to stretch it to a week. It was a top tune, you could tell it was going to do something. I decided to keep it just like them, not to over produce it. I shortened the arrangement, it was quite a lot longer when they first brought it in, and turned it into a pop song. They were very amenable to the changes, very easy to work with.'

The session went well except for the guitar solo that Baker fluffed, a solo that Rob had come up with, picking the notes out on his keyboard. Nagle got the band to record to a click track and keep things tight. 'Rob and Martin seemed to be the main creative people in the band at the time. They would dash off to their collection of obscure 1970s prog records and nick the tunes, just reversing the chords!' he laughs.

Tim just wanted to get the vocals over and done with as fast as possible, but Nagle made him work a whole lot harder than that. Recording the vocal is the most nerve-wracking point of any session. For a start it's the most important component of the song, putting a focal point on it, and it's also the hardest thing to get right. You need the tuning, the feel and the intonation all at once – a voice can't just be switched on, it has to be coaxed.

As Burgess stood in the lonely vocal booth he looked up at Chris Nagle, who was doing the prompting and prodding that all producers have to to get the best out of their charges.

'I just wanted to get more out of him,' says Nagle. 'I pushed him, made him do things a few times. The backing vocals were really sharp. They went down really fast.'

A solid production job, Nagle captured a young band cutting their breakthrough single perfectly. Youthful vigour and good times soak from its Hammond-soaked grooves. There is a total joy in the power of pop pouring from the single, a fab slice of psychedelic smoking pop complete with a knowing cool and a great chord change that just makes the track. Jon Brookes also whacks down a great shuffling drum beat that hints at Reni's awesome drumming in the Stone Roses. 'The Only One I Know' sounded like a hit record the moment your ear first copped its lazy luxurious pop rush.

The press were generous. *Melody Maker*'s Paul Lester thought, 'Like all top Manc outfits, they sing and play like they're doing you a favour. Like they're blessed with international superstar arrogance even when they are playing to five mates.' He also pointed out that they sounded like the Stone Roses, but dug the record anyway.

Ian McCann at the *NME* felt the band were destined to go all the way, *Sounds* pointed to the record's run-out groove, the etching on the inside of the record, where it said 'Good, aren't we?' and couldn't fail but to agree.

One strange quirk with the single is in the songwriting credits. The band's names are all there but like some of their early releases, Jon Baker seems to have disappeared and his name has been replaced by 'Day'. This isn't the same Day as the key Prisoners man Graham Day. Jon Baker picks up the tale. 'As a joke I once put my name down as Jon Day and it was something that stuck and even ended up in some of the songwriting credits.'

On its 2 June release 'The Only One I Know' flew out of the shops. Word had been spreading fast about this hot new band. A youthful sexy version of the big Manc bands – they really had it. As well as great songs, they played brilliant gigs and had an instant rapport with their audience.

On the Sunday, they were headlining the Town And Country Club in London, a much bigger venue, the next rung up the ladder after the Boston Arms, the first proper show on the rise to the toppermost of the poppermost. It's a signal that something really is happening here.

It's also the point that the backlash usually kicks in. The single had slid in at number 24 its first week in the charts – would it do the usual indie thing and fall straight out again or would it keep moving with the full steady momentum that was now apparent?

Backstage after the soundcheck, Alison Martin kept a steady vigil by the radio for the Sunday-night chart countdown. There was an expectant tension in the air; sales had been good but where had they gone in the charts, had they even crashed into the hallowed top 10?

They had sold out the Town And Country Club, and the press was beginning to bite hard. *Melody Maker* dealt one, claiming that the gig was less of 'a happening and more of a game of "spot the reference"'. The journalist went on to claim that he could only spot three modes of rip-offs: 'complete and utter Stone Roses rip-off', 'complete and utter Stone Roses/Inspiral Carpets rip-off', and 'complete and utter Stone Roses/Inspiral Carpets/Monkees rip-off'. Oh, and not to mention 'complete and utter bollocks'. This, I guess, was someone who didn't enjoy the band!

It was too late. The Charlatans were now unstoppable; as the pop kids paper *Number One* pointed out, 'The Charlatans will be the one Manchester band who will remain long after the bandwagon has collapsed.'

The night was already buzzing enough without Alison Martin being hunched over her radio. Backstage in the cold brick corridors of the Town And Country and the narrow dressing rooms they waited. The countdown seemed to last for ever, and as it got higher it felt like the band had dropped out of the top 40.

15-14-13-12-11-10 . . . it looked like a dead loss, but then, with a rush of adrenaline, the rundown announced that the band were number 9, and Alison rushed through to the soundchecking to break the great news.

'It had gone in at number 24 the week before and we knew that it had done really well that week, but as it got closer and closer to the top 10, I remember getting more and more nervous. When it was number 9 I remember telling everyone and there was this great rush of excitement,' she recalls.

Looking For The Orange One fanzine also remembers the excitement of the band's first hit. 'Listening to the chart before the Town And Country gig, only catching it from number 18, by the time the chart reached number 11 I was sure that it had fallen out. The shock was something to see when it was announced that it was number 9, everyone was phoning their mums and dads!'

Tim Burgess was crackling with excitement. 'I always knew I would be famous, everyone has doubts, but I knew I would do something. I mean, if you're going to do something, do it properly.'

The following week, they recorded their debut *Top Of The Pops* appearance, always a great moment for any band, no matter how cool they like to think they are. After the recording they went out for a massive celebratory curry and, this being the Charlatans, it could only go all awry and mad, as a bleary-eyed Tim explained, 'I was up till 6 o'clock last night. We went out for a curry and everybody was having this massive argument about what the next single should be, except for me, of course, and about not doing interviews any more because we have got bored of all that!'

There was no damage done, though, the air was cleared and the band were ready to enjoy all the fruits of success that they had slogged for.

Not that the cynics were having their comeuppance quite yet. 'They are so cynical' claimed the usually quite astute DJ and record maker Norman Cook, feeling that the Charlatans had manipulated themselves on to the bandwagon and there were many pundits who were calling their tune.

'The Only Song They Know' became the jokeline on the band, cynics claiming that they were one-trick ponies. The Charlatans, though, weren't only becoming one of 1990's key new bands but were also consolidating their success with a series of barn-storming big-venue gigs.

At the end of the year in the *NME*, one of Tim's heroes, the acerbic Fall vocalist, Mark E. Smith, was asked to review the year's standout singles, including 'The Only One I Know', and as expected didn't cut any corners. He said, 'All these Manchester bands when it comes down to it, they're just a bunch of jessies. Just young businessmen into dressing up and Echo And The Bunnymen. I'm very happy for them, you know. Making a bit of money by funking up Echo And The Bunnymen.'

Smith almost sounded favourable. 'They get accused of copying the Stone Roses. I wouldn't say they're doing that. They're just copying all those 1960s bands. Good luck to them, they were in the right place at the right time, but all these bands they're bloody interchangeable, the High, Ride . . . the Charlatans . . . he does try that singer, I'll give him that!'

Also on the panel, the Farm's Peter Hooton snuck in, 'But they're not the sort of people you'd want to go to the match with. Any of you lads I'd be happy to stand by at the match.'

Smith cut in quick, 'I wouldn't go to the bloody match with you, pal!'

Overall it was a much more positive reaction than when the first single came out, as everyone knew the plot now, and the *Manchester Evening News* – at first all reticent and coy about the band – was now all over them like cheap perfume. The reviews were glowing and it looked like the band had been given the official thumbs-up, not that they cared, as 'the kids' were backing this one all the way, and how!

Steve Harrison was definitely smiling at this unprecedented reaction when he told a local Northwich paper, 'Last week they did their first *Top Of The Pops* and they were Radio One's record of the week. They appeared on the front cover of the *NME*, ousted New Order and Erasure from the top spot of *The Chart Show* and saw the new single enter the top 10 after coming straight in at number 24; it's been a good week.'

It would be fair to say that the Charlatans were the first Northwich band to reach such dizzy heights.

SCALLYDELIC ACID CASUALS AND THE DEATH OF THE WEIRD

Acid casuals, psychedelic scoundrels, scallydelia – funny phrases made up by northern journalists in the twilight zones of burned-out club nights. Whatever the label, the scallies had won the great pop war.

Since punk the freaks and the kids had been redefining the great pop culture fallout and now the freaks were well and truly defeated, and indie was becoming mainstream. At first this seemed like a victory but soon it meant that pop was going to crush all resistance and everything would be blanketed by a normality.

When the Charlatans burst into the big time they were quite often called scallies. Although they never paid much lip service to the football-soaked culture, they had copped the look and mixed it with a loose approximation of modishness. Tim, being the youngest, had gone deepest into the new baggy look.

Scally culture was the key culture of the time and any association with it wasn't going to do the band any harm. In many ways it was the late 1980s equivalent of mod. Obsessed with clothes, pop and football, it was streaked with occasional violence and abrasive attitudes, and has dominated British culture right through the 1990s.

The Charlatans could never be described by any stretch of the imagination as scallies; these weren't match lads or football yobs. They were far more firmly rooted in mod culture and sparked by punk.

Most bands in the wake of the Stone Roses and the Happy Mondays adopted the dressed-down baggied-up look of the street scally culture, much to the amusement of so called spokesmen of the original scouse scally scene, like Liverpool's fairly amusing *What's The Score?* fanzine, a loose cross between football and pop put together by Peter Naylor and very much influenced by Peter Hooton of the Farm's highly influential *The End* zine. With great hilarity, the printed the back street in Ancoats shot of the Charlatans, all sloping around being as street as possible, with Tim looking sharp, lean, spiky and young-haunched.

The heading screamed 'Manc Scals! What?' It was the voice of piss-taking scousers perturbed that their arch rival city was getting all the credit for a youth movement they claimed as their own.

Scientists of street culture will argue the toss over who invented the term . . . the clobber . . . the idea, in pubs for years. Mancs could make claims for the Perry Boys (so called because they wore Fred Perry shirts) of the late 1980s, whilst their scouse counterparts would point out the European shoplifting expeditions in the wake of Liverpool FC's endless cup conquests of the early 1980s, trips to the continent when their fans would return home with pockets stuffed full of sports gear, precipitating the casual sports look of the late 1990s when every fat-arsed malingerer squeezed his or her flaccid non-sportsmanlike frame into designer sports gear.

The article screeched with laughter, pointing out that ten years after the initial model ponced around Liverpool, Manchester was experiencing a 'scally phenomenon', and it went on to add, 'At one time the term "scally" was a badge of honour. Always more to do with attitude than expensive clothing, something the so-called casuals could never come to terms with. As the 1980s went on and every snotty-nosed kid with a Tacchini tracksuit started calling himself a scally things went really downhill. Travelling outside Liverpool revealed strange graffiti like "Birkenhead scallies", "Maghull scallies" even "Wigan scallies", but they all beat Mancsville to it.'

The beauty of this parochialism is etched into the words. The guardians of the Liverpool scally flame arguing the toss over which town was first. It's the coolest thing about youth culture – the originator is always the god.

For most of the late 1980s and early 1990s the music press used to rage to the great debate over who wore flared trousers first. Aggrieved scousers would howl as the Mancs got all the credit of their great invention and there were serious accusations of fashion piracy. In Manchester the Happy Mondays go down in history as the first band to wear flares, buying them off their soon to be manager Phil Sach's stall underneath the Arndale centre. The fifth Stone Rose Cressa, a man who in his teens was a sharp and angular mod, introduced them to the Stone Roses camp, giving Ian Brown his bottle-green cords, the hugest pair of flares in Manchester.

All this fashion shift wasn't going to miss a group of ex mods and pop culture freaks like the Charlatans, and it wasn't long before Tim Burgess could be seen flapping around Northwich in the biggest pair of flares he could lay his hands on.

'I got these trousers from Identity in Manchester,' he told the *NME* in early 1990, alluding to the shop that invented the 'and on the seventh day god created Manchester' t-shirts which was a prime mover in the whole look of the city in 1989-1990. 'They were about 30 quid, but I got some similar from Walsall market for about a fiver. I think Cressa from the Stone Roses was the first to wear them in Manchester. In Liverpool they used to wear them with a little cut up the sides and they'd wear them right over their trainers and that was in 1984 or 1985.'

Attempting to back out of the fashion debate he added, 'When you wear your flares on the street you're the same as everyone else but when you wear them on stage then you're part of a specific scene.'

The Stone Roses were an influence on the Charlatans but then they were an influence on nearly every band in Britain and as the years roll by their effect seems vaster and vaster. They really did re-invent the blueprint for British pop, how it was made, how it was played; they copped the walk, the look, the attitude and the tunes. For a band like the Charlatans to have not been touched by the Roses would have been unthinkable.

Tim conceded, 'The Stone Roses did break down a lot of barriers and made it a lot easier for us to be noticed. But I think the only similarity between us is the actual looseness of the band. Two years ago when acid house was massive in Manchester the Roses were probably going to the Hacienda like the Happy Mondays and the Charlatans. They all developed from this brilliant beat. It changed people's minds about how free and easy music could be. People in Manchester are really positive-thinking people. They're always looking for something exciting.'

The baggy thing may have been expedient for the Charlatans, and at first when they broke through they definitely struck a bit of the look, but it was never something that they were that comfortable with. When someone asked Martin Blunt if they were part of a movement he just looked blank: 'We've always had respect for the individual to be honest. On the last tour, there were loads of people with Hawkwind t-shirts and stuff like that, y'know, with all different tastes.'

When asked if they were just a typical student band, Blunt didn't flinch. 'I think it's quite a cross section of people but, yeah, it does include a lot of students, especially a lot of people with "suss".'

The man that had once been at the heart of a mod scene was displaying a remarkable lack of snobbery; pop after all is for anyone and fashions come and go, and the true survivors are the ones that can get past the fashionable stage.

Meanwhile his vocalist had this to say on the matter. 'We're not a total lifestyle package like the Farm or the Happy Mondays, with clothes and drugs and soccer and a whole attitude. We don't say, "Well, we're not playing a gig tonight because there's a big soccer match on TV." I've never been into sports anyway.'

'WE'RE IN THE MONEY!' (NOT!!!)

By June, it was becoming pretty damn clear that the Charlatans were fast becoming one of the best bands of the year. Like the way that the Roses had burst on to the scene the year before they were making the same sort of tracks. Despite this, on paper, mass success, the band were reported to not be exactly coining it in. The *Daily Mirror*'s pop gossip page claimed that the band members were only earning £65 a week, even if the single was at number 9. Not that the band were complaining, as Jon Baker explained, 'We've all been flat broke before so it's great to be on a wage for the first time, even though it seems low. We get £65 a week, which we all feel is really quite sensible. It's actually a figure we all worked out ourselves. My last band starved and we had to break up, but that was four years ago.'

What Baker's former band, the Liquid Egg Box, had found out was that hardly anyone in rock & roll makes a fucking penny. Every musician starts to play for love, and with a bit of talent and a whole heap of luck they get their hands on the publishing rights and the money starts to flood in. Some bands go crazy and blow the lot fast, encouraged by the hoary old rock & roll myth of crazed decadence, and some, like the Charlatans, have a long-term handle on things and stretch the money out for as long as possible.

For a group like them the music comes first and to keep open the space to create is the first and foremost priority. The wage may have sounded crap to some but for a musician to get any money at all in the 'filthiest business known to man' is such an incredible buzz that it seems churlish to complain.

That summer things went mad, and the band went from doing any gig where they could get one to being a band that was as busy as fuck. Rule one in pop is that when you get your money you have to work like a dog to maintain it; it's bastard difficult to get to the top but the top is even more difficult to hold on to. You have to work like crazy to take full advantage of what you have got.

Jon Baker thinks of that summer as a total blur. 'I remember it was really mad, we seemed to be in the studio all the time, recording the album and then we would be off down to London to do a John Peel session and then back again, and then straight back down to record a Mark Goodier session for Radio One, five weeks in the studio, and then we would be up all night and down to London. It was really tiring, there was no sleep. It was good fun, excellent. I was off on tour all the time. All of a sudden from being a member of a band doing nothing to being in a *Just Seventeen* photo session, from being an average Joe Bloggs to being a centre spread.'

The Peel session transmitted on 9 April had four tracks: 'Then', 'Always In Mind', 'You Can Talk To Me' and 'Polar Bear'.

On 3 June their first Mark Goodier session was transmitted with another set of four songs: 'Some Friendly', 'Indian Rope', 'The Only One I Know' and 'White Shirt'.

Pop success brings its own stresses and strains, the pot of gold that we all dream of is nowhere near as brilliant as the dream always paints it. It's damned hard work, a full-on stress that no one on the outside ever appreciates, believing that bands wallow in some sort of pop nirvana, whilst really they are burning up the motorway from one end of the country to the other desperately attempting to consolidate their one moment of fame.

That summer saw the continued rise of the surrounding 'Madchester scene'. The Mondays blew Glastonbury apart with a crazed party performance at the never-ending bastion of hippiedom. The festival with its dull bill and great vibes was open to runty hordes of newcomers ready to party, with the Mondays being the central motif to a weekend of getting wrecked. Even the Farm were briefly hip – getting the cover of *NME* – posing with *Brookside*'s Harry Cross character in a celebration of the scouse end of the new scene.

New Order's 'World In Motion' football anthem was at number 1 as the World Cup groaned into action. With its hip moves and archly funny lyrics with references to E ('It's one on one' they sang on the song, originally entitled 'E For England') it was a witty and cool commentary on the current pop climate and a respectable football song (an unlikely event in itself). Spike Island came and passed where the Stone Roses hit their zenith; their gradual unwinding from this so-called 'baggy Woodstock' would open up the scene for every other chancer. Even James were now big bucks with their *Gold Mother* album, their most successful yet. It seemed like no one affiliated with the north who had got themselves organised was going to fuck up.

Whilst all this was raging the Charlatans were about to kiss Northwich goodbye in terms of playing there. The small Cheshire town that had been their hub since their formation a year previously was now too small to accommodate their massive fanbase. It was their version of the Beatles' last gig at the Cavern, a goodbye to the struggle and clearing the decks for the next phase.

This was a measure of just how far the band had come in a short space of time – the upcoming gig at Northwich Memorial Hall was pronounced to be their last gig in the town. It had been a matter of mere months since the band had been hustling gigs in Northwich and its environs, and now it had become totally impractical to play the town any more, although some group members still lived there, as Martin Blunt pointed out, 'We've got no regrets about moving up here. This is where we always had the biggest following.'

But Steve Harrison said, 'With the national support that we now have the band should never be playing Northwich. But they wanted to say "thank you" for the loyal following they have received from the town over the last six months.'

For the Charlatans it was the closing of a chapter as no longer were they small-town hopefuls (I know some of them come from Wolverhampton but that's not a pop epicentre) but major-league players who had inadvertently given the small Cheshire town an unlikely pop footnote.

The rest of the tour was in the sort of 1000-capacity venues that definitely marked a band's upward progress.

These certainly were the salad days.

'I GOTTA TV EYE ON YOU!'

Whatever happened to Granada TV? The pride of the north, at one time the best in exciting telly with a bang-on taste in pop music, making documentaries like *The Doors At The Roundhouse* and *The Stones In The Park*.

Now come the biggest guitar pop revolution since punk rock, right on their Mancunian doorstep, and Granada seemed to be nowhere.

Precious footage was going to waste as most of the local Manc media like radio, press and TV seemed to be totally wide of the mark. Still hanging on to the Smiths' myth the city's commentators seemed to be ignoring the biggest thing ever to happen right on their own fucking door steps!

Maybe as an attempt to readdress the balance, Granada was throwing a pop party with the Charlatans and the New Fast Automatic Daffodils kicking out the new jams. The New FADs, who were plying their great frantic funk punk that had somehow got caught up in the whole Manchester thing by just happening to live in the city after they had left university, were the latest band to be getting some deserved attention. Their best track was a song called 'Bigger' which they played that night, and readers are urged to check their music out.

They were followed by the High, whose crafted and cool guitar pop, for some reason was falling between the cracks and disappearing.

So on 12 July 1990, as part of their occasional *Celebration* series, a cultural extravaganza concentrating on north-west youth which had the usual crap loser groups and unfunny comedians, Granada plumped for a homemade gig to showcase what was really happening in the city.

Ian McGregor, the mad kid writer for the *Melody Maker*, who was covering stuff in the north for the paper was righteously enthusiastic and machine-gunned a review in staccato speed speak. 'Bass thuds low and drums keep up a monster dance beat. Drummer looks cool. Organ prods the rhythm then blossoms out into swirling psychedelia. Tim sings, eyes shut and alluring. Bass and tambourine chug out alone before the organ swirls in and wigs out totally with shrieking freak-out guitar squirting across the massive groove.'

Aaah, great hyperbole and enthusiasm – where the fuck is McGregor nowadays?

The concert was in Studio 12, the huge Granada complex in Manchester city centre. The last really cool band in there had been the Stone Roses and they had confused technical staff with their surly arrogance. This time the band got a telling off. When the Charlatans took the stage the floor manager told Tim to take his fag out of his hand whilst the singer was doing his five-year-old with an arrogant swagger thing announcing 'hooray hooray, get the cameras on me' at the suitably bored-looking crew. There was a pause but when the band kicked in, it was business as usual, ending with a great mad drum and feedback exit.

Great TV.

'SUMMERTIME AND THE LIVING IS . . . FULL ON!'

For their first date abroad on 10 August the Charlatans played in Sweden at one of the biggest Scandinavian festivals, alongside the Buzzcocks, the great Joan Jett, the Waterboys and the fab Jungle Brothers.

Hultsfred is the main rock festival in Sweden, a typically Scandinavian affair – well organised, efficient and with a killer bill. Sweden has always been very receptive to the vagaries of British pop music; bands clamouring for chart attention in the UK can also find themselves worshipped on the other side of the foul and dirty North Sea.

The festival itself was in a small town 100 miles away from Stockholm. It really was well and truly in the middle of nowhere, having only one hotel, and most of the bands had to stay at the next town along, in the too-clean environs of Vimmerby.

The Charlatans were making their Scandinavian debut to 8000 people in a tent and they were going to be having it large. To the Swedes this was a true slice of Mancunian pop from one of the coolest bands on the scene. Six months into their trajectory the Charlatans could complain as much as they wanted about being confused with being a Manchester band but it was giving them excellent mileage. Their Manchester credentials were reinforced now that Martin Blunt had moved up to Northwich from his Black Country bolt-hole. It was like the further the band were trying to move away from their musical connection with the rainy city, the closer they were actually physically moving closer to the place. But as Tim told Andrew Collins in the *NME*, 'I'd like to say we're from England, I fucking would. We're all English chaps and we're fed up of having to apologise to the people who know that we're not from Manchester. Manchester was the first place to champion the band but now people from Manchester say, "You're not from fucking Manchester!"'

The gig was a blast, despite the front falling off Rob's hired organ, not that it mattered as the valves were still cranking it and the Hammond was on fine wheezing form – the band were cooking it and the crowd was having it large enough for Tim to proclaim, 'This is the best song in the world by the best band in the world,' the sort of announcement that he was prone to make.

AND . . . 'THEN'

On 3 September 1990 the Charlatans released their third single, 'Then'. It hit number 12 on a five-week run, a slightly deflated chart profile compared with its poptastic predecessor but a big hit nonetheless. Backed up with the fabbly titled 'Taurus Moaner', it was punted as a preview of the soon to come album, from which 'Then' was culled.

Many pundits felt that 'Then' was an odd choice of single, with the *NME* feeling that it was like 'Emerson Lake & Palmer with a cocaine enema', suggesting that the record sounded like, 'at its worst points a progressive rock track.' But Tim Burgess was pretty adamant about this being a cool record when interviewed in *Sounds*.

'No, we wanted it that way,' he said. 'We wanted to record "Polar Bear" [at one point mooted to be the third single; would they ever give up trying to release this as a single?] like it was more of a dancy sort of thing but it would have been too light to put out as a single. We decided that "Then" was good to back up the first year of the Charlatans. A lot of people thought that it wasn't commercial but if you start pandering to that sort of stuff . . .'

Although it isn't as instantly catchy as 'Only One I Know', 'Then' is by no means the let-down that it has always been painted as, in many ways it was just copping the backlash that the band were almost inevitably going to get. Too much success too soon is always a recipe for disaster, with the punditry always prepared to shoot down a successful new band.

The accompanying video for 'Then' showcased the band poncing around a hill in darkest Shropshire, semi-obscured by a bilious cloud of smoke.

Only a handful of dates were lined up to promote this single, although the band played a show at Warrington Legends as a thanks to Gavin the promoter for supporting them in their early days. The tickets were available through the *Looking For The Orange One* fanzine and all 800 were snapped up fast. It was typical of the rootsy vibe the Charlatans always projected; Warrington was hardly a flash or a fashionable town but it was the heartland of the band's support, the backwater small towns seeking some sort of pop magic on their own terms.

Barbara Ellen reviewed the gig for the *NME* and captured Tim in her own hilarious and cutting way. 'My first meeting with Burgess leaves me in a state of shock. I was expecting an ordinary Joe. Who is this geezer with the straightjacket smile, over-boisterous eyebrows and nervous tic? My immediate thought is that Tim Burgess is either a born star or a long-term inmate from an asylum. Only later does it occur to me that a combination of the two is closer to the mark . . .'

SOME FRIENDLY

Released on Monday 15 October, *Some Friendly* was doing big business from the off. This was obviously going to have a very different chart career from the Stone Roses' debut album which had never hit higher than 19 in the charts and had relied on word of mouth to sell its half a million copies. By the Wednesday the Charlatans had gone gold, selling over 100,000 copies.

Inevitably the album went in at number 1.

'The build up, the buzz, everything was right for it to go to number 1,' a proud Steve Harrison beamed. 'On the strength of the three singles, they had sold out every concert this year, our agent had never worked with anyone who had done that. And when we went to Europe it was the same. And that buzz became evident on this record.'

The album does indeed have that; it captures a youthful optimism and innocence but is also scoured with a realism that twists into melancholy given half the chance. The album, though, was the perfect 1990 record, sound-tracking the youthful pop vibe of that year.

Some Friendly did well across Europe (although not quite to the same extent as in the UK, despite managing a top 10 in Greece). In America the record would eventually do 140,000 copies, a respectable start for a British band in the early 1990s when the US was in the midst of the grunge wars, and hit number 1 in the US independent radio and retail charts. In fact Stateside they were considered the main northern baggy band; it wasn't long before Ian Brown was getting compared to Tim Burgess, and the Stone Roses to the Charlatans. It was an irony of ironies, the runts of the litter had truly arrived!

But even though it was selling in boxloads and made a great attempt to capture the flavour of the times, *Some Friendly*, although a cool record, wasn't quite the classic that, say, the Roses had dealt the year before.

The Charlatans knew they could get something better together, they knew they were capable of so much more. It was this restless search for the ultimate album that they knew was in their souls that would come to dominate their career. No matter what trials and tribulations there were, the search was all.

This was something that Martin Blunt agreed on later. 'It could have been a better album, yeah. Some songs like "Flower" and "Then" are a year and a half old. But yeah, it's pretty good. We're getting ready for the next one. I mean it's done now, that was our first offering.'

But carping aside, *Some Friendly* still has a lot of great moments.

This was the band's Hammond album; the record was stamped with Collins' brooding complex personality and just beyond the record's poppy vibe you can hear the great crashing keyboard played with an intense passion by a young man working out his inner turmoil through rock & roll.

Manchester saw the Charlatans as the Stone Roses that were still available, the Inspiral Carpets that were cooler, the pure pop version of the baggy beat – the outsiders had entered the inner sanctum, and the album was all that was needed to cement their hard fought for status.

The record was vital for them. The main Manc triumphate of the Happy Mondays, Stone Roses and the Inspiral Carpets were established stars, and it's very rare in pop for the second wave of bands to come through and beat the masters at their own game.

If the Roses were already playing the mysterious card, the Mondays the yob rock card, and the Inspirals were being considered less than cool, then the Charlatans had a wonderful opportunity to take their whole thing into the realms of total popdom; they had the tunes, the swagger and the pouting frontman. There was a whole different audience to be checked out, one which was already buying into the Charlatans' myth.

Not only were they pure pop, *Some Friendly* also hinted that there was a serious band lurking in there. The music was Hammond-heavy driving acid pop, the sort of stuff members of the band had been listening to or playing for years. Even if it does sound a tad lightweight there was definitely an edge.

Again Chris Nagle was at the helm producing, even if certain band members were being coy about who was at the controls.

A couple of months previously, when asked about who was going to produce the album Tim had this to say, 'We don't really know much about that. How about Sid James? Hattie Jacques, Wilfred Bramble, Eric Sykes, Una Stubbs. Actually I'm almost sure that Una Stubbs hasn't produced anyone. Although she could have produced one of them Russian heavy metal bands for all we know . . .'

In the meantime Chris Nagle had got the call again and the band set off for the Wyndings in North Wales for a return trip, this time to record the album, before moving north up to Stockport for mixing at Nagle's preferred Strawberry Studios. With more money in the pot due to their deal the band could afford to stretch out a little more, and spend a few weeks on the record.

Like most bands in 1989-1990 plying a guitar pop they were still feeling the aftershocks of the Stone Roses' debut masterpiece, as Chris Nagle remembers, 'At the time they seemed to be really paranoid about the Stone Roses' album. They were trying to copy it, be better than it and be completely different from it all at the same time.'

The Stone Roses was the album of the period and the one that a whole generation of bands was having to measure themselves against. Most of them would be using it as a yardstick for the rest of the 1990s – not even the Roses could equal their own debut.

Nagle remembers that the Charlatans had 'about four or five weeks' to record *Some Friendly*, which caused a different set of problems. 'The band had never worked in a residential studio before, and when one of them was working the rest of them would get really bored and there was some damage done!'

Not that it was all rock & roll hi jinks, as some members of the group were now pitching in at the mixing stage. 'The group was getting a lot more confident now, they had ideas of what they should sound like, stuff like asking for the keyboards to get more distorted,' says Nagle.

Fucking around with the band's hard and tight formula, there was some space for experimentation, and Nagle took Burgess outside for a couple of tracks and recorded his vocals in the open air.

It may have been a touch too early for the band to be in the studio recording the album – in existence for barely a year and on the road for most of that time, they hadn't really had, let's say, the five years in isolation that the Stone Roses had to come up with their debut. In some respects the Charlatans were short of songs, and for every good song on the album there is a track which if not quite a filler, isn't a killer.

But strong songs abound, including 'The Only One I Know', already a classic that still gets heavy radio play to this day, and evoking the carefree summer days of youth it's the song's almost naive charm and apparent simplicity that does it every time; several other tracks work within the same sort of optimistic pop rush.

If many felt the record was an up-beat pop statement there were others who didn't, including, of course, Martin Blunt who saw things differently, believing the band were tying themselves into a northern pop tradition that went back a lot further than the too obvious Stone Roses' comparisons or positive pop connections. 'It's a pretty melancholic album. Not romantic. There's quite a dark side. A lot of "highs" are on there, but there's quite a lot of, not depression, but moods. We've always been influenced by sullen bands coming out of the north-west like the Bunnymen, New Order and the Fall.'

These bands were the anchor to the band's sound; never getting too flamboyant or too flash, they worked well within the northern pop framework, a framework that dictates a sullen coolness soundtracked with minor-key, down to earth songs written on a rainy day, but armed with fantastic uplifting choruses that can't help themselves leaping out of the self-imposed gloom. Northern pop may be the soundtrack to a gritty city's frankly rather shite weather but, like the north itself, it can never help its exuberance overcoming the crappy surroundings.

But even Blunt couldn't let the melancholy ooze through all the songs, and the set-ending 'Sproston Green' was the Charlatans' equivalent of the Stone Roses' 'Resurrection' – a long, sprawling classic that despite being tight as fuck and learned to the note, sounded like a loose sprawling jam, capturing the live vibe. It was a great signing-off note and a climactic exit to gigs and the album.

'Sproston Green' is one of those classic tracks that the fans know but which has never made it into mass consciousness. Never released as a single in the UK, it has come out in America and France, and there was even a video made for the record, filmed at the Manchester Apollo.

Sproston Green itself is a lane in the tiny mid Cheshire village of Sproston which is just to the side of junction 18 of the M6 where it meets the A54. The road was set up for some mega zealous fan to steal the sign, and in January 1990 the road sign was half-inched. The sign was quickly replaced but the same fan returned and stole that as well. The sign thief was at early Charlatans shows like the Glasgow Mayfair and waved it around at the front of the crowd.

Some mad people follow this band around!

Behind the superficial pop sweetness of the album there were some heavy sticks being carried, as Tim explained when talking about 'Flower' to *Sounds*. '"Flower" is about wanting someone dead. It's a death threat. It's directed at somebody who did me over when I was young,' he mysteriously alluded, giving little else away.

Other songs were about specific incidents that the singer found easier to talk about. 'Opportunity' was about the poll tax riots in London and Burgess's accidental involvement in them. 'After I'd been to a rehearsal I came down to London on the train. I came out of Goodge Street tube station because Tottenham Court Road was closed, and it was towards the end of the riot. Everyone was running about, police were on horses and windows were smashed and some people were still smashing them. People were all walking in one direction, dragging stuff behind them. I was just planning on looking for the best shop from which to steal. I just thought it was fascinating.'

Imagine the buzz as you wander out of the tube still half asleep from your train journey down from the north, you exit the ticket machines and there is this massive mad commotion going on in one of the main streets of Britain. If in your youth you had been a fan of anarchist punk bands, suddenly those record sleeves and lyrics seemed to have come to life.

Tim was asked if he took part in the brick throwing. 'I might have. But I wasn't arrested for it. I just got overawed by all this violence. I probably threw the last stone of the evening.'

The poll tax riots were one of the biggest demonstrations against the Thatcher Reich, and were back in the days when people used to go on demos; the poll tax was the lowest point of a low-point government. The Tory scum were digging up ancient laws to screw money out of people. The Poll Tax march was a justified and great moment in street protest and Burgess was right there in the thick of it. It was the first time for a long time that people had stood up against the Tory bastards. You can trace a direct line from these riots to the Conservative's eventual defeat – it was a great day for the people.

'Opportunity was about as directly political as the Charlatans ever got. In the baggy wars the bands were fairly apolitical. The punk revolution had taught most people that no one was listening, nihilism was the result of punk, and by the 1990s dole-bound decadence was the flavour. Agit pop was replaced by dope-smoking bedsit dwellers and bands sang of their personal pain and depression. 'Fuck the world, let's get stoned' was the battlecry instead of 'stone the world, let's get fucked'.

'Opportunity' also looked at the more sensitive side of the lyricist. 'Being an outsider to the group, or an onlooker,' Tim tried to explain his role in the band, a band that he joined a few months before they took off and one that had been slogging away for two years without him, 'a lot of the time the music is already written. I mean the arrangements still need to be done. I mean I feel so proud of the music, it's really uplifting. It's just that I feel on the outside sometimes.'

Sometimes in the beginning when Tim talked about the group he sounded like he was a fan sitting on the outside looking in. It's never easy being at the front of a band, especially a ready-formed one and the young singer was still finding his feet within the group.

Despite the band's runaway success which saw them marked as the biggest and best newcomers in Blighty in 1990, the Charlatans felt that it was still important to keep things moving, to keep their feet on the ground.

'With the next album there will be a progression definitely. We have no interest in sitting on our laurels. We are committed to getting on the road and keeping on touring – we're into travelling, we're visiting, you know, seeing places, meeting people. We want to keep it there, you know, on the ground, cookin' . . .' noted Martin, a man never satisfied and someone who knew from past experience that getting the breaks in pop is pretty damned difficult and not something to be easily discarded.

But, looking at the album almost as an outsider looking in, Burgess was digging his band's creativity, 'I think *Some Friendly* is a brilliantly varied album. They are lasting songs. There are tracks that will be dated in years to come. It's got quite an industrial feel about it, even though it's so pleasant and free, sort of an urban feel. The organ is used in a really warm way that keeps the bottom end and adds a bit of top as well.'

When Tim looked back on the album in *109* fanzine, he summed up the album beautifully as the keyboard player's baby. 'Rob's LP was *Some Friendly*. He was driven by pain, determination and he's fucking mad for it and he got our first LP to number 1. He covered it all, deep into it, it was a Hammond. I wish it was produced better, I wish we'd done it. If it was done five years later it would have been terrific.'

The Charlatans 1988. Baz Ketley, Rob Collins,
Martin Blunt and Jon Brookes. (Note Rob's
upper-lip — moustache Tipp-Ex-ed out!)
Baz Ketley private collection

'Get on the pitch lad, I'm pulling Ketley off. Just
do your stuff.' Top manager Steve Harrison
prepares to play the teenshag superstar in the
late Eighties as the Charlatans go Premier
League. *Ian Tilton*

Ah! The glamour! Photographer Tom Sheehan
shoots yet another *Melody Maker* front cover
shot in a makeshift bedroom on the road, 1990.
Ian Tilton

Oozing star potential and buckets
of sweat... The Charlatans' Jon Baker
line-up, 1990. *Ian Tilton*

'You'll be able to spot Tim. He's the
one with the massive flares on,' a local
Northwich paper once stated.
Burgess, in full turn-of-the-decade
fashion flow. *Ian Tilton*

Burgess chews on the lyrics to 'The Only One
I Know' in some cheapo hotel on the threshold
of stardom. *Ian Tilton*

'Black and White'… In a session based on the
legendary Stranglers' album cover.
Ian Tilton

Two funny little Baggy men. Jon and Tim looking
like dolls, mid 1990. *Ian Tilton*

Back in the limelight. The Charlatans, with new
guitarist Mark Collins, return to Top Ten pop
stardom with 'Up To Our Hips'. *Rex*

Still skinny after all these beers… Iggy and
Keef… Mick and Ron. Hang on, its Tim and Mark,
Up To Our Hips in cool rock posing. *Ian Tilton*

A snap that speaks volumes about the personalities of the band. Martin's innate modishness, Tim's pop star oozing, Rob's surly couldn't-give-a-toss, Mark's Keefness and the drummer being the drummer! *Chris Floyd*

Pheeew. Rock 'n' roll. 1995 stadium gods
packing a cheeky face at T In The Park.
Chris Floyd. Opposite: *Rex*

The Charlatans: 'We are fucking rock.' *Rex*

For a debut album recorded under the stresses of sudden pop arrival and without the usual gestation period necessary to make a classic work, it was a damn fine intro to the band, and one of the records that caught the real flavour of 1990.

PRESS GANGED . . . REACTIONS TO THE ALBUM

The music press was still in a bit of a tizzy when it came to dealing with the 'Manchester thing', the whole scene had happened without anyone's permission. It was the first time since punk that a fully formed music craze had emerged in what was basically music paper territory and stormed the charts, and bands had for the first few months arrived without their permission.

By late 1990 the Roses and the Mondays were accepted as part of pop folklore, and the two bands between them had supplied a fistful of rock & roll tales that filled column inches and bar rooms with a drugs, sex and hooliganism quotient to keep any publicist grinning with a crazed satisfaction. The Charlatans themselves were getting favourable press, especially hooked around Burgess's neat media persona, but there was still plenty of uncertainty about the music.

The reviews of *Some Friendly* were generally okay, grabbing on average three out of five stars, but there was very little of the full-on five out of five treatment. People weren't sure – the band were undoubtedly big, one of the bands of the year, but their debut album wasn't quite firing on all cylinders; there was something missing, preventing the record from being a drop-dead classic.

Mind you, that's what most people had been saying about the Stone Roses debut the year before . . .

Some claimed that the Charlatans were too often style without content. *Q* pointed out that they were still getting bogged down with the Roses' steals. The watchword was Rob's Hammond organ, which was giving the band a definite individual edge which combined brilliantly with their love of the more mod-orientated end of the British late 1960s pop boom. These were small differences but enough to mark the Charlatans out from the pack.

Where the Roses songs hung heavily on John Squire's intricate guitar work, the Charlatans' first album saw far simpler constructions but wasn't the less effective for it. Sure, they still retained some of that shuffle beat that dominated indie drums at the time and Tim's vocals had that Brown-copyright hoarse and light intonation, and *Q* was impressed enough to note 'the album's twin peaks of "Sproston Green" and "Polar Bear" reveal that the Charlatans possess enough wit, style and personality to transcend mere nostalgia and produce something vigorous and exciting . . .' – it was hardly slavering but the band weren't worried as the record was a dead cert number 1 due to the massive fan base that was out there greedy for this type of music.

The 6 October *NME* was pumped with the album, and alongside the up-to-our-hips-in-murky-lakewater classic shot Terry Staunton, long-term staff writer and a man who had rock & roll thundering through his veins, gave them an 8 out of 10 in the *NME*. He dusted off the regional pigeonholes that were thrust upon the group (Terry knew all about the Midlands, having lived in the backwater town of Stafford) and pointed out that the band were now travelling a very different road from the Stone Roses, with none of their former mentors' aloofness in evidence. He felt that Tim Burgess was more likely 'to tap you on the shoulder and share his packed lunch with you'. The 'low-key' production from Chris Nagle was given top marks, and mentioning stand-out tracks like 'You're Not Very Well' and 'Believe You Me', he felt the band had made a remarkable album after just one year together, not just relying on the hit singles to tide them over.

Sounds raved about the album, giving it four and a half stars, and claiming that it buried any preconceptions about the band being also-rans on the Manchester playing field. *Sounds* claimed that every track on the record was a 'positive gem' and got off on all the moods the album presented, from 'upbeat songs to dreamy melancholia', and decided that the record was one of the 'finest and most challenging records of the past two years'.

The thumbs up were coming in thick and fast from the national press, but the local papers were a tad more suspicious. Many of the regional reviews, and there are heaps of them in the dog-eared press clippings box, started off by claiming that the band were aptly named, being bandwagon jumpers, and that all their songs sounded the same. Then they gradually wrote about how good the group were, and finished off by saying what a great band they were – confusing, eh?

ON THE ROAD (AGAIN) PART THREE

October 1990, with an album at number 1 and the band big news, the Charlatans set off on the first big-time national UK tour. The support came from Intastella, who got the shows after manager Caroline Ellary played Tim Burgess a tape of their tunes. He fell in love with their stuff immediately and put them on the tour, no buy ons (the ancient and dishonourable rock & roll art of charging the support band a fortune for the privilege of opening the night), no rock star bullshit; the Charlatans were the perfect hosts.

Intastella's space-age disco pop sounded like it was constructed for the top 10 and front woman Stella Grundy oozed the star thing perfectly. Kinky afro'd drummer Spencer looked like a renegade from the MC5 and was one of the best sticksmen in Manchester. Along with World Of Twist they represented the best two possibilities for the third wave, both bands playing a twisted pop that avoided the endless pratfalls of lad culture and scallydom. Little did they know that new lad thing would be the enduring culture of the 1990s (boosted by James Brown's *loaded* magazine and Noel Gallagher's footballing, boozin', brawlin' Oasis – a return to the great British values of fumbling inarticulate and drink-sodden goofiness), making their pure pop difficult to break into the mainstream.

Intastella were an inspired choice of support band and if the mass audience chose to not eventually put Intastella into the charts it was their sad loss.

The October tour went off like a rocket. Tickets were sold out virtually on announcement of the dates. This was the group in their heyday, number one and still selling fast; it was a time of triumph for the Charlatans.

The gigs were so packed that they weren't without problems. At the Leeds University show 1800 people crammed into the University's Refectory Hall and a girl was squashed at the front over the crash barriers, getting a crushed windpipe. Stewards managed to pull her out of the sweaty throng and to the side of the stage where she was treated by a first aid team. It was a small blip on a great night, but a signal that the band was now quite definitely in the pop first division.

The local paper loved the first 20 minutes and then felt that there was only 'one drum beat and one tune', but despite this they decided that the band had the style to blow 'bands like Northshite and the Inspiral Cartoons away'.

Mid tour, surrounded by the mayhem of sweet success, Martin Blunt was asked if there was any danger that things were happening too fast. 'We've always tried to hold back. We've always had the chance to oversell ourselves but we never really wanted to, y'know. I mean, we were doing no press for this tour really, but there'll be some publications who'll say, "Oh they've gone all bigheaded."'

Maybe *Smash Hits* were suggesting that just then as the band had just turned down a feature with them.

'A lot of people have come to trivialise the band. I think that's one step up from slagging us off, y'know,' Blunt added.

It was this kind of blunt pride that was serving the Charlatans well and keeping them away from their potential early grave.

When asked if there was a chance that the band could become 'pompous' or 'ego ridden' like 'certain other bands' Martin was cool. 'No, not at all – our egos don't stretch that far – we're not into that "superstar" thing. We don't want the "red rocks" thing. We like the small halls where you can still see everybody and hear the abuse!'

At the Birmingham Hummingbird the local reviewer sent down by

Sounds was distinctly unimpressed, calling Tim 'a cuddly pyjama type of guy' and claiming that the band were 'a man at C & A version of the Joe Bloggs Stone Roses', signing off with, 'At times like these, you just wish their horizons were as wide as their trousers.' Predictably the crowd just went mad.

'People really did love the Charlatans,' long-time Brummie gig-goer The Bat pointed out, contradicting the gig review.

On 19 October the Charlatans popped out over the Channel for a date at La Cigalle in Paris. For a mere 89.50 quid you could get a two-day coach trip to Paris organised by travel agents in Northwich. Everyone was at it since the Roses fans had instigated the following your favourite band like a footy team lark the year before, running coach parties of baggied-up and drugged-up pop kids to Paris and back. This run was always the favourite, and countless coaches made the trips, countless customs were duped by barmy Brit kids with drug stashes hidden all over the joint (ha!), pissing in lay-byes, robbing service stations, shagging in hotel corridors . . .

The fans were far wilder than the bands could ever be, although their boisterous hi jinks were just yer average Brits on the piss Euro foolin'. The chic Parisian youth could only look on aghast and stare at what crazed pop buffoonery 'Les Rosbifs' had come up with now, as hordes of ruddy-faced drunk teens fell off the coaches, bleary eyed and foul of mouth, looking for some action.

La Cigalle was bang smack in the centre of Paris's red-light area, an expensive student disco that every couple of weeks played host to the cream of new British pop talent; they all came through here, from the Manics to the Mondays, a whole new generation of yobbish bands cutting their Britpop teeth on foreign soil.

And the Charlatans were just the latest in the long line of new bands. The baggy Manc thing, although not mainstream pop culture in France, was a hit with the hip kids in the French capital. Every week Manchester DJs were imported to the city to play a clutch of cutting-edge indie vinyl and very chic kids were flapping their cute new flares to the baggy shuffle.

The Northwich boys had it large!

Tim swaggered round the stage, claiming that the band were playing the best songs ever and oddly introducing one new track as 'The Birth Of A Cripple'.

The *Melody Maker* wasn't sure at first, wondering if the band were being a bit too blatant in their steals, but eventually decided that the band were too much fun and the kings of the zeitgeist to even bother about being original.

Meanwhile, the coach parties all climbed on to the stage only to be thrown off by the bouncers.

What a great weekend out!

*

Back home the tour was gathering thunder, the band bonding tighter with their audience, a bond that would serve them well for years to come.

'Glasgow Barrowlands was brilliant. We travelled up in a car from Manchester to see the show,' remembers fan Ian Patterson, 'I'd seen them before but now things were getting really big the atmosphere was like a giant party.'

Glasgow had always been kind to rock & roll groups, and people's bands have always prospered in the city. From day one it had supported Manchester more intensely than the home city itself, recognising the very streetness of the bands and it was paying off well for the Manc-associated groups. The Roses had played their last ever British show there and the whole Manc baggy flared-trouser scene was huge in Glasgow: 'The crowd loved them no matter what they did,' points out Patterson.

On the other hand the elder statesmen of the local media, being pretty well out of touch by the new scene that had all but bypassed their too cosy consensus, were baffled by the new bands like the Charlatans, writing, 'They've got the crowd, they've got the star, all they need now is the songs.'

Ouch!

At the Brighton Event on 5 November the local (male) reviewer was enraptured by Tim, pointing out that the Charlatans managed to threaten on a sexual level whilst Manchester's rival bands were mere lightweights messing with rock & roll folklore, and then went into raptures about Tim. This was the reaction that a pop star was meant to get from an audience. Total lust!

In keeping with the psychedelic haze that surrounded the coolest British rock bands at the time, they had a light show with slides showing the album cover and a masked face. Interspersed with this was a very hip heated-oil set of images bubbling up from the well of a Captain Trips effects unit.

The light show was a direct connection to a psychedelic past, the sort of genuine full-on trip that 1960s psych fans like the Charlatans could have only dreamt of in their days of unavowed fandom. This was the sort of groovy oils and weird shit that had freaked out the heads at the UFO, the Avalon ballroom and the Fillmore West. In fact not only was it an approximation of those days, it was the real G-E-N-U-I-N-E thing, as the bearded freak controlling the barrage of cranium blowing visuals was Captain Whizzo, the man who had conceived the original skull freak visuals in those trip clubs in the first place. He was discovered doing the visuals at a Deee-Lite (remember them and their divine 'Groove Is In The Heart' single . . . glam disco at its best) and Factory records party in New York during the New Music Seminar. The party was one of those totally hedonistic experiences from the period and a melting between Manchester and New York, two places that had musical connections at the time.

Staggering around with your mind blown on top-notch grade As and bizarre chemicals made the party seem like some sort of modern-day freak show, and to get a bit of that flavour into the burgeoning UK psychedelic pop scene was a smart move and a neat connection with the rock & roll past. Captain Whizzo was rumoured to be living in a treehouse in California, and had worked with the likes of the Chocolate Watch Band, Jimi Hendrix, Quicksilver Messenger Service and Hot Tuna, the sort of rollcall that would have made the Northwich record collectors slaver with excitement.

It was on this tour that the Charlatans found a novel way of dealing with Rob's pesky Hammond keyboard, which would break down at regular intervals; it had always been the bane of the live set. Now, if there was any problem with the organ Collins would pick up a large bell and clang it away frantically until the road crew made it on to the stage and pasted the rickety thing back together.

Well, it was better than booting it into the crowd!

On 12 November they played a packed out Rock City in Nottingham, where fan Betty Taylor caught them. 'The atmosphere was brilliant. I remember Intastella playing and they were pretty good but the crowd was really waiting for the Charlatans. They had the backing intro tape of "Imperial 109" which then went into "Only One I Know", and the place went mental then. People were massively into them; they had become so popular so quickly.

'They ended the gig with "Sproston Green" which seemed to go on for ever, just peaking, peaking, and then left the stage. Of course everyone went mad and they came back and did "Polar Bear" and a longer version of "Everything Changed". Tim muttered "Ta very much" at everyone, and that was it.'

In October vital new press allies were getting on board: *Melody Maker*'s Stud Brothers were won over by the band, and in a feature on the band they described the album as 'beautiful' and almost 'feminine', whilst finding Tim the perfect star – no longer was Bob Stanley alone at the *Maker*. The Studs would become virtually the Charlatans' biggest champions on the rock press.

In an amusing piece they encountered the band lying on their backs in the lobby of a hotel when conducting the interview and confounding the waiters. They checked on Tim's ebullient optimism and contrasted it with Martin's determined pessimism, 'his head bent forward in what's either a sombrely Kafkaesque posture or a polite attempt to keep up with this floor-level conversation'.

The Studs loved Tim. 'Tim's lips are so romantically lush, his eyes so wide and innocent, his whole demeanour so sweetly mischievously androgynous, it's impossible to imagine anyone else fronting the group.'

The Burgess star thing was still paying the bills!

The band themselves knew this and in the pictures that accompanied the article, like all pictures of the band, saw the rest of the group skulking in the background whilst Burgess threw the rock star shapes.

It was a simple formula but it was hitting pay dirt.

BRITS AWARDS

That December the Charlatans were nominated for a Brit award in the best newcomers category. In a move seen as getting away from the stuffy past of the awards ceremony, acts such as the Happy Mondays, the Stone Roses and the Beautiful South were all picked. The awards are chosen by 150 members of the British Phonographic Institute which is made up of high-ranking record executives.

The Brits had, over the few short years of its existence, gathered a reputation for being old-fashioned and out of touch. The awards ceremony itself was broadcast live and was usually a laughable mass of errors, with turgid, creaking, shite groups walking off with the honours whilst all the cool new talent was left on the shelf.

The main reason for winning an award was that it generated more record sales – no one forms a rock & roll band so that they can fill their mantelpiece with cups and shields; how square is that? Any award picked by 'experts' is always going to be fraught with difficulties, and most groups recognise that awards voted for by the fans alone are the only ones that have any real meaning.

But because of the TV coverage and the big fuss made about the award ceremony on record sales, isn't it laughable what crap really pushes the music market along? I can't think of anything as tedious as a televised back-slapping ceremony – it's the sort of crap nightmare that the dullards who run the music industry delight in.

The Charlatans, of course, didn't win, and I haven't got a clue who did, it's that important.

LONDON IS MINE . . . THE KILBURN SHOW

The Kilburn National is a big one, a further rung up the ladder, with a 5000 capacity. Selling this out was the perfect nightcap to an amazing year which had seen the band come from playing gigs in huts around Northwich to being one of the biggest groups in the country; that's a fast rise to the top and it looks like it was done with the minimum of fuss.

The Charlatans' show at the Kilburn that December was a triumph. Reviewers talked of Tim Burgess, the perfect pop star with drooling girls at the front and sweaty boy fans digging the band just behind, proper pop, an overt appeal to all sexes and tastes. Burgess may have epitomised the star and the sex needed to get the teens juiced up, but it was the tight-ass band featuring a 'thunderous Hammond' running through the hits with ease that tapped the positive review space.

This was a band during its triumphant ascendance. The Charlatans were making pop look easy. They were tight and they were drilled and they had Tim giving it the 'X' factor.

AND FINALLY 1990 IS ALL OVER

The year end saw the Happy Mondays' Bez dressed as Father Christmas smoking a spliff on the front of the *NME*. Manc bands dominated the year-end polls, although there was a pointer to the future with home counties with some acts dubbed so-called 'shoe-gazers', such as Ride, getting votes as well. Maybe there was, at last, an opportunity coming to overthrow this northern thing after all.

The new pop hierarchy of the 1990s was now gathering momentum away from the tail end of the baggy thing which was already becoming stale and dull, a retarded parody of itself after just one year. With real bandwagon jumpers and useless outfits fighting over the scraps of attention, its cultural worth was that now everyone seemed to smoke dope, dress in baggy clothes and be a 'lad'; it wouldn't be long before *loaded* was launched and Chris Evans would take over the world.

At a badly attended gig in Manchester's International, the Manic Street Preachers stunned a totally unsupportive crowd into silence with their ferocious poppy glam punk rock whilst supporting Flowered Up. Very few people saw the awesome potential in the band, but those of us that got it were already in love with them.

The post Stone Roses-influenced bands were in their rehearsal rooms getting ready to take over from the decimated 1980s acts, baggy pop was the flavour and 12 months after they burst on to the scene the very satisfied Charlatans could sit back buzzing after an incredible year.

They were figuring heavily in the end-of-year critics' lists. *Melody Maker* had *Some Friendly* at number 6, calling it a 'glorious collection of modern pop songs – charismatic, sweet and handsome'; *Sounds* pegged it at number 25 – detailing the album as 'a likable, joyous romp through the buzz of 1990'; and *Vox* claimed that the 'hit singles were no fluke'.

It was a pattern repeated everywhere: the band was the name to drop, critically acclaimed with a massive album that had set them up nicely for a good innings in the 1990s.

A solid line-up, sensational easy success, a mad for it fanbase, pop naturals . . . what could possibly go wrong?

1991
Becoming Unstuck

1991 looked good at the start. If 1990 had been the year that the Charlatans had exploded from nowhere on to the scene, 1991 was going to be the year that they would easily consolidate on this success. There was a trip to the States planned, a whole world to go and tour, and cash tills were ringing merrily in the main western pop markets. In those early months of that year they looked a dead cert to be the only northern band to break out of the UK and go truly global.

All they needed to put together was a second album that was a step forward from the first, and in the early months of that year their thoughts turned to new tunes and the scraps of ideas that were lying around.

Already 1991 was picking up from where 1990 had left off. That February the band were winners of the *NME*'s best new band section of their annual poll. Winning the poll was confirmation that they were winning over the punter's respect. Celebrating, the band held court with *NME* journalist Andrew Collins in hometown Northwich.

Relaxed, as you would be after a great year, they jumped around in a half-frozen lake near their hometown for Kevin Cummings' series of brilliant shots. Then they sat back and tried not to laugh when asked if they were the coolest band on the scene, with Tim declaring, 'It takes more than 19 fags to make a packet of 20.' He then proceeded to chew up the interview with a series of hilariously daft quotes, finishing with the fact that they weren't going to take a track off *Some Friendly* for the new single because 'we want to go forward, do something new, make it a bit more difficult, get an erection out of it'.

It was also reported that brothers Steve and Andy Woods were finishing the *Looking For The Orange One* fanzine after five issues because 'the band had grown away from the zine'. Feeling it was too small to cover the band left the task of being the band's main fanzine to Jon McGee's *109*.

McGee was an unabashed fan and, slightly older than the band, he had known Steve Harrison from the manager's punk days, and since the late 1970s had witnessed some of the greatest rock & roll bands on the planet kick some righteous ass. When he saw the Charlatans he was totally blown away, first becoming a fan and then working for them on and off; his tireless enthusiasm via his zine was a vital connection between the band and their fanbase.

Phase one of their world domination plan was clearly over – no longer were they a small cult band, no longer were they indie strugglers. This was a serious concern. The tunes from the first album were clearly baggage for the band now, they were moving on as fast as possible, changing quickly, looking for other things to do with their sound, rehearsing new tunes and finding a new way to work their music.

The band knew where they stood and they understood their audience.

Only a year on the road, they had bonded tight with their fans, and this had set them apart from some more arrogant contemporaries.

Burgess related to his audience perfectly; he knew they were like him, lovers of music, just beyond fashion, these people were here for the band and the song. Looking out, Burgess declared his audience as having 'no fixed haircut!'

THE DEAD GOOD DEAD DEAD GOOD LABEL

Encouraged by the Charlatans' success, Dead Dead Good, the label that they had set up to put out 'Indian Rope' was beginning to take on a life of its own. Quickly established, it became one of the biggest labels in the country. Based in a high-street record shop in Northwich, it broke all the music biz rules that dictate virtually everything has to be run from London.

There had always been independent record labels in the north, like Zoo in Liverpool in the post punk days, and Factory in Manchester for a good 15 years after punk, who had been key players in both city's musical developments. Dead Dead Good so nearly pulled it off to become a similar big-time northern underground label, run on a shoestring budget, enthusiasm and a fan's nous for exactly what's going on. But after some initial spectacular successes it burned itself out ironically, by trying to push new bands instead of concentrating on its run of dance act chart smashes.

It was Andy Woods, fresh from his *Looking For The Orange One* fanzine who ran the label. 'I had got into dance music in a big way, I was going down Quadrant Park in Liverpool and picked up on "Katherine E" which was like the anthem down there.'

Surprised that no one had signed the track, he picked it up for himself. The single, released on 6 April 1991 peaked at number 41 and hung around the charts for five weeks. It was the label's follow up to 'Indian Rope' and things were boding well. The next hit was their fourth release, 'Insanity', from Oceanic, which turned into one of the biggest hits of that year. It was starting to look like they were minting money.

'"Insanity" sold 500,000 copies. Labels down south couldn't believe where the label had come from and where we were finding all these hits!' laughs Andy.

Oceanic crashed in at number 3 after its release late August 1991 and was in the charts for four months. Their follow up, 'Wicked Love', the label's fifth release, only got to number 25 on a three-week chart run when it was released that autumn, but the following June they hit the top 20 again with 'Controlling Me' – it looked like Oceanic had found their feet (having bigger hits than their parent group the Charlatans), but that autumn 'Ignorance' only got to 72 and that was the end of their chart career.

The label also had a minor hit (number 72 on a one-week run) with

Rhythm Eternity's 'Pink Champagne', although that outfit would spring a few surprises yet.

'We found Rhythm Eternity in Crewe and they did all right. They were really a front for Dario G, who has gone on to greater things,' explains Woods. (Dario G is in fact not a hip Italian DJ, as his name suggests, but a northern born and bred Crewe Alexandra fan who took his pseudonym from Crewe's long-serving (second longest in the league as this book went to print, the longest being Port Vale's John Rudge) manager Dario Gradi!)

Dead Dead Good also put out a couple of singles for 2 For Joy which although not getting mass chart action, kept the pot boiling. It looked like it would become a cred dance imprint as that side of things was going swimmingly.

It was the rock side that they fucked up on, backing That Uncertain Feeling, Rig, Kerosene, Manta Ray and Orange Deluxe . . . bands that showed plenty of potential but were just in the wrong place at the wrong time. It was money down the drain; breaking bands is difficult at the best of times and in the early 1990s dance was rooling the roost, the live circuit had nosedived and straight guitar music was in the gutter – Dead Dead Good lost a fortune on its rock & roll bands.

By 1993 the label experiment was over.

OVER EASY . . . 'OVER RISING'

'Over Rising' was the first of the new material released by the Charlatans, put out on 25 February and backed with a Flood remix of 'Opportunity' from *Some Friendly* and coupled with new tracks 'Way Up There' and 'Happen To Die'. The three tracks apart from 'Opportunity' were produced by Dave Allen and the EP was recorded at RAK Studios and at Ray Davies from the King's Konk Studios (a great place to make a guitar record).

'Over Rising', mixed by Mark Stent, was a funky piano groove that was shackled to that sort of off-kilter council estate swagger that the Happy Mondays had been making their own for the last couple of years. The verses are all smartly struck sevenths on the guitar, nailing the lolloping beat, and the chorus is understated and anthemic. Not as instant as their previous hits, repeated listens are rewarding as the song is one of the best tunes in the band's early canon.

The other three tunes on the EP were long, hypnotic, funky grooves and the closest that the band came to marrying their sound with the mesmerising acid house rock crossover, three underrated songs that actually pulled off this difficult task a lot better than most of their rivals had managed.

They included the bass-driven English psychedelics of 'Way Up There'; 'Opportunity Three' was the band mixing the fat narcotics of a near acid house groove into their sound and tripping out in the vocals in Beatles'

'Tomorrow Never Knows' style – the song has that sort of keyboard pulse that the genius Spacemen 3 had been experimenting with for years whilst being totally ignored by most people. The final track, 'Happen To Die', was closer to rock with Blunt's bass getting back to the driving seat, gelling with crashing guitar chords and trad Charlatans swirling organ.

The whole EP is strong as fuck. To think that they were throwing songs as good as these away on B sides shows a young band confident in their abilities. At this point of time the Charlatans seemed to be making pop music effortlessly.

Bagged up in a sleeve that was the latest in monochrome shots of the band, featuring this time Jon Baker, open mouthed before the camera, the euphoric young guitarist monging out in pop star best.

Press reaction was mixed. 'Well-formed lips are not enough,' declared the *Melody Maker*; the *NME*, though, was well into the record, deciding that even if the verses were 'perfunctory' the chorus had a 'great swelling hook' and although the record 'wasn't the Charlatans at their best' it was still a cool pop record.

The single was a hit, getting as high as number 15, enjoying a five-week run on the charts.

The Charlatans were looking to consolidate their success with the new single, and there had been a remixed version of 'Opportunity' available in clubs for a few weeks. The remix itself had been meant to be one of those groovy club-only things but had crossed over to national radio playlists fooling many people into thinking that it was a single. The demand had been pretty good for the track and it was decided to couple it with the brand new track 'Over Rising'.

The 'Over Rising' EP still saw chart action but the heat to some extent was off the Charlatans. Instead of being the hot new band on the block, the brightest and the shiniest penny from Manc land, they were now old-hat, the pop kids and the *Smash Hits* kidz had moved on, and the band were now down to a core audience.

The single's title meant 'rising above, up and coming, taking over . . .' explained Burgess, who added that the band weren't trying their damnedest to stick to the formula and grovel to daytime radio schedules. 'We definitely wanted to make the song more guitary, the piano sounded quite beautiful, so we decided to find the most disgusting guitar sound we could and muck it up a little. The producer kept trying to turn down the guitar sound, saying, "The radio won't like it." We just said, "Fuck the radio, this is the first EP from the Charlatans in 1991 and it's going to fucking kick and burn." By the 14th attempt, we finally got what we wanted.'

The band were pretty busy in the studios that February as they also recorded their second Peel session at Maida Vale, putting down 'Can't Even Be Bothered', 'Between 10th And 11th' and 'Opportunity 9' for the great man's show.

Then it was time to shoot some videos for the single on the Yorkshire Moors and at the Apollo theatre in Manchester; this they did at the same time as shooting a video for 'Sproston Green', which was their American single released on 4 February (the B side was 'Opportunity 3').

On 10 February they set out on their first coast-to-coast US tour, a real jaunt that would see them on the road into early March. By now 500,000 copies of *Some Friendly* had been sold in the UK, and the band shared a split cover on *Rolling Stone*, the old timers' music mag that was always so damned difficult to get into, let alone waltz around on the cover of. The august organ was tipping them as one of the bands of the year to come . . .

Following on the heels of that tour there was a jaunt to Australia and New Zealand, and then in April some big shows in Japan – Northwich Memorial Hall was starting to seem a long way away.

First, though, they had to go and make their debut Stateside.

SPAZ DANCING IN THE USA

Full of ourselves in the UK, we Brits tend to think that the world of rock & roll totally revolves around us. Of course this couldn't be further from the truth.

The US is where it's at.

In the hot house of pop fashion we may churn out more bands per capita than anyone else in the world, but because of this intense fashion-fired music scene a lot of our groups make very little sense to anyone else in the world nowadays.

Conquering the UK is one thing but to really prove you have got it, you have to break the US, the epicentre of rock & roll. And things weren't going very well then for the Brits over the Atlantic; by 1990 UK bands had pretty well given up with America, although the likes of EMF and Jesus Jones may have been chalking up their one-hit-wonder status.

But the Charlatans were already off to a good start as their debut album was the biggest import album of 1990, reaching number 73 in the charts and selling nearly 300,000 there, and they were one of four bands on the front cover of *Rolling Stone*, tipped as a band to watch in 1991.

There was an attitude gap that was knackering a lot of UK groups. Back on home turf up-coming British bands revelled in their bad boy status, and every detail of their lurid yob lifestyles was hot copy and flogged records. But cross the Atlantic and there was a very different set of rules in place. In the US there is a distinctly harder work ethic in action – bad behaviour is still good copy but it seems to have its place and sometimes it seems almost cartoon-like in its unreality. Most Brit bands went to the US, did a couple of gigs, were rude to their record labels and stomped off home again. It had become a tradition. In America, the music business is a business, and bands were expected to press the flesh and play the game. UK bands brought up on being surly were hardly going to suck corporate cock.

America is the country that invented rock & roll and is the world's number 1 market (Japan is 2, Germany 3 and the UK 4, fact fans), and isn't always that hospitable to outside acts looking in. In the 1950s it was only the occasional British rock & roller that got the taste of the hi life US style, with very few of our homegrown stars making it over the pond.

So when the Beatles broke the whole market open with their astounding success it was more of a surprise than anything. After the Beatles the floodgates were opened wide and the 1960s and 1970s saw the US market dominated by UK acts, a supremacy that lasted until punk started to put the blinkers on things.

The Americans, all nice and comfy, didn't 'get' punk, and despite a mini revival for the UK bands with the new romantic shite of the 1980s it's been downhill all the way since them. The situation hasn't been helped by UK bands falling apart before they could score the US success that seemed inevitable. The Smiths were, perhaps the main band here, as in the mid to late 1980s they were gradually building in the States, and then fell apart on the verge of the breakthrough. Lacking the work at all costs attitude of their transatlantic rivals, UK bands were wont to blow it at the last minute.

If the Smiths had made it stateside, then the Manc bands of the next decade would have found a far easier path to US success than they have.

The occasional band still gets through but for mainstream US the British bands don't really rock enough to assault their marketplace. American mega bucks success is built on rock – rock rools over there in a way that it never really has done here. By the late 1980s the cultural reference points between us were beginning to spin miles apart. The Stone Roses may have been making pristine pop but their seriously laid back attitude completely flummoxed the workaholic Yanks, whilst the Happy Mondays made very little sense outside the UK.

The Charlatans, though, had a better chance than most as their music had that universal appeal – pop that could rock – and they were a tight touring band who didn't come equipped with the big surly attitude of some of their contemporaries.

So, whilst the UK was rocking to their shimmering sexy beat, it was time to turn attention to the US. Five dates were lined up, hooked around a mini festival called 'The Gathering Of The Tribes'.

BUT FIRST A BUNCH OF OLD HIPPIES MAKE THEM ADD 'UK' TO THE END OF THEIR NAME!

It's one of those bizarre twists in rock that a British band will storm the UK and then take their schtick over to the US only to find some clapped-out bunch of old hippies have already *staked a claim to the name* and are prepared to go to court to hold on to their monicker.

Suede would have to trade in the US under the ridiculous name of the London Suede and US band Dinosaur when challenged by the Grateful Dead spin-off band of the same name swiftly changed their name to the rather witty Dinosaur Jnr. The Charlatans found out pretty soon that there was a bunch of old-timers who were already trading under their nom de plume.

'Fans should note that there is no similarity in our trouser width,' a spokesman for the Cheshire Charlatans cracked as the band added the rather dull 'UK' on to the end of their name.

'It's not a problem really,' intoned Jon Brookes. 'When our record was first played in England on the John Peel show, John being a man of many records said, "And this is the Charlatans from 1968." It was another band called the Charlatans which we didn't know existed. Apparently they wanted to sue us for loads of money for using the name. We put the UK on the end, so if they decide to be silly, we've got it covered.'

Tim seemed almost glad that there was a controversy over the name: 'Luckily it's caused a bit of controversy, which is excellent for us. Apparently there is another band called the Charlatans, it makes us seem even more like a bunch of charlatans, which is really dead good. You know what I mean?'

The question that remains on this pundit's lips is why are no American bands ever made to add US on to the end of their names in the UK market?

The original Charlatans were a West Coast psychedelic band formed in 1964 and, pioneers of the new freak scene, they had the whole US band works, including their own band house at 1090 Page Street in San Francisco. History paints them as San Francisco's first drug-orientated rock band who by all accounts were a pretty whacky bunch, as reported in such an unlikely paper as the *Scotsman*, 'In 1965 the Charlatans could be found at the Red Dog Saloon, Virginia City, playing their first residency . . . dressed as Mississippi gamblers and playing to an LSD-crazed audience who would show their appreciation by emptying their 6-guns into the ceiling . . .' It may be a tad exaggerated but it still sounds like one hell of a gig!

The original Charlatans played good-time blues and country, with songs like 'Codeine' and 'Long Comes A Viper', and a brilliant cover of Van Dyke Parks' 'High Coin' and the woodwind-driven 'Time To Get Straight'. Signed to Phillips they struggled to record a Dan Healey-produced eponymous album, which had the band on the cover dressed in their 19th-century gambling threads, a pic which looked remarkably like the bizarre vaudeville sleeve of the great lost band of the Manc scene, World Of Twist (another note to the reader – please check out World Of Twist as they were brilliant and should have been massive with their hard-edged psychedelic pop). Then the old-time Charlatans' drummer Terry Wilson got busted, and by mid 1969 the band members had gone their separate ways.

TAKING THE COALS BACK TO NEWCASTLE . . . THE CHARLATANS BECOME THE ONLY UK BAND OF THEIR GENERATION WHO CAN BE ARSED WITH BREAKING THE US!

The Charlatans, unlike the Stone Roses, had decided to work the US, a move that made them, initially, the biggest baggy band there, a curious state of affairs that eventually saw the Stone Roses getting compared to them! The Charlatans were lumped in with the Americans' warped perception of the 'Manchester scene' where bands like the Soup Dragons and EMF were pulled into the northern city's ever-expanding music scene.

In March 1991 they debuted at the Ritz in New York, a fair-sized venue which they managed to pack out, even adding a proper pop star touch with excited teenage girl fans down at the front screaming at Burgess. The gig went well, even if it did receive mixed reviews. Out of its home-based context this sort of pop mystified people, and as the US was in the middle of the grunge wars, British pop sounded lightweight and carefree. Separated from its drugs and pop culture roots and placed in the middle of a full-on rock & roll battle the band sounded pallid and underfed. 'Haircut bands' the hipsters sneered.

The Charlatans also hit the US the same week that Oliver Stone's *Doors* film was released, and got unfavourable comparisons with the original kings of the keyboard-driven freak pop.

The next show was the Ackerman Hall at UCLA, a student union hall bang smack in the heart of Doors country, being the same Californian college as the Doors themselves formed at. The Charlatans were the first of a fistful of Manc-related bands to play the city, and the local press pointed out that they were rushing in where the Stone Roses feared to tread; this would be their story in the US.

Playing to a half-filled hall, the band were disheartened but ploughed on regardless; the reviews here were much better, one even referring to Burgess as being a 'frenzied disciple of Mick Jagger'.

The way that the music scene in America works is so different from the UK. In Britain a band can be swept to the top by a sudden twist in the fashion stakes but in America it can take years of grinding it out on the live circuit until a band gets anywhere near to breakthrough. It takes much patience and a lot of work, two qualities that British bands aren't always endowed with.

Melody Maker went over to the US to cover the band on tour and documented the usual band and media stand-off that occurred when a young and hot British band were interviewed live on air in the US. Although not quite in the same ball park as the Pistols or Oasis swearathons, the Charlatans' disarming honesty must have caused some confusion. In LA the DJ offered to play 'White Shirt' or 'Polar Bear' from the album, but Burgess decided that he should play 'Flower' as the other two 'were shite now'. In a climate of rampant self promotion this sort of no-bullshit-norf-of-England honesty quite often caused bafflement. Tim also went on to describe the *Some Friendly* album as '60 per cent good and 40 per cent below par', hardly the stuff of arrogant chest-beating plug-plug-plug that the US pop business was used to.

For *Melody Maker* Tim looked back on *Some Friendly*, giving them a deeper perspective on the album and the initial interviews that accompanied it at the time. Even now, only a few months after its release, the band felt that they had advanced a long way forward.

'The LP was pretty much influenced by what was going on in Britain last year,' said Tim. 'But the songs were strong enough to stop it from seeming like a fad album. We were naive. We were part of the street culture of the time because us and all our friends were going to clubs and enjoying it. The mistake a lot of groups make is to copy from the past too heavily. We may have stolen a few chord progressions from the 1960s, but we've brought it through the 1970s and 1980s until it's slap bang where we are now.'

Tim also pointed out his influences, with one telling name that was going to have a profound effect on their songwriting in the future – Bob Dylan.

'I've got millions of records. Far too many records to be influenced by just one thing. I've admired and had exposure to so many people, from Iggy Pop to John Lydon, from Joy Division to Donna Summer. Oh, and Bob Dylan – I'm reading his biography at the moment. The only thing most people that I admire have in common is that they're just slightly to the left field of mainstream pop. It's all pop, it's only pop. But pop's still important, a reason to kill yourself for, or dream about.'

Sitting in the US hotel room gave Burgess a chance to kick back and look back on the last barmy 12 months. Honest enough to check his own shortcomings, he noted that the band were willing to shed their egos for the good of the band, and he admitted that he used to throw 'tantrums and things like that, claiming that I was the greatest thing!' Burgess felt that the band were now on the right track but 'wait till two years time, we'll be unstoppable'.

'I definitely hope to be seen, be heard and be thought of,' he said. 'It's important that we do mean something. It's very easy to become trivial. We're not performing monkeys and I hope we make people think about things. I want them to come away from a Charlatans gig feeling horny, brilliant, dramatic and meaningful . . . not particularly in that order . . .' Then with a typically bizarre Burgess mindwarp he went off at a tangent, 'The human brain only weighs two or three pounds, but there are over 500 trillion synapse connections. Each of those can invent or create something, from the combustion engine to literature. If everyone in our audience could use just one of those connections then we've achieved something.'

Confused? Burgess wasn't, as he then added, 'The Charlatans are sex and threat and dark corners where you can do things you want to keep quiet. There has to be a corner where the mistakes are made.'

The mutha fucker certainly knew how to talk up a great battle.

'On the record there is more sex, live it's more direct and more emotionally charged. There's also violence and threat but it's quite subtle and depressed. What we do is clearer than a direct socialist Billy Bragg type of thing,' he added.

The Charlatans were in that Doors-style position of being a critics' fave band, a boys' band and a 'serious' band that little girls certainly understood!

Burgess had by now taken to the habit of carrying a notebook around with him in which to write lyrics, and he showed *Melody Maker* a phrase that he had woken up with that morning – 'Today, I'm happy, you're a weirdo'. *Melody Maker* jokingly wondered if it would be the title of an upcoming single.

Clairvoyance was in the house!

The real world made one of those occasional intrusions into the fantasy world of rock & roll when Tim flicked on the TV and the gulf war was droning on.

'Operation Desert Storm is a fucking serious thing because people are dying, but here it looks more like an American "Saint and Greavsie",' he muttered darkly as the almost cartoon-like unreality of war flickered across the cathode ray. The war seemed like an MTV pop video, less real than pop; the world was getting weirder.

The Charlatans were making tentative steps in a country where there was no chance of the instantaneous success they had achieved in the UK. It was going to be a different sort of haul here, a haul that Steve Harrison understood well. At the annual huge New Music seminar in New York City he was spotted looking calmly confident in his Manchester City top and flares.

Could America be about to go their way as well?

GATHERING OF THE TRIBES

A sunny day in LA and the seeds of the infamous travelling festival Lollapalooza are getting sewn, in a too-plastic amphitheatre lost in a maze of roads somewhere in the huge sprawling city of Los Angeles. The Cult's Ian Astbury has arranged a bill of bands that smashes boundaries and crosses genres, and it's a measure of the Charlatans' potential success Stateside that they have been chosen as one of the bands on the bill.

The 'Gathering Of The Tribes' was a strange spectacle, deep in the heart of poodle rock country in LA, with an eclectic bill of bands in an attempt to focus on the wide range of styles on the current music scene.

People like Public Enemy, the Cramps, Iggy Pop and ex Pistols Steve Jones were strutting their stuff along with the Charlatans, on a baking hot day in the quarter-full stadium at Costa Mesa Pacific Amphitheatre.

In America at the time the whole idea of these sort of gigs was bizarre anyway as people just didn't go to festivals with mixed bills – this was a European ideal, and you have to doff your cap to Ian Astbury for trying to break down these barriers, which exist in the US due to radio programming which seeks to split all bands into marketable divisions.

It was precisely this sort of segmenting of music into different boxes that confused the more eclectic British pop mind, as Martin Blunt observed. 'I watched a lot of MTV. It was mainly rock and rap. It's really homogenised. Apart from an hour after midnight when college radio plays what you would call the independent type of stuff, which is pretty good, stuff like Jane's Addiction, Pixies, the Breeders, it's mainly rock and rap. After eight hours it all sounds the same. There's not such a "thing" going on over there.'

The 'Gathering Of The Tribes' was the prototype Lollapalooza, an early incarnation of the roving festival that was to dominate American underground rock for most of the 1990s. In the States, despite the 1960s hippie fest Woodstock, the festival had never really caught on.

For the Charlatans, though, it was a great day. They connected with the small crowd who had vague notions of the Manchester thing; they were prepared to do the work and were getting ahead of the Roses and the Mondays in the US. This was the fourth and last date on their first jaunt across the pond, one that had seen them take in New York, Toronto and San Francisco.

Arriving at the stadium an hour before show time, they hit the stage running, playing to the spoilt-brat rich kids of California. They were the quintessential gang of spotty, pale-skinned Brit pop kids out in the mean midday sun.

Tim was doing his full-on Jagger frontman bit, flapping those pop star lips, dragging on a cig, spazz dancing and leaving the stage to let the crowd check the band out during their instrumentals and as the band extended the now traditional set-ending 'Sproston Green'. The Charlatans were great that day, playing their hearts out completely, belying their low billing (next band on was The Quireboys!).

When asked, Martin Blunt saw behind the bullshit. 'I think the idea behind it was really good. I don't particularly like the Cult but I've got respect for him [Astbury] for what he tried to because it had a lot to do with political feeling within the States. They've got a big censorship law over there and you have to register to vote. A lot of young people now, they aren't bothering to register. I know they ain't got much choice over here, they can either vote for a conservative government or one with a few different ideals, but they should still use the vote.'

When asked if they had time to fraternise with some of the other stars on the bill, Martin looked a bit nonplussed. 'We played and then we went basically. We were asked to go back on later in the night just after or before Iggy Pop but we said people should have been there at 1pm in the afternoon when we were on, y'know.'

Sat backstage in the caravan after the show Tim explained, 'I've got that ego that makes me want to jump up and down, you know, to be like a spazz . . . that's me. I've always had that. I always wanted the attention.'

The Charlatans were fired up anyway from a great response the night before in San Francisco. There was a real feeling in the camp that the US could be theirs, that they had the best chance of breaking the US out of all the so-called baggy bands. But with that typically British attitude to the States they didn't seem to care.

'It's no big issue,' said Tim. 'It doesn't make any difference to us. I mean the record label will probably release three tracks off the album and all those sort of things that we're not into, but we don't really care. It's no big thing to us because we don't really see it.'

When asked if he had any fear of the US, Tim explained, 'Yeah, I suppose so. I mean some bands come over here and they disappear. They forget England. We definitely won't be changing our sound for America.'

Aaah, America, the crock of gold and the curse, the place where they invented rock & roll and where a band can make a huge pile of money if it breaks there. It's also a music scene that is totally dominated by the business, and a huge continent that can easily chew up a band and spit out its aspirations. Many a time a huge British act has gone to the States and found that their love for the birthplace of rock & roll hasn't been reciprocated, and have had their careers broken trying to get in there. Just look at Slade, the biggest band in Britain in the 1970s, who came back from a year trying to break the US to find that they had been replaced by the fickle pop public.

America was still trying to make up its mind about the 'Manchester Scene'. The Happy Mondays were making little sense or headway there as the standard explanation that had sold them in the UK, of being mad football scallies who had calmed down on Ecstasy and got into dance music, was incomprehensible in the US where sports fans didn't riot, didn't take Ecstasy, and rock fans had never really got into dance. The brilliance of the Mondays freaked-out music-hall funk punk was going over a lot of heads. The Stone Roses could have had it, but they kept delaying tours and seemed totally nonchalant about the whole business; whilst the Inspiral Carpets were plugging away in the clubs attempting to do things from the grass roots up.

The Charlatans had been in a lot of interviews and were confused by the angles that the Americans were coming from.

'Over here they keep asking us about Manchester and the Hacienda and the drugs. I don't want to talk about it. Too many people want to go on about it. But they seem to think that the Sundays are part of the Manchester scene as well,' said Tim.

Whilst the American media was a bit confused by the geographical details of the UK scene, Tim was trying to make some sense of the US. 'It's in a bit of a bad state really. All the different places you go have separate identities. Every place you go to is a contradiction of the place you just left,' he rapped.

In Washington, though, they managed to flesh out this apparent sameness, visiting the Georgetown steps where *The Exorcist* was filmed, a veritable tourist stopover for lovers of anonymous looking steps and fans of heavy-duty populist terror flicks.

Musically, the Americans were bagging the Charlatans into a weird loophole of their own making. In the confusion of where exactly to place the band the US press were hooking them in with groups like the Bunnymen. On paper it made some sort of sense as both groups were from the north of Britain, where that Doors tradition of dark-hearted pop had long ago taken root, and they both seemed not that interested in making career grinding pop moves. It was hardly an insult but it was a comparison that rankled nevertheless with Burgess.

'Everyone thought for some reason, I haven't got a clue why, it's really poxy actually, the new Echo And The Bunnymen is what they call us,' said Tim. 'That's what really bugged me about the whole American thing. That they have to have something to relate to before they see something new. They thought that England was London a couple of weeks ago and now they think that England is Manchester. They can only relate to one thing at a time. Can't relate to two separate cities, so to all the new bands that are going over, they all say, "Oh, the somebodies from Manchester, the Shamen from Manchester" or whatever.'

It was part of the confusion of the time, as going to the States was a sudden explosion of UK bands which they weren't totally enamoured with, and they were fingering Manchester for the blame.

'They take everything very seriously over there. How talented the musician is or something like that. We've never considered ourselves to be musicians anyway, just a collective doing good songs rather than individuals,' said Tim.

The American media scene with its go-for-it extrovert presenters and fame-hungry bands was probably as confused by Tim's approach as he was by theirs.

'They keep trying to get us to do things. Like on MTV I had to read these lines, but because I can't read that well I couldn't do it, it's like I've got dyslexia or something. They threw us out in the end. They aren't very patient, these people,' said Tim.

America means big tours, the whole slog, the total hog. Rather quaintly the Charlatans believed that they were going to make it by sheer talent alone.

'The Soup Dragons are bigger than the Charlatans over here,' Tim pointed out. 'I don't feel competitive. I don't want to get into any bitching. We just want to create our own space. If it works out that's great but we're not a piece of meat.'

The Charlatans were too cool to bend over backwards for the US market. 'We're using this tour to warm up new material for the British tour,' half joked Burgess.

He was asked what he thought about New York. 'I felt really small in Central Park. We met the most morbid man in the world when we were there. He took us on a guided tour of all the sights and the famous murder places, including the Dakota building where John Lennon got shot.'

Did he get off on the insane energy of the big apple? 'Yeah, it was really intense. When you leave, though, you feel relieved. But you can't help thinking, "Fuck me, what a brilliant place!"'

As ex Sex Pistol Steve Jones started to grind out some waste of time (and his talent) solo stuff onstage, the oddball couple of Burgess and Blunt sat in a caravan, the lively frontman talking in tangents, one moment wise, the next a village idiot, and the deep bassman, his fingers knotted tightly together, with an introvert intensity that cloaked a fierce pride and a warm heart. Tim looked up, their relationship was vital to the band's chemistry and he knew it: 'Secretly I agree with him and he agrees with me, and we both agree to differ . . . us two, we pull in totally different directions but we meet in the middle. It's that brilliant,' he attempted to explain, making total sense in the midst of nonsense. 'I never like thinking too much, in conversation you should never have too much to think.'

Typical Charlatans – north-country boys to the er, man. Take it or leave it, like it or lump it. There was none of that big star attitude to 'do this, it's good for your career guff' with this band.

The venue was the vilest I can ever remember being in: clean, safe and sterile, body searches before entering and a too-keen security forcing your ass into your hard plastic chair – it was more like a military exercise than a rock & roll show.

Backstage was full of bored rock stars waiting their turn to hang around in the hospitality caravan, the Charlatans seemed out of place as they didn't have that sort of fake-tan, limp, bored look that some of the older hands had. Rob Collins wandered around looking surly and unimpressed, threatening to headbutt any of the rock royalty that came too close, muttering insults with a drunken Midland slur whilst someone told an apocryphal tale about him: 'When Rob was younger he was addicted to glue. He shoved a binliner of the stuff over his head. It stuck to his hair and he collapsed. When he awoke the next morning his dad was kicking the fuck out of him.' Probably a bollocks tale but one that was easy to believe as the Charlatans' wildest man of rock stomped around.

It was a mere fistful of months since they were playing gigs in Northwich and Crewe, and here they were in LA, the capital of the rock & roll world, and it wasn't fazing them the slightest.

'LA, it's just like Blackpool, innit?' sniffed Tim Burgess to a passing *Sounds* journalist.

What a Charlatan!

INDIAN ROPE . . . AGAIN!

Back home from the American tour there were some side problems of success, which often face bands when they reach the limelight. If there's one thing a whole new batch of fans love to own more than anything else it's the out-of-print early releases from their favourite group, and if the record label has no intention of re-releasing these singles then prices soar. The collector's market in pop is massive and the Charlatans fans were about to fall foul of the unscrupulous bootleggers who thrive upon such a situation.

Unavailable for about a year, the band's debut single 'Indian Rope' had in time-honoured style become a collector's item. Money was to be made on the record that, because Dead Dead Good didn't actually exist as its own separate imprint, wasn't on the shelves. Unscrupulous bootleggers through-out Europe had been pressing short runs of the track and cashing in on the fans' hunger for it by charging swollen prices for their bootleg.

In early June the band re-released 'Indian Rope' in an effort to counter the inflated price of 40 quid that the record was changing hands for. The original had now sold 20,000 copies but there were still plenty of people out there who wanted it.

The single was available now on 12-inch and for the first time on CD, via the band's fanclub and *109* zine and in specialist shops, a low-key release for the hardcore fanbase.

Despite this the record still reached number 57 in the charts.

TAKING THE MUSIC TO THE PEOPLE, THE BAND GET BACK ON THE ROAD UK STYLE!

With new tunes in the can and a starving fanbase to satiate, the band announced a short sharp shock of a tour in June. The venues were again upgraded, this time to the likes of Manchester Free Trade Hall, St Austell Coliseum in Cornwall, Bridlington Spa, Edinburgh Playhouse, Wolverhampton Civic Hall and on 15 June, the biggest of the lot, the Royal Albert Hall in London.

All very grand, these were the sort of venues reserved for the big league and the Charlatans effortlessly sold them out.

Support on the tour was from post-shoe-gazer outfit Catherine Wheel and Johnny Male, the man behind Republica, an excellent, underrated dance act, with songs outfit Soul Family Sensation at Manchester and Wolverhampton, and Soul Family Sensation and fab Manc based New Fast Automatic Daffodils on the rest.

The New FADs are another one of the great lost Manchester bands, and their initial bursts of scratchy frenetic funk pop should have developed into bigger and wider pop monsters. After 'Big' they had an air of confidence about them, experimenting and stretching their sound as far as they could, and, intelligent and questioning, they were the experimental end of the Manchester thing. Who could forget such cool songs as 'Fishes Eyes', 'Big' and 'Partial', quirky idiosyncratic workouts and genius-warped tunes from a band that was fated to be an also-ran in the baggy fallout? Formed by four students at Manchester University, the New Fast Automatic Daffodils, named after Liverpool poet Adrian Henri crossed a car maintenance manual with the famous William Wordsworth poem, were one of the unexpected small-time success stories thrown up by the late 1980s pop putsch. Caught up in the heady rush of the times, the band had been destined for indie obscurity but were cast briefly into the open glare of the pop spotlight, where they flowered (ha!) into a great pop unit.

It was typical of the Charlatans to pick yet another cool band to support them, doing what any band who gets the big break should do and take the best bands they can find with them.

After the tour they went out to Europe to play the Roskilde festival in Denmark and the Belfort festival in France. By mid 1991 the Charlatans were slotting very nicely into the big-band chug of UK tours in the spring and autumn, and slots at the big summer Euro festivals.

From the outside the band was in its strutting prime, a rock solid unit casually grabbing hits and selling out tours. It's a nice life if you can get it, and one that it would be heart-breaking to lose out on.

LESS THAN SOME FRIENDLY . . . THE EXIT OF JON BAKER

A day after the triumphant packed-out gig at the Royal Albert Hall, Jon Baker left the Charlatans.

Or that's the story that has floated around the press for years.

In fact Baker remembers the Albert Hall gig as his personal high point in the group. 'My best memory, my fondest memory was when we did the Albert Hall, it was an amazing day and night. Shitloads of my friends came down. There was about 50 people there that I knew from the Midlands on the guestlist – they came down and we had a brilliant time. We went back to the hotel and it was like a party.'

Instead of quitting the next day, as the myth has propagated, Jon Baker went on tour in Japan with the band. 'It was weird but really good. You had to go onstage at seven o'clock and by the time the gig was over it was straight back to the hotel and sit in the bar and get pissed really early. It was totally confusing. Three or four of the shows were in Tokyo and one was in Osaka. We then went back home and started writing the second album,' he pauses for a moment . . . 'and then it all started going pear-shaped.'

Baker had started to feel like the outsider. It may have just been a personal paranoia but he felt like he was being shunted on to the far edges of the circle.

'It began during the last tour. I felt like I was always the last to know anything. In that sort of situation it made things difficult. My confidence as a guitarist started going as well – I was in a top 10 band and it was beginning to turn into a nightmare. The inter-band banter that was always there was starting to get a bit more full-on. We had been living in each other's pockets for ages and it had got to the stage where it had got a bit much. We needed time out, as frustration with each other had started creeping in. Like I said, my confidence had started to slip and I was afraid of suggesting ideas for new songs.'

Baker started to feel that there was an inner core to the band. 'Rob, Jon and Martin had been together a lot longer and they were like a unit, those three would talk to each other. I'd only been in a year and so much had happened in that year, but I still felt excluded and I started to feel paranoid.'

Baker spoke to Martin. 'I asked him what was going on. I said, "You don't tell me stuff I should know about, I'm feeling left out. Is it because you feel that I'm not right for the band?" He didn't say a lot, he just told me not to worry.'

They continued to rehearse for the second album for a couple more weeks but things still didn't feel right.

'One day I turned up for rehearsal and Tim and Jon left early to go round Jon's house. Martin and Rob sat down with me and said that they thought I should leave the band. I was shocked. I thought, "What do I do now? What can I do?" It fucked me up for six months.'

Jon Brookes looked back on the split: 'Something had to give at that point and Jon Baker was the weak link in the chain. Not him as a person or a musician . . . But something had to give.'

Martin remembers the fateful day when Jon left. In a later interview his version of the events was slightly different to how Baker remembers it now: 'At the very outset of those dates that we did in June he came to us and said, "Look I don't think I can contribute anything else to the group. I think I'm holding you back and it would be better for everyone if I left."'

Whatever, Baker was shellshocked; he knew there was a problem between him and the band but he didn't think that it was going to go as far. It was a bombshell – from being in a big band that was going places, he was down on his arse and back to square one.

'I didn't tell anyone for three months,' he confides. 'It changed my life; one day I was in a successful band and the next I was nothing. The band didn't give a reason. I felt crap, and I thought that everything that I played was crap. I had just bought a house and I couldn't afford to pay for it. I had major money worries so I just hit the bottle – my life was in a bit of a mess.'

Some members of the band were shocked as well. Tim remembers the departure differently from Jon Baker's version when asked by the *NME* what his reaction was, 'I thought, "What are we going to do now?" That's what we thought. But we understood. In fact I thought it was a really brave thing to do cos he could have said nothing and milked it for a while.'

Tim Burgess was saddened by his departure but quite logical about the situation. 'It's no big deal,' he told the *Melody Maker*, 'he just didn't want a record contract, he didn't want any of the hassles. You know, the touring, the interviews. He just wanted to make music, which is fine, it's what he's doing now. The only bad thing is that I haven't seen him since and he's a mate.'

So there you have it. Jon Baker thinks he was told to leave the band, and the rest of the band claim that he left on his own accord. That's the way with these painful situations – each side always has a version of the rift. However it was, Baker was no longer in the Charlatans.

At the point the Charlatans were at then, most of their contemporaries, once they had settled in the limelight, had solid line-ups, and members leaving so soon after a breakthrough was something that didn't happen very often. So it raised a few eyebrows when Jon Baker left. To Steve Harrison, though, it was something he was resigned to – the second line-up change in 18 months and the second guitarist to leave the band since its inception was something he could sense was on the cards: 'It was inevitable really. We could see it coming. Jon left and we decided that we would have to advertise for a new guitar player.'

Jon Baker never really spoke to the band again, apart from occasionally chatting to near-neighbour Jon Brookes.

For Baker it was all over; he felt that Martin Blunt had made the decisions in the band and 'the rest of them would agree with him'. It took about a year to get over the sacking but he doesn't hold any grudges.

He looks back on his last days with the band wistfully. 'Most of that second album that we were working on didn't turn out that good, did it? But I really like the band, and the last album [*Tellin' Stories*] is really great, isn't it?'

Baker had worked on about three tracks on the *Between 10th And 11th* album, tracks like 'Weirdo', which was finished before he got the chop, and '(No One) Not Even The Rain', which was well on its way to being finished.

After a year of being down in the dumps he pulled himself back together. 'I woke up one morning and made a decision not to wallow any more and just get on with it. After a year I formed Spin Playground; I had still been in touch with the Liquid Egg Box people during the Charlatans thing, so me and the drummer Sean Ratcliffe put a new band together with a singer called Mac and a keyboard player called Darren that I had met in Brum.'

Soon however Sean left and the band started to work with a DAT backing track providing the rhythm parts.

Spin Playground lasted a couple of years on the local circuit. Their demo tape was thrust into your narrator's hand about a year later in some crazed Manchester gig night. It was a lighter take on the Charlatans, guitar psyche pop infusing the tunes in a fine manner.

Eventually Jon went to college and passed an advanced media and communications course. 'I got amazing grades and that was only finished in mid 1997, and then I started doing photography, taking pictures of local bands.'

With that, combined with his love of playing, he's put a new band together called Polanski. 'We've been together for 18 months. It's full-on guitar music without being Neanderthal, with good tunes, you know. We released a track on a compilation called *Camden Town Gigs* on Jellybean Records; the second volume is due soon. We got a lot of gigs off being on that compilation . . .'

WANTED: A GUITAR PLAYER FOR HAMMOND-DOMINATED GARAGE BAND

Steve Harrison started searching out a new guitar player.

Although Jon hadn't exactly written every song for the Charlatans, his contribution had been large in tunes like 'You're Not Very Well', 'The Only One I Know', 'Polar Bear', 'Flower' and 'Sproston Green' – about half of the first album.

This time around they needed someone who was going to go the whole way, a proper guitar gunslinger, a rock & roller to put the fire into their bellies.

Harrison put in a call to Alison Martin, who mentioned it to Anthony Bogianno (the Inspiral Carpet's manager) and they had a chat about it and came up with two names, Mark Collins and Noel Gallagher. Mark Collins because he was recognised as being the best guitar player on the local circuit, and Noel because he was roadying for the Inspirals (after failing his audition for the singer's job he kept the Clint Boon haircut and was about to embark on a career that would make him the most famous ex roadie of all time) – and he was just down the corridor at New Mount Street, and was known to strum on guitar a bit . . . Remember that this was before Noel had really got Oasis going, although he knew how to play everything just by setting up the gear for the Inspiral Carpets. Sitting in before soundchecks, jamming out tunes with whoever was there, and shaping up ideas (not that this was appreciated; the Inspirals nicknamed Noel 'Catnap' because he was always asleep on the tour bus, avoiding as much real work as possible).

Maybe Noel was confident enough with his own untested tunes to turn down the chance to join a band that was already at the top of their game, on paper a mad decision if he ever was asked directly to join the Charlatans. A friend of Alison Martin's ponders, 'It's weird to think it now that Noel is so confident and everything, but I don't think he was confident enough to go for the audition. In those days he was quite shy. In some ways it's good that he didn't go for the audition because we've ended up getting three really good bands [Oasis, Charlatans and the Inspiral Carpets] out of it.'

It also meant that after years struggling away hacking through the Manchester undergrowth Mark Collins got his deserved break.

HAVE GUITAR WILL TRAVEL . . . MARK COLLINS STEPS OUT OF THE LOCAL CIRCUIT

The moment that Mark Collins walked into the rehearsal room with his guitar was the moment when any chance of a Charlatans downward curve was arrested.

For a band so tied in with the myth of Manchester, his arrival into their camp brought with it a bizarre irony; Collins was, in fact, the first member of the band who actually lived in Manchester.

At last some geographical credibility!

Brought up in a pop environment, some of his earliest memories are of the Beatles being played in his family home. 'I think George Harrison was my first influence. He's still one of my favourite guitarists now. He had a very good ear for a melodic solo. I wanted to be George when I was 14 or 15.'

Harrison was the definitive melodic lead-guitar player, and instead of using the guitar as some sort of ego trip, the quiet Beatle would wait his turn and help to define some of their classic songs with a deft lick. It was an understated but vital craft, and something that he has never been given full credit for.

Harrison wasn't the only influence on the young guitar player. Mark Collins was also digging Neil Young. 'My elder brother used to con my pocket money out of me when I was about nine so he could go out and buy Neil Young records. But of course nine-year-olds don't really "get" Neil Young, so I didn't really appreciate those records till I was about 20,' he told *Total Guitar* magazine.

Mark Collins had certainly payed his dues for, unlike Burgess for whom success arrived at a relatively young age, Collins had been down rock & roll's mean and winding road. A pupil at the same school as Bonehead from Oasis, he had spent his teens in the usual drifting and dossing around mode. He had social workers on his case as he skived off school all the time and left it early, although after having an IQ test where he scored highly, he was reinstated. He was drifting, going nowhere and it was only by discovering the beauty and power of music that his life suddenly made some sort of sense. He knew he was cut out for more than the usual grind but couldn't see how he was going to get the break.

Whilst trying to make it through the local band scene he had spent eight years on the dole or working in a kebab house, shit jobs paying for his rock & roll habit. At the kebab house he had to crush frozen mince with his bare hands, moulding the little balls into a bigger ball, making the vile-looking slab of shitty meat that gets put on the stake. Being a natural perfectionist, he would spend an age on the allotted task.

He also spent years playing in bands. In the tangled maze of Manchester groups in the mid to late 1980s Mark played in the Waltones and finally with Candlestick Park (named after the San Francisco stadium where the Beatles played their final gig in 1966), and then the Medelark Eleven.

The Waltones played a bright upbeat guitar pop and built up a really healthy following. 'Of all the bands that played around Manchester they seemed to have the most girls following them around at the gigs,' remembers one eye witness.

The Waltones were one of the last remnants of the sorts of bands that were around in Manchester before baggy burst in and kicked everything aside. Their press release at the time described them as 'a post-Smiths Merseybeat group' and they were certainly pop classicists; they knew their shit. Frontman James Knox had a voice that hinted at the heavyweight voices of the post-punk era, people like Weller, Billy Bragg, Morrissey and Elvis Costello, the sort of voice that betrayed a sharp intelligence.

The Inspirals' Clint Boon remembers them as the band that he used to rub shoulders with whilst making friends with Mark at the same time, before his own band took off. He pinpoints them as one of a whole bunch of Manchester bands that missed out on the looming baggy thing. 'They were all guitars and fringes, bands like them and the Bodines and maybe Laugh [who would become Intastella] were really good bands but they didn't have the right sort of attitude that was needed when the baggy thing took off. Everything changed then and those bands were left out.'

The Waltones though had a loyal coterie of fans, including future Manchester faces.

'Noel Gallagher really looked up to Mark,' remembers one scenester, 'he bought the same guitars. I remember after one gig he was backstage and picked up one of Mark's guitars and said, "This is the only one of your guitars that I haven't got yet!"'

Noel and Mark knew each other from the Inspiral days where Collins was the occasional van driver and Noel the roadie, although they never actually worked together at the same time with the band. Mark would do a few odd jobs for the Inspirals and ended up doing a bit of driving for them.

The Inspiral Carpets seem to be the Almost Men of Manchester, as they are there at every twist and turn in the plot, although mainly famous now for being the group that spawned Noel Gallagher. They were the first Manchester band to break through and the first that were critically slammed. They had a knack for knocking out catchy as fuck pop records, and grabbing chart hits when everyone wasn't looking – their problem was that they lacked the sort of drop-dead cool that classic bands require.

Inspirals' keyboard maestro Clint Boon played his Vox Continental on five tracks of the Waltones' *Deepest* album, and it was from this connection that Mark worked with the Inspirals. 'He only did a few things for us, he wasn't employed all the time like Noel was.'

So he wasn't working for the Inspiral Carpets like Noel was.

'Well, Noel was hardly working for us either! Didn't everyone in Manchester work harder than Noel!' jokes Boon, adding, 'Mark was a cool geezer, we just used to get him to come down for a few days and move boxes around in the offices.'

Mark didn't put enough time in with the Inspirals to end up in Noel Gallagher's legendary roadie band, a loose jamming ensemble that the upcoming songwriter would roadtest his new songs to whatever road crew were around whilst out on the road with the Inspiral Carpets.

Meanwhile off the Inspiral Carpets tour and back with the Waltones things were getting serious. They had recorded their debut album and were hoping for some way to break out of the local circuit with it.

The *Deepest* album came complete with a poncy sleeve painting from John Everett Millais called 'Ophelia' that hardly hinted at the pop guitar workouts inside. Collins' stamp is quite definitely on the record, from his slide work on the title track (also released as a single) shows. The melodies had the traditional Beatles stamp on them, as tunes like 'When It All Turns Sour' and 'Smile' proved that the band dug the Fabs' guitar-led melodic strokes and were using them as a template for their sound.

One of the Waltones' greatest moments is the visceral guitar pop rush of the autumn 1987 single 'She Looks Right Through Me'; the following single was 'Spell It Out'.

Releasing their records and managing the band was Anthony Bogianno, who by now having met Clint Boon, would soon be moving to manage the Inspiral Carpets. The son of an ice-cream salesman, Bodge or Boggy was of Italian descent. Labelmates with the likes of the Popguns, the Waltones didn't ever get the breaks to come through and the label fizzled out when it was sold and fell apart. Left without a label the Waltones were stuck in that dreaded no man's land and soon split up.

Every rock book you read has someone cockily announcing that they are going to be a massive star and then succeeding in making their doubters and detractors suck eggs – but what about those that fail? How stupid they must feel! At this point in the late 1980s Collins must have felt like one of those people, but instead of caving in and giving up, he just hunched over his guitar and worked hard at his craft, checking the great and copping their timeless licks.

'At the time I was really into Paul Weller and Roger McGuinn's [the Byrds] 12-string. I really liked the look of their guitars. Roger McGuinn was my first guitar hero, then I went through a big Pete Townshend phase, I graduated on to Jimi Hendrix, and later Johnny Marr was someone I really admired.'

Collins recalls his big call-up which plucked him out of the local hopefuls. 'I met the Charlatans through a mutual friend, she introduced me to them, then the next thing I knew, I had a phonecall inviting me down to a rehearsal. I didn't know anything about it, I just went down thinking the Charlatans wanted a second guitarist. I turned up with my guitar at a rehearsal room in Birmingham, and there was no other guitarist there and they just said, "Do you fancy joining the band?" I said, "Oh. Go on then, why not?" I didn't have anything better to do. It was just sprung on me really. I had a phonecall on the Monday and I was in the band on the Wednesday. It all happened really quickly.'

It must have been pretty tough fitting into a band as tight-knit as the Charlatans, and being in the Ron Wood-style outsider position was something that Mark had to handle.

'Obviously I was on some sort of trial period. I knew I had to perform and not conform. They asked me to join on the understanding that I'd be an active member of the band – they didn't want a shrinking violet in the corner just playing what they told him to play and, to be honest, I don't think I would have joined if they had wanted that. I said from the outset that

I wanted to be part of the songwriting and that was exactly what they wanted anyway. I think they welcomed me with open arms and they were very helpful to me from the word go. It was never very intimidating.'

The band knew that Collins was a great guitar player, fitting perfectly in with the Manc guitar hustler tradition, but they can't have guessed then that his songwriting and some of the classic influences he would bring to bear on the band were going to make great positive changes in their sound, and help them to make the big jump forward out of the so-called baggy rut that they could have so easily found themselves flailing about in.

Between 10th And 11th, although featuring Mark, wasn't really his first proper input to the group. Most of the songs were ready and he just added guitar, giving the songs an edge and added flavour. However there were some songs on it that he helped to write from scratch: 'I'd only been in the band for a couple of months and I'd only really got involved in writing about four of the songs. It was a bit weird. I had to learn the songs really quickly and write a few of the songs as well. Recording *Up To Our Hips* was a lot different to the second album, definitely.'

After years of struggling in local Manchester bands, Collins was buzzing from the lifestyle change. It was a dream come true, and Jon Baker by leaving the group had unwittingly answered the prayers of one of the city's more talented musicians whom, it had seemed, was never going to get the break he deserved.

'It was quite a change in lifestyle from sitting around in local rehearsal rooms, wondering what was going to be happening next week, if we were gigging or not. All of a sudden I've got 90 shows to do in six months, tours of the States, Japan and Europe. I was blown away, it was totally amazing; it's an experience I can well recommend. Playing live with the Charlatans is a total buzz experience, just the sense of power that you exude on the stage, you get it back straight in your face from the audience.'

Mark Collins bumped into Alison Martin at the Cities In The Park festival in Manchester where he told her the good news. He was there playing his last gig with Candlestick Park before his promotion to the pop Premier League.

As Collins kissed the local band scene goodbye, and the Heaton Park festival marked the final death knell of the Manchester with its definitely vibeless flavour, the Charlatans were once more a functioning unit.

Back firing on all cylinders, they were ready for anything. The only problem for the new guitar player was that the band spoke in thick Black Country accents.

'I spent the first six months getting Tim to translate everything that they said!' says Mark.

THE DEATH OF BAGGY

The band that Mark Collins was joining had by now subtly removed itself from the pop mainstream. Being fashionable is a double-edged sword – it can make your band storm to the top of the pile, but it can also see you dumped equally quickly. The new faces breaking into pop stardom can disappear back to pub life and football as quickly as they arrived.

Every burst of excitement in British street pop has seen the same sort of 18-month reign at the top before fucking off back to a core of true believers, and the baggy/Manc thing was no different.

By the autumn baggy was dead on its feet, ridiculed and mercilessly parodied, and the music press was having a field day killing it off. Damon from Blur announced that their *Leisure* album would finish it, whilst Shaun Ryder smashed up mirrors in Manchester's Dry Bar after false stories of him being a rent boy were printed in the tabloids.

This, in turn, led in November 1991 to the legendary Swells piece on the Mondays in the *NME*, where Bez went into his infamous anti-faggot tirade. The Happy Mondays sales would collapse as the pre *loaded* generation of students were bothered by such prejudiced talk, and quickly went off the band. The fact that the Mondays' last album *Yes Please* wasn't much cop didn't help either. The Stone Roses had disappeared from view, and the whole scene was in disarray.

The music press replaced baggy with 'shoe-gazing' and no one took any notice, and the 1990s, for a few months, seemed suddenly to go all stale and dull.

The Charlatans were well aware that the scene that had helped to propel them to the toppermost of the poppermost was falling apart in front of their eyes. They explained, 'We weren't victims of the end of the Manchester scene. We were just keeping away from it all. You just have to keep out the way.'

Unusually among their peers they found very little reason to slag off the scene that had nurtured them.

'It would be so easy now to say that the Manchester scene was, in fact, a hindrance and we're now pigeonholed or misunderstood or whatsoever. But it's been no hindrance at all, it's been a great help,' Tim told the *NME* a couple of years later.

Martin agreed. 'We were in the right place at the right time, like a lot of bands are. There was nothing calculated about it. It's so easy to be cynical now but there was something really important and good about the Roses and the Mondays. They did have a real effect.'

Suddenly perceived as being awash with line-up difficulties and a scene that was no longer flavour of the month, many commentators felt that the Charlatans were surviving on borrowed time. Many of the second-wave bands did fall apart in the next 12 months, and it was a tough time for the northern groups.

But the Charlatans were still a big band – they had just sold out the Albert Hall, for fuck's sake – but the days of sailing in at number 1 in the album charts suddenly seemed really distant. As they approached the tail end of 1991 they were still working on their second album, as well as breaking in a new guitar player and peering anxiously over their shoulders at glories past, and they felt the cold chill of doubt descend upon their operation.

All they needed now was for the backbone of the band, Martin Blunt, to feel the pinch as well.

'GONNA BREAKDOWN . . . YEAH'

Even though most people look on being in a band as a total doddle, an excuse to do no work and put your feet up, in reality the pressures are immense. The lifespan of a group can be dictated by fashion, the whim of an audience, running out of tunes, bad luck or the wrong hair at the wrong time. The road brings another set of pressures: being away from loved ones for months on end, crap hotels, shit food and abysmal drugs, the adrenaline rise of playing live back-to-back with the misery of motorways and the mind-numbing concrete of Mway service stations, living on your nerves, and getting on everyone else's.

It takes a tuff hide to survive the road, and a sensitive soul can get ground down by this odd existence. Martin Blunt was more sensitive than most; an intense and quiet man, distrusting of the false bonhomie and wreckage that floats around the music business.

At the end of 1991 he was hit by severe manic depression, compounding the Charlatans' problems further. Manic depression is a condition that's far more common than most people would like to admit. It's a state of mind that's the likely result of working like a dog on the rock & roll circuit, and the exciting highs and despondent troughs that this tough lifestyle assaults the musicians with.

The *Melody Maker*'s Dave Simpson remembers once meeting Blunt and noticing the bassplayer's demeanour: 'He was friendly but he had the air of someone who was really damaged, someone who had looked into the eye of the devil. He said that he had gone out for a beer and come back with 30 cans of dog food, and that was the point that he knew he had problems . . . that really freaked him out.'

At one point Martin decided that he was going to leave the band, which would almost certainly have been the end of the Charlatans as he was considered by his colleagues as being the backbone of the whole affair.

As he told the *Melody Maker*, 'Yeah, I was in hospital, I was totally fucked up seriously. It wasn't to do with the group but I needed time out really badly. It was like I was on this treadmill, it was getting like a job. It wasn't self pity or anything, just insecurity and an attack of paranoia brought on by personal stuff I can't talk about. It was a bad time. I was over-thinking, over-analysing, and Jon was leaving, and I always thought the whole thing about the group was keeping it together . . .'

The band as a gang, that crucial tenant of great rock & roll – once that chemistry has cracked it can never be the same again. It also means, in effect starting all over again.

It looked, to many at this point, as if the Charlatans were about to split up.

'Well,' Tim Burgess admitted, 'the press said we were and I don't blame them either cos it might have seemed that way. But no, never.'

'We just had a rethink,' explained Martin.

HIT SINGLE NUMBER 5!

The band had been through the wars, but they were determined that they were going to survive. Lying low for the close of the year they had quietly gone about their business despite the mass upheavals and problems that were threatening to tear them apart.

Ensconced in Monnow Valley Studios in Wales they started work on recording their second album which had a working title of *Normality Swing*. A bunch of tracks culled from these sessions were put together for the band's next single, the first that would feature the guitar playing of Mark Collins.

Originally and fairly cheekily entitled 'Hit Single No 5', the title of which was released to the press and was even prematurely reviewed as that in a few regional papers, a spokesman for the band was quoted as saying that the single was 'one of 18 tracks that the band are working on, we have enough material for a double album; we don't even know if the single will be on there as yet'. They were probably fobbing for time whilst they sorted out the record's title!

They retitled it after record label pressure – you can be a bit too cocky and tempt fate! – 'Me In Time' was released on 28 October, peaking at a lowly 28 and sliding out of the chart in a three-week stint.

The single's lack of success was a disappointment for the group; it seemed like the hiccup in the middle of the year was starting to effect their status. They had even spent a few bob on the video which had Tim doing his best pin-up shapes. But it had been ten months since the top 20 'Over Rising' EP, their last release, and things had moved on, so in some ways getting to even number 28 was an achievement in the fast and mean world of pop. At least it proved that they had a hardcore base of fans who were likely to support them through thick and thin.

The lack of daytime radio play didn't help either. But the evening DJs were still sticking with the group, and the Evening Session on Radio One put out their second session, with 'Weirdo', 'End Of Everything', 'Me In Time', and '(No One) Not Even The Rain'.

The vultures were out waiting for them to fail, and after Martin Blunt's breakdown and the line-up shuffle, there was even talk that Mark Collins had turned into an alcoholic already, although that was a tad premature! This seemed like a band that was about to be on the skids, reacting to success in as many extremes and different ways as possible.

For some reviewers 'Me In Time' was the band's worst yet and they were already consigning them to the rock & roll dustbin, along with all the other bands that appeared in the Manc baggy wake.

This was a bit premature as 'Me In Time' didn't do disastrously, although it wasn't quite the hit single no 5 that the band's bold prediction had touted!

1992
The Wilderness Year

CRASH AND BURN, THE FINAL DEATH OF BAGGY!

By 1992 the Manchester scene was burnt out, its rude intrusion into the cozy fallout of late 1980s pop already celebrated, catalogued and then spat out. The bands themselves weren't really helping in the scheme of things. The Stone Roses were lost in the fog of making *The Second Coming*, and already people were wondering just where the hell they had disappeared to. The Inspiral Carpets may have kicked the year off with 'Dragging Me Down', their biggest hit, but they were starting to turn the corner on their pop career, and the Happy Mondays were falling apart – their *Yes Please* album had sold badly, their tour was floundering and their last two singles, 'Stinkin' Thinkin'' and 'Sunshine And Love' were both missing the top 30 – the second wave of bands were all faltering, and the Charlatans too were about to enter a dark zone.

In pop it's very rare that a band can ride the zeitgeist; you may ride up with a wave of bands and get thrown into the mainstream as part of a new craze but when that craze fucks off and is replaced by a shiny new toy it takes a rare talent to survive. Like the dinosaurs wiped out by a meteorite, the Manc bands were looking high and dry by 1992.

Even the hot new demo tape floating round town from Noel Gallagher and his new outfit Oasis was getting the thumbs down from the music business. Manchester bands were finished, shoe-gazing was in and Suede were the hot new thing. At last there was a London-based band that knew how to press the right buttons, speak the right language; they were scoring the hits and making the Manchester bands seem fat and lazy.

This was the situation when the Charlatans were launching their new material. With *Between 10th And 11th* recorded, pressed up and ready to go, a plan was put into action. 1991 had seem them adopt a low profile, with two singles and a handful of gigs, so the plan was to go in with low-key gigs, get a single out and then launch the new album, one that they were already hinting was a bold step forward, a changing of the sound and an attempt to escape the 'baggy' tag.

BACK ON THE ROAD . . . THE SMALL SHOW COMEBACK

Typically of their generation of bands the Charlatans seemed to have grasped success and then be almost prepared to throw it all away by playing the low-key card. Getting to the top in pop is tuff enough but holding on to it is nigh on impossible, a fact of life the band had discovered already. After the apparent ease of their early success they were now fighting for their pop lives.

The vibe had quite definitely gone and there was a bad air in the town; the loved-up E feel of the previous years was over and a monstrous downer was kicking in. Dealers were the new stars and gangsters were causing difficulties in the clubs, and the pimp roll was ousted by the mugger shuffle. The streets were getting meaner – Piccadilly bus station giving out a mean midnight menace – there were scuffles in clubs and you could see guns being pulled, the bullets occasionally getting sprayed, all in the name of a night out.

Weird.

The party was over and the hangover was kicking in.

Not that the Charlatans were to do with any of this but it seemed that the decline in the city's music scene was being matched in the decline of its standard bearers.

The February 1992 edition of the *Melody Maker* where the Charlatans met the Stud Brothers (who would be consistent supporters of the band for years to come) saw the Studs waving the Charlatans' flag, one now rarely waved by early 1992. The band were deemed by others as unfashionable, and it was pointed out in *Melody Maker* early that year that the very language used to describe the band was changing: their records were no longer billed as 'straight in at number 15' but as having 'stiffed in the lower reaches of the top 20'.

The Studs instead were enthusiastic about the soon to be released 'Weirdo' single, saying it was the sign of a creative renaissance, and the song pointed to a tougher and yet more melancholic band emerging from the shiny pop sensation of their early period.

Before 'Weirdo' was released the band embarked on a club tour. These low-key tours can be great tools when used by bands in the Charlatans' position, as it means face-to-face eyeball contact with the core fanbase, potentially sweat-stained jam-packed gigs and an opportunity to break in new material before the old much-loved set gets broken up with the new, as yet, unheard of, tunes.

On 29 February and 1 March they played two warm-up shows at Glasgow's King Tut's, the sort of small venue that they hadn't rocked for two years. These shows were the debut gigs for the 26-year-old Mark Collins. King Tut's is the premier small-club venue in Glasgow, and of course has now entered rock & roll folklore as the place where Alan McGee would eventually see Oasis, and is notorious on the touring circuit for its steep wrought-iron steps round the back where you have to lug your gear in from the car park. Wonder what the roadies were cussing between their clenched teeth as they brought the Hammond in!

The dressing room is a small space round the back, more like a homely sitting room than a rock dressing room. The venue is the perfect size for a band of the Charlatans fame to swamp out with sweating fans and start on the planned road back to the supa nova, a supa nova that seemed to be slipping out of their grasp. The Charlatans perhaps were too idiosyncratic or lacked the brutal arrogance required for mega success, or maybe they wandered too far away from the Beatles greatest hits albums for inspiration!

Of course the kidz were totally satisfied with the gigs but the critics were still not sure, and the new songs caused a few furrowed brows. Dave Bennun noted for *Melody Maker* that the band's new material sounded unfocused, but that the 'Tremelo Song' stood head and shoulders above the rest, something that they should be worried about. He decided that the new material was 'too oblique for the new teen fanbase' and that the combination of changed line-up and new material was something that made the whole gig a cliffhanger. It was always very difficult for a band to break in their second album, and it was looking increasingly so for the Charlatans.

The 'secret shows' were announced in the local press only, in keeping with the low-key aspect of the gigs. The shows were a definite attempt to move forward, and to try and throw off the past, and the band didn't even play the screamed-for 'Indian Rope'.

They still encored with 'Sproston Green', though; some things are impossible to resist and a song like that, the climactic explosive exit, is something that could never be missed.

It was a relaxed and assured performance, and perhaps now it would be plain sailing from now on.

Of course life is never quite that simple.

When the going gets weird, it's time to release 'Weirdo'.

WHEN THE GOING GETS WEIRD THE WEIRD GET PRO . . . 'WEIRDO'

Arguably one of the finest moments in the Charlatans' career, 'Weirdo' was just a few minutes of prime-time early Charlatans, playing to all their strengths. In many respects the track, overlooked at the time, was the start of something new for the band. It was the first time that they had married the new technology of sequencers to their live band sound, and the moment when they started exploring different passages that would result in some of their best work in the future.

Released on 7 March with a variation of flipside tracks, including 'Theme From "The Wish"', 'Sproston Green (US version)' and 'Weirdo (Alternative Take)', a rejigging of the track by Peter Walsh, the single reached number 19 in the charts, although it had been expected to go higher. 'Weirdo' is considered by yours truly as perhaps the finest song in the Charlatans' songbook. It really kicks ass, proving that the band always considered weedy by pundits who weren't really listening, could break out the jams when they felt like it. Riding on a fat and ferocious keyboard lick, Collins pumping the Hammond hard, 'Weirdo' is the sound of a band hitting their own groove and not paying much attention to the niceties of the pop rulebook.

The video was great as well, a black and white affair featuring a Dalmatian dog, a dancing girl and the band sat on a settee; it ends with the Dalmatian doing the dog thing and jumping up on to Martin's knee.

Musically this was a powerhouse of a song, riding roughshod on Rob Collins' zig-zigzagging Hammond riff, a Hammond that you can feel the power oozing from, with the beautiful clatter of the keys that's its hallmark. The phat and powerful Hammond chops marks out the song, but it's underpinned by a damned funky bass that makes the record a dead cert for the dancefloor.

The Charlatans might have been getting 'weird' but they were making sure that you could dance to it. Tim's wispy vocal held its own as well, nailing down the subtle melody.

The single hinted at a stronger-sounding, new Charlatans and boded well for the upcoming album. It said that they had nudged at their sound and come up with something very interesting indeed.

With this new flurry of sonic confidence the band took to the road again for a big-venue spring tour of the UK, followed by the whole of May rocking the fuck out of Europe.

Even if the single had only scraped into the top 20, in theory at least, they were back in business.

CAUGHT BETWEEN A ROCK AND A HARD PLACE . . . *BETWEEN 10TH AND 11TH*

Long regarded as a blip in the Charlatans' career, *Between 10th And 11th* may have been their worst-selling album (released 4 April 1992, peaking at number 21, spending four weeks in the top 75), but the record's contents stand up pretty well when compared to any of their other albums, and the outrageous sleeve which featured a bunch of bananas is hard to forget (the picture was Tim's idea; it was part of a deal with Martin Blunt who insisted that the vocalist allow his lyrics to be printed on the album cover – Tim said that was cool if he could have his way with the artwork). The sales blip was probably more due to a backlash amongst record buyers who were growing tired of what they perceived as the Manchester thing than the band not delivering. Within 18 months the Charlatans had gone from being a band who had been pumped up by fashion to number 1 to being a band dumped by fickle fashion to number 20.

Originally mooted for release in September 1991 the album was glitched when Jon Baker walked out during the rehearsals for the album, and this was followed by Martin's breakdown. It all hitched the album's natural flow, and the long delays in the release schedule saw the band removed from the hothouse of media credibility and questions asked as the record moved further and further back on the schedules.

Maybe these frustrations combined with the disasters that were falling around the band's ears accounted for the rather subdued and depressive air that surrounded the album.

Tim Burgess was never that forthcoming about the state of affairs around the band, but said, 'It's difficult for me. The intensity of everything is very difficult for me to talk about. There's a lot of personal stuff that I don't want to mention.'

The group had set out to change their plot with this album as there had been a feeling that they were getting too restricted by a formula. Their first move was to change producers from Chris Nagle to Flood, a man who came with a fistful of production credits.

'Chris Nagle had done some Joy Division stuff and we thought that he was really cool,' remembers Jon Brookes. 'But you've got to work with different people. Chris was all right, but I think we've moved on and so has he, and he'd be the first to admit it.'

Also Nagle was deep inside producing the Inspiral Carpets and had to turn down the new Charlatans project.

Flood's track record included the likes of U2, who were at the pinnacle of their career at the time before slumping down to the paltry 10 million sales or whatever they shift now.

'I never knew he had done U2,' claimed Jon. 'I knew that he'd done Depeche Mode and Wolfgang Press and I thought that was really good. Then when he was doing the album I found out that he'd done U2 and been offered all these massive stadium groups. I was quite chuffed really that he was working on our poor little group.'

In his career Flood had seemed to work with every interesting group in existence. Real name Mark Ellis, Flood earned his nickname whilst working as a tea boy at Morgan studios in London in the late 1970s through his habit of overfilling cups of tea; it was a studio in joke that stuck.

From the very keen tea boy he graduated to being an engineer and at the beginning of the 1980s moved to Trident Studios, where he met Daniel Miller, the head honcho of the upcoming Mute label. It was a mutually fruitious meeting, Flood engineered a whole stack of acts for Miller's booming label, groups like Depeche Mode, Erasure and Nick Cave, as well as countless smaller bands – extra curricular stuff included Soft Cell and Jesus & Mary Chain. Eventually, at the invitation of Brian Eno, he went to work on U2's *The Joshua Tree*, a break into the biggest league of all that can hardly have ruined his career.

After working with Eno and having his engineering CV stuffed full of great credits, Flood decided to move into production and went on to produce some of the biggest records of the era like U2's *Zooropa*, Depeche Mode's *Songs Of Faith And Devotion*, plus Erasure, Pop Will Eat Itself, Renegade Soundwave and the Wolfgang Press. It was a hell of a CV.

Flood had a very different way of working to Chris Nagle. He dropped the click track that the band had been made to play along to for *Some Friendly* and went for a far more live feel whilst making the band sound slicker.

Playing live and loose in the studio is something that all bands love. For a start it's a lot more fun and it feels far more natural. Unfortunately not all bands are capable of keeping themselves tight enough for this way of working but the intense roadwork paid off for the Charlatans and they were more than ready.

'Flood went for a more open, live sound,' explained Jon. 'With Chris everything had to be on the dot with the click all the while. It sounded good, but it took away the raw edge. Flood would start with the melody and sort of build the song. I think, in retrospect, the first album is a bit linear compared to this one.'

Flood's contribution was to make the band's sound more spacy. Not as raw, they were less like a garage band and more polished in an experimental sort of way; whether this actually suited them has been a moot point over the years.

Enthusing about the 'liveness' of the record, Brookes added, 'We'd set up and play live, and he'd maybe keep the drums or the organ and replace everything else. The last album was like three weeks of drums, two weeks of bass, a week of guitar . . .'

That's the traditional way of recording, the poor drummer flailing away to a click track till he gets it right whilst the rest of the band fuck off down to the pub. The method gets results: it can make a band sound tight, albeit a tad clinical, but many bands find it makes their music seem cold.

Flood, though, wasn't hanging about.

'He pushed us a lot, we did 11 backing tracks in about eight days, straight through. We didn't actually work long hours. We just didn't stop during the hours that we were actually doing it,' Brookes told *Making Music*. 'It was dead spontaneous, like tightness and feel all at the same time. Songs like "The End Of Everything", "Ignition" and "Can't Even Be Bothered" sound as if they have been done live in the studio. There's a few mistakes that have been kept, quite a lot of rough edges – it just adds to the whole feel of it. You always want perfection but you can stand back and think, fucking hell, that mistake makes it sound all right.'

Despite this much-vaunted liveness the overall feel of the album is strange: on one level there is a rasping rawness and a great drum sound, on the other some of the song arrangements sound a tad empty, and the band almost wander into Talk Talk country, a sort of thinking man's pop, when their key strength is exuberantly joyous pop rushes. Maybe they were trying too hard to break away from their pop roots and prove themselves as a band with 'depth' or whatever disinteresting properties 'real' bands possess.

Not that they were scivving when the choruses were required: 'End Of Everything' has a great stumbling explosion of a chorus complete with yearning backing vocals in the build-up, and 'Tremelo Song' is no slacker either. When they were in the mood the Charlatans were still writing great pop.

For Mark Collins the album was his first recording with the band and it gave him the opportunity to cop a bunch of songwriting credits whilst adding flourishes to generally half-finished tracks that had been rehearsed up before he joined, and although there are some songs that he worked on from scratch his overall contribution is less than it would be on future records. Here he is warming up, and now and then his guitar slashes out; you can hear him down in the mix, but he's there and he's adding a different flavour to the band's music.

His guitar, when it cuts in, is razor-sharp, like taut wire. A rasping and great sound, devilish licks lash across the tracks. There is a real aggression here and it gives the Charlatans a spikier edge. You cop it right from the album's top 'I Don't Want To See The Sights' intro, which has some prime-time Collins, a driving, yearning guitar figure with a hint of Dylan – its sneering rasp instantly sets up the track, welded to the sort of groove that made the band such a success story in the first place.

'End Of Everything' has a great cascade of filthy feedback guitar, nagging, driving it along. Mark may have been working on his first album with the Charlatans but he was already getting right into the middle of the sound, and some of his interplay with Rob Collins' consistently invigorating Hammond is already a key hallmark of the band's sound.

Not that every track has the young buck guitar player slashing and burning his way round the 6-string riffology. On 'Can't Even Be Bothered', one of the first paeans to total laziness from the vocalist, Mark intros the track with a guitar tremmed-up warble that sounds like it has been copped from the Beatles' 'Flying' (an instrumental from *Magical Mystery Tour*, a much maligned doodle that was the only track where all four fabs got a credit and an egalitarian four-way split – a split between all the members of the band had always been a Charlatans' constant). 'Can't Even Be Bothered' is one of the album's highlights; the guitar is great (you can hear it being sampled or lifted and being made into a Beck-style lazy hip hop pop track), and the chorus itself explodes in, making it one of the album's highlights.

Collins was quite definitely an exponent of the school of keefing it raw, relying on feel, and his puritan streak even meant no headphones.

'I hate wearing headphones,' he reported to *Making Music*, highlighting that great bugbear of all studio-bound musicians. 'I always take a big long lead into the control room, leave the amp in the studio. You can get more of a feel, if you've got the big speakers on in there, we did all the guitars like that, except for the acoustics. It's just a better way, it's a lot more natural. Also it's not as lonely, not as paranoid.'

As befits a band recording their next album after a big hit, the Charlatans were doing things their way this time. This meant attempting a combination between playing live as a band and experimenting with their sound. They ended up making a record that was both looser and more polished, as if they had tugged away in two directions at once.

In the new regime of just taking a chance, 'Subtitle' was probably the closest they came to walking the creative tightrope.

'It was just set up with a keyboard and a microphone in the middle of the room, and I just sang the first thing that came into my head,' said Tim, 'based on the sort of mumbo jumbo feeling you get from like a huge crush on someone. Basically, that simple. It sounds pathetic, but it's true.'

'Subtitle' is just that: Tim plainly howling his love poetry in that curious sort of English folk melody that most British psychedelia seems to wander into (maybe the very weirdness of tripped-out states of minds makes us reach deep into our stabilising folk roots) over a superb fucked-up keyboard warble, which is further freaked by Martin's bass cranked weird through a Zoom fuzzbox (the bassplaying on this record is, of course, solid as fuck, Blunt driving, propelling the songs with simple shapes that give the band their much vaunted danceability). You can feel the dirt sloshing off the Hammond and as the track builds Mark slashes in some Townshend chords, spaced out and freaked.

But it's 'Weirdo' when the record explodes. Jesus, that's one of the greatest Hammond signatures that you're ever going to hear; Rob makes the organ sound like a total weapon. When you're in a club and that sound comes on, that great explosive rush of pure keyboard violence, it still gives one hell of a rush. Great guitar from Mark, and Jon copping Reni's funky drummer lick, and you've got a track that really rocks. This really is one of the best tunes that the band has ever come up with.

The following song, 'Chewing Gum Weekend', is one of Tim's best, with a title that sounds like his hero Mark E. Smith from the Fall at his descriptive best, capturing that speed-induced jawing that marks the 48 hours of freedom-from-work grind on fast drugs. There's a great melody on the chorus on this one and Rob really goes to town on the keyboards; here it sounds positively euphoric!

This was the backdrop against which Burgess was laying down his mostly world weary snippets of lyrics. Shards of words and phrases would tumble out of the vocalist's perfectly formed Jagger lips, hiding behind lyrical weirdness and charm. He was trying to articulate something without giving anything away, a very British pop trick that most Britpop bands would explore over the next few years.

Despite history painting the album as the low point in the band's career, some of the reviews were actually very positive. In the *NME* it got an 8 out of 10, the band described as 'a user-friendly Happy Mondays, a sexy Inspiral Carpets, a successful High, they have in effect pulled off a triple and they're not even from Manchester!'

NME dealt with the Stone Roses' comparisons pretty smartly. 'Four fifths unfashionable west Midlands, the Charlatans might have been the Stone Roses idiot half-brothers to the purist, but who beat Ian Brown's lot to America? Who kept their noses clean? See you in court, Stone Roses!'

NME decided that this was an album that wasn't exactly stuffed with great singles and that it had been made for the band's own sake and not the fans. But that the band had decided to stretch out and make some great interesting music instead was something to be cheered about in the gaping post-baggy vacuum.

Select, though, felt that the Charlatans had gone an album too far, that this was a record that stretched their capabilities just a little bit too thin. They looked at the album and felt that it was the chance for people to indulge in some 'swift revisionism' with the band: 'The problem with *Some Friendly* was that there was a suspicion that Tim Burgess just didn't know any tunes, that he was making everything up as he went along, but at some points he sounded like he may have cracked it. Subsequently such happy accidents have remained few and far between.' *Select* felt that 'Tremelo Song' and 'I Don't Want To See The Sights' were cool single material but that the rest of the album lacked the vital core items that made songs great – 'Tracks stagger around in a miasma of sound, choruses evaporate, solos turn up announced and then bugger off inexplicably.'

Steve Sutherland, then at the *Melody Maker*, was disappointed with the record. 'Don't let anyone tell you that the band took too many risks. The band just fucked up, okay?' he opined, finding the record ill-focused and lacking in any sort of energy, valid points in an album that seemed to pride itself on rubbing its sleep-shod eyes and yawning at the world; it seemed at some points that the band were going to fall asleep.

Sutherland also questioned Burgess' oddball credentials. 'Like that other would-be eccentric has-been, Julian Cope, Burgess appears to think that if he acts obtuse enough, we'll think he's a genius,' before going on to scratch his head at some of Tim's more bizarre lyrical excursions on the album. He found that Burgess's lyrics were 'freely associative bilge', pretty meaningless lyrics that didn't seem to hit home at any point.

It was a criticism that hit home with Burgess.

'We're not like that really,' he told Q. 'I'm fucking angry about a lot of things, but I was never angry about people knocking me. I knew that in some ways there was a lot of truth in it and in some ways it was just stupid. I don't feel as if we've proved a point to the people that hated us.'

Maybe people felt that there was more to the band than they were offering. Now it was down to the Charlatans to prove that they were one of the great British rock bands of the 1990s and not just the bunch of chancers that many felt they were, hitching a ride on the baggy bandwagon.

On listening years later *Between 10th And 11th*, although not a classic, has fine moments on it. Maybe the overall sound is a bit too flat and clean, maybe some of the songs are doodles and some of the attitude is just that bit too fey, but any album that has a track as great as 'Weirdo' on it, as well as 'Tremelo Song', isn't one for the dumper.

In retrospect *Between 10th And 11th* is the album of a band trying to find their direction; it's the sound of a group of people caught up in the maelstrom of pop attempting to find their own identity in the fallout; it's also the sound of a band with a new line-up trying to gel in the public eye.

The fact that saleswise the record hardly set the world on fire led many to believe that the band were soon to be consigned to the baggy dumper. But the Charlatans were made of tougher stuff than that. A combination of gritty northern confidence and Midlands non-interest in the winds of fashion would see them through. Despite being thought of as the wimpy younger brother of the Manc gangster bands, they were made of far sterner stuff than their contemporaries.

Not that everyone was seeing it that negatively. Jon Harris, who now edits *Select*, spoke to Tim Burgess at the time and was championing the band. 'I thought *Between 10th And 11th* was a very underrated album, people thought that they were just a crap Stone Roses rip off, but they were obviously much more than that. Maybe it was because of Martin Blunt's mod background but they certainly understood dance music, and this helps to explain why they eventually got the Chemical Brothers in later on. They were always looking so much further into music than bands like Ocean Colour Scene. Tim always had great taste and really knew his music.'

Not that the second album was without its faults, admitted Harris. 'That packaging was pretty crap, the sleeve really lacked any sort of focus. It made it look like a Northside record. I think the thing about them, though, was that they were always a huge people's band without being as leaden musically as someone like Oasis, but they were also trapped in people's minds as not being flamboyant enough to be truly big rock stars.'

Between 10th And 11th was between a rock and a hard place for the Charlatans, the big full stop on their rise.

Rock & roll can be a tough life.

Many bands would have fallen apart at this point. The future, on paper, seemed bleak; it looked like they were going to slip away from the musical consciousness of the nation.

But for the band themselves, armed with an enthusiastic new guitarist, this was only a new beginning. It was felt, in some quarters, that the worst was over and the decks were now cleared for action. They had stabilised the line-up, it was their best yet, and they were coming out fighting.

After all the shit that they had been through, things would surely improve.

PUTTING BUMS ON SEATS . . . THE BAND HIT THE ROAD AGAIN!

Even though the album wasn't churning up the expected sales, the Charlatans were still holding tight on to their fanbase on the road. People loved the band; there was no way that this thing was going to go belly up, as the Charlatans attracted the sort of perverse loyalty that is evident in, let's say, Man City fans – the fans were sticking closer and closer by the band throughout everything.

The worse the band seemed to do, the more that fans seemed to support them. For a band with an album that didn't scrape the top 20 (going in at number 21, then slipping down to 43) they were still selling out some pretty decent-sized venues on the tour promoting it, where they were supported by Burnley's Milltown Brothers.

The Manchester Apollo show was reviewed by that tosspot John Robb for *Select*. The band sold out the gaff and proved that they were still a force. 'Oozing teen Jagger sex appeal' claimed *Select*, talking about Burgess, noting that he 'played to an audience of screaming girls and screaming boys'.

Other bands from the scene would be lucky to fill small clubs but the Charlatans could still sell out places like the Manchester Apollo, a cavernous hall that takes a lot of filling. Surprisingly after such a great gig the band were later found skulking around Manchester's Britannia Hotel post show with a severe case of the blues.

The Britannia at the time was Manchester's premier rock & roll joint, it was the closest the city got to the notorious Chelsea Hotel in New York, and often when you slunk into the bar at about 2 or 3 in the morning there would be a bizarre collection of touring heavy metal bands with their crap nylon tour bomber jackets, B-list soap stars looking frayed around the edges, and frazzled businessmen with bog-eyed leers checking out the over-dressed prostitutes working the room. The bar would stay open all night and it was here that the Charlatans were sitting quietly contemplating what they figured was a crap gig.

If that wasn't bad enough there was someone there from their parent label Beggars Banquet suggesting that they should tour the US supporting the former Bauhaus singer Peter Murphy, a bizarre idea as the two acts were hardly compatible.

This was a band with high standards, and just turning up and playing wasn't an option. If it didn't go off for them they could get very despondent, so couple this with what Steve Harrison reported as a 'huge row backstage', which resulted in Rob Collins storming off back home and the 'fourth Hammond of the tour to be blown up, you know that when he really gets into it, he just overloads it,' added a nearby Martin Blunt.

The destroyed Hammond keeling over due to the intense keyboard player's incessant pounding meant that the band would have to find another keyboard before their show the next night at Birmingham's Hummingbird club, not so easy when you consider the uniqueness of a great Hammond.

The album's under performance in the charts didn't seem to be having much effect on the vocalist, as he told Q magazine. 'Chart placings are for marketing departments aren't they? Records are records. They're there to be treasured. When they get analysed or criticised and everyone talks about "product" it sort of ruins it for me.'

Brave sentiments maybe but harder to say when your record crashes in at number 1!

The band, though, were in a defiant mood.

'Something's got to happen this year,' admitted a not too forlorn Burgess at the Britannia Hotel. 'Everything's either going to turn around and get better or we will be the most hated band in the country. Whichever one, we can live with it.'

As ever it was business as usual with a sold-out tour of big venues clashing with an album that refused to get into the top 20, as usual the Charlatans were trading in contradictions. This was a band who never made anything easy for themselves.

SEARCHING FOR THAT ILLUSIVE TOP 10 HIT . . . 'TREMELO SONG'

One of the few songs that didn't take a critical battering on the *Between 10th And 11th* album was 'Tremelo Song', with many pundits tipping it as a future single, and for once the band were only too willing to comply.

'Tremelo Song (Alternative Take)' was released on 6 July. Mixed by 'Spike' Drake, extra tracks included 'Normality Swing', the original title of the album now reduced to licking its wounds as a B side, along with an unedited version of 'Happen To Die' and live versions of 'Then' and 'Chewing Gum Weekend' from the recent Manchester Apollo gig; this was the first time that the Charlatans put live stuff on to a record.

'Tremelo Song' bounces along an almost house-style jazzy keyboard break, an up-tempo song, it sounds like a perfect radio tune. On paper it should have been a hit as it was doing nothing that their previous singles hadn't done – sly chord changes, an insinuating chorus with great towering backing vocals, and a cool, brisk, laid back feel, and that damned keyboard digging deep into your memory. Maybe the song was just too downbeat for the pre-misery indie times.

The single's video was typical of the band's era with an arthouse look and a young man sleeping rough who wanders, Reggie Perrin style, into the sea, but before he disappears slips into a pub and hey! there's – I knew they'd be in there! – the band.

The single only got to number 44, the band's first real flop. The writing was now on the wall, and it looked like their pop career had burned out already. In the mean world of pop you usually get two years to prove yourself and then the scrapheap beckons; with fashion against them and a whole heap of problems inside the camp, many were predicting their imminent demise.

It was going to have to take some guts to get this shebang back on to the road.

But as the single was released in the UK, the band were slap bang in the middle of the biggest North American tour yet, starting out in Ottawa in Canada on 24 June they remained on the road until 22 August when they finished at Dallas. Supports on the tour were from the Wolfgang Press and the Catherine Wheel, the latter about to springboard to some sort of success in the States themselves.

The tour also saw them drop that ridiculous 'UK' suffix from their name over there and revert back to being 'the Charlatans'; maybe no one had been confusing them with a bunch of old hippies after all!

Following the American jaunt, they were briefly back in the UK playing second on the bill at Reading festival (fellow Midlanders the Wonder Stuff were headliners), before fucking off to Japan for a bunch of dates in September. They could hardly be accused of slacking!

For Mark Collins it was marvellous to be on the road proper after years of small-venue work in Manchester, and for the rest of the band it must have been a relief that they were still holding on to some semblance of their status after their recent flops.

LIVING IN THE CITY . . . MANC LIFESTYLE 1992

Arriving on the plateau of pop success meant that the good times could be enjoyed, and for Tim this meant trips up to Manchester to enjoy the city's booming club scene and there were certain clubs he often went to.

'We would bump into Tim all the time at clubs like Most Excellent, he was always really sound, talking about loads of mad things,' remembers local comedian and poet, the excellently named Qwerty Asop.

Tim would hang in the club with a bunch of muckers from Northwich with none of the arrogant pop star crap that usually hangs on the skinny shoulders of pop stars. There was none of that parking the black BMW outside and ordering champagne crap that went on with some of his contemporaries. Burgess was just taking the opportunity to have a cool night with his mates, no airs and graces. Maybe when you know you've got that star thing you don't have to flaunt it.

Most Excellent was a great club, following hot on the heels of Spice, another eclectic club for the flash glam end of the house scene. In the early 1990s, after the initial rush of excitement of the house explosion had started to wear off, many venues were quickly turning into generic handbag clubs, losing the edge and the flash of the initial hedonistic, almost illegal fervour of the early clubs and illegal raves.

Spice was an attempt to put some edge and glamour back into the scene and Most Excellent was the club born from its ashes. It took place every Saturday night at the Pavilion on Portland Street, which eventually mysteriously burned down ending all the revelry. The club was promoted by Ross, the Inspirals manager Anthony Bogianno, who was moving into the club scene at the time, and Justin Robertson. It attracted a well known crowd of party heads, people like Nigel Pivaro (alias Terry Duckworth from *Coronation Street*), footballers like Ryan Giggs, as well as the city's musicians, scallys and beautiful people, a weird mixture that just about worked, and one of these was Tim Burgess.

'He would talk to anybody but he didn't hang around with the stars. He would usually be sat in a corner with some of his oldest mates from Northwich,' remembers a local music journalist from those times.

After the club Tim and other revellers like Alison Martin would head back to their flats in Salford. They had a few parties around her flat which she was sharing with the currently homeless Rhys Hughes (Rhys is now a top Radio One producer). Tim would always fall asleep on the floor in the middle of the party, usually curled up inside a massive coat.

Tim had moved into Manchester, buying a flat in Acre Court in the block of reconstructed flats on the edge of Ordsall, just ten minutes from the city centre. He painted the inside of it black and red, and settled in ready to party in the heart of UK party central.

His place may have been in a bleak setting but the flats were well built and many of the city's media folk had their perches there; with a massive supermarket across the road and the city centre within walking distance they certainly had advantages, especially for the newly sociable singer.

Maybe the album had relatively failed but the pop life was fun. The band had turned the corner, the line-up was gelling more and more, and there were cool new songs in the can . . . and a bright future to look forward to.

THE CURSE OF THE CHARLATANS STRIKES AGAIN

After a bumpy ride everything seemed to have stabilised and the band were in a position where they could start to get positive about their work again.

They reckoned that they had hit rock bottom and that things would now improve. Plenty of bands have a dip after that initial surge of success; it destroys a lot of groups, their ego is dented, and the god-like status is removed as suddenly as it arrived. From living like a millionaire when you're on the dole to living like a dole-ite when you're a millionaire – it's a weird lifestyle change.

The Charlatans believed that they were turning the corner.

Mark Collins was a good close-season signing, his presence already felt in the band, with a more rocky, harder edge.

After the crisis of most of 1992 they were beginning to find their feet again. But then the Charlatans' curse erupted again and this time it was in a heavy duty mood.

On 3 December Rob Collins drove the car in a getaway from an armed robbery from an off licence in Great Wyrley in the Midlands. It was the beginning of the worst disaster to befall the band so far, and one of the oddest chapters in rock & roll as the Charlatans' keyboard player was committing a crime that he possibly didn't even know that he had done.

Fresh back from a tour of Japan and in a band whose career, even if it had dipped wasn't in what could be described as a free-fall, it was pretty obvious that even for a wild card like Collins, robbing an off licence was strictly off the agenda. He hardly needed the dosh or the adrenaline rush! On paper it looks like he was the unwitting accomplice in a bungled burglary.

The Charlatans, who had been perceived as being the 'nice boys' of the Manchester scene, a scene that made great play of its street connections, with groups glorifying gangsta-style cred at the drop of a hat, were in for a nasty shock.

Tim Burgess remembers the moment when the bombshell was dropped. 'We got a phone call on 6 December saying don't go and rehearse today, Rob's in prison and he's going to be there for a few days. He's been arrested in connection with an armed robbery. It was the worst feeling I've ever had in my life.'

For Rob the evening had started off innocently enough. He and his friend, Michael Whitehouse were out on an easy-going night on the tiles, checking out a few local pubs. After a couple of pints in Cannock, Rob drove them back to Wednesbury to meet Jon Brookes for last orders.

At a quarter past nine Whitehouse asked Rob to pull up at an off licence.

'As he got out of the car he said, "I might do this off licence over, you know." And then he went in, leaving the car door open. So I closed the door and waited. Next thing I heard this bang and he came running out of the shop and past the car,' Collins told Stuart Maconie from *Select* in the only full interview he ever did about the incident.

He added, 'Of course, as everybody said, I should have left him. But I'd known him a long time, so I picked him up. As we drove away I was saying, "What the fuck did you do that for?" And he was saying, "Oh, I need the money." I said, "forget the money, what if someone saw me? What if someone got the car number?"'

Whilst in the shop Whitehouse had pulled out an imitation handgun and asked for money from the till; the man working in the shop had refused and had had a go at the gun-toting desperado. Whitehouse left the shop fast and jumped into Collins' car.

Collins dropped his friend off at his house, drove home and parked up. Getting out of his car he was jumped by the Serious Crime Squad. It was a ridiculous state of affairs.

He recalled the arrest in *Select*. 'Anyway, we got to Wednesbury and I went home at about quarter past 12. As I was parking the car in the garage, a Fiesta pulled up and two blokes got out and asked me where I had been. As it turned out they were plain-clothes police officers. The next thing I knew they had pulled a gun – at that point I thought, Wooah! And I'm under arrest and on my way to Cannock police station.'

Collins spent the next five days at the police station. For the first two days he denied everything. 'Then on the third day they told me that my co-accused had admitted to it all, so I told them everything.'

It was hardly like Collins needed the money, and would a getaway driver, let alone a high-profile local musician, use his own car to rob a shop?

Jon Brookes was as shocked as anyone by the whole state of affairs. 'The whole thing was almost comical. He took a mate he hadn't seen for years out for a drink and somehow got caught up in an armed robbery. It was such a farce seeing him in court. It was like, "What are you doing here, you pillock?"'

Martin Blunt was equally confused. 'The first thing I thought was this is unbelievable – anyone but Rob. Rob has always been so quiet, you know, so self assured. He'd always sort of been the anchor of the group. I first got the call at eight in the morning and it was completely unreal.'

Tim Burgess has his own theory why the keyboard player did it: 'For the buzz, he's into danger, he's just like that.'

Alison Martin remembers Tim and Mark coming round to her Salford flat to tell her what had happened. The two Charlatans seemed surprised but not too shocked as they related the story; the implications probably hadn't sunk in yet.

The original charges that Rob faced were attempted robbery and possession of a firearm. Heavy-duty charges that would result in five years in prison if they could be made to stick in court, but Collins' solicitor got the charges adjusted to 'assisting an offender after a crime'. They then hit the judge at the bail hearing with heaps of stories and statistics about the Charlatans' success in an attempt to question why the hell the keyboard player in a successful rock & roll band would bother robbing a small local off licence.

As Collins told *Select*, 'The idea was to prove to the judge that, seeing as I'd had a number 1 LP, I was hardly likely to do over an off licence for a couple of hundred quid, plus the fact I'd been using my own car.'

Rob was released on a bail surety of twenty five grand (paid by his dad) and his passport was retained.

1993
In Limbo

REELING FROM THE BLOWS BUT STILL ON THEIR FEET

1993 stumbled in, bleary-eyed with shock, as were the band with a keyboard player who was going to spend the year wondering whether he was going to jail or not.

Down but definitely not out, the Charlatans needed a big gesture to prove that they were still serious contenders. They needed to be seen to be doing something hip and something grand, to prove that they were still a big-league band before everyone else forgot.

Perceived to now be in dire straits with tumbling record sales, the end of the scene that had helped them to the top and a keyboard player battling a jail sentence, on the outside it looked like a pretty fucked situation.

Wouldn't it be smart to play a one-off or a couple of big shows in big venues, just to look the part on the big stage in front of the big crowd?

The answer was a double bill with Ride, seaside gigs that would do both bands' profiles a lot of good. Sparked by a chance meeting between Burgess and Ride's Mark Gardener at the previous year's Reading festival, the gig looked like the answer to a lot of problems.

At one point the shows were thrown into confusion because there was doubt when Rob's court case was going to be. But an application for bail proved successful so the keyboard player was free for the concert.

The two shows, the 'Day Tripper' gigs, one in Brighton and one at Blackpool's Empress Ballroom, were both 5000-capacity, no nonsense venues that would take some filling – the bands sold them out easily.

Luckily for the Charlatans they had a brilliant manager in Steve, who was a sort of Brian Epstein type of figure, the small-town shopkeeper who really, really understood . . . This was where the smart move came from. Ride were perhaps one of the best bands to slip out of the shoe-gazing melee, although they were closer to a pop band than to the naff scene, basing the rudiments of their sound on the guitar dissonance of the genius My Bloody Valentine and even the feedback rush of prime-time Jesus & Mary Chain. Allied to this they had brought along saccharine pop melodies and had hit upon a perfect pop combination, scoring several hits since they burst through in 1990, including their biggest, 'Leave Them All Behind', a top 10 that previous February.

The two bands had several connections, they were both dealing in a guitar-heavy psychedelic take on three-minute pop and had lush-lipped frontmen with dishevelled mop-top hair who were indie pin-ups; they talked the same sort of talk and loved the same records. Although they came from different scenes the two bands were a lot closer than at first they seemed.

And Burgess and Mark Gardener did look remarkably similar – two shaggy-mopped pouty indie frontmen, straddling the worlds of the *NME* and *Smash Hits*.

It was also a great excuse to escape the 1000-capacity venues and put some proper big-time shows on. For the Charlatans it was a chance to showcase themselves as a big-scene band, and hopefully springboard themselves back into the mainstream, whilst Ride were getting to play a huge venue c/o the Charlatans' loyal fanbase.

Something in the south and something in the north, two seaside towns, one big, bold and brash and one small, quaint and media friendly; it was north meets south. And don't forget the Empress Ballroom in Blackpool was the scene of the Stone Roses' crucial breakout show three years previously, something that neither band, stuffed full of Roses' acolytes, could have ignored.

In Blackpool, the Charlatans naturally headlined, being on their home turf. It must have been a great moment to hit the stage in front of the keenest party faithful to fill the beautiful hall since the Stone Roses had played their classic gig.

Ride acquitted themselves well too with the feedback-drenched huge pop soundscapes; never as lightweight as history remembers them, they were easily the best of the shoe-gazers, their pop heart never too far below the surface.

In Brighton the Charlatans hit the theatre at 8.15. Burgess, who had spent the afternoon being chased around the beach by screaming fans, gave it his full-on punchy-armed Jagger take, and the band were tight as fuck, pumping out their soulful pop, rooted by Blunt's pumping solid bass, the bassman becoming a solid rock of fours stringpower onstage, quite a spectacle!

Leaving the stage to the ever-triumphant 'Sproston Green', the massive crescendo of whirling keyboards and whirring helicopter blades was a mighty climax.

The Charlatans were definitely back, all the old swagger was there, and the band were believing in themselves again. One of the most unlikely pop revivals was under way.

JAIL GUITAR DOORS

After the two tremendous seaside gigs, it was a return to the studio to continue working on the great batch of new songs for the third album.

With the band ensconced in the studio, putting together the album they were convinced would put them back on the track, their keyboard player was facing an additional pressure. Waiting for his eventual trial, Collins was desperately trying to get his organ parts down before the case came to court.

The Charlatans camp was quietly confident that he would get off, as after all he had hardly instigated the robbery.

With most of his parts down Rob Collins went to trial at Stafford Crown Court in September, where he admitted to being the getaway driver during an attempted robbery at the store in Great Wyrley. The uncertainty to whether he was going to get jailed or not remained to the wire. On the day Rob went for his sentencing he spoke to Martin Blunt, as the bassman remembers, 'He shook me by the hand and said, "I'll see you next week. Or in two years."'

It was with this mixture of apprehension and pessimism that Collins went to be sentenced.

And the result was a shock.

Despite the fact that the initial charges had been reduced in seriousness, Collins still copped an eight-month stretch. Whitehouse got four years.

It was a personal disaster for Collins and a massive blow for the Charlatans who were working hard on *Up To Our Hips*. The band returned to the studio, shocked and numb.

The errant keyboard player had already been carted off to the clink, but in some ways the waiting around had already broken him in for the sentence, as he recalled, 'The worst part was being on bail. I was held for five days and then it was nine months before I actually went to court.'

The band was nobbled, and a projected tour of America had to be put on hold, even if there had been talk of a temporary replacement for Collins, such as James Taylor.

No one had really expected Rob to go down. The whole thing was so obviously a farce and it seemed that he had been caught up in events beyond his control, an unwitting bystander in someone else's crazy scheme.

Collins in the *Select* piece recounted the stress of the court case and the trial. 'I think the band thought that I'd get a slap on the wrist or a suspended sentence. It really came as a shock, although I had my worries cos I'd been reading reports of similar cases in the local papers. Halfway through the trial the judge adjourned to consider all these reports and when he came back he said, "Well, I'm going to have to give you both a custodial sentence." My co-accused got four years and the screws had to hold him up. Then he turned to me and said, "Eight . . ." and he paused. I thought he was going to give me eight years.'

Tim Burgess told the *NME*, 'When he went into court the first time and said he'd been accused of armed robbery but he'd have to come back to be tried for attempted armed robbery, without intentionally knowing about it or something, we thought, "Brilliant let's get back in the studio." So we went back and did a little more, and then when he had to go back only Martin went with him because we thought he was getting off. Then we get this call from Steve and he's going, "All right Tim, it's over." So we're like,

"What time are you getting back?" and he replied, "We're not, it's over. Rob's in prison."'

It was a tense and difficult period; the band were loyal to their keyboard player, this was family after all. 'If Rob had gone down for four years there was no way we would have carried on without him,' Tim claimed.

Mind you, it may have been family, but it wasn't a particularly happy family. Tim never visited Rob in jail. 'I apologised to him at the time but I didn't approve of what he had done. Because he put my life in jeopardy and I wasn't asking for it. But we survived and I love him, he's spooky but he's a good guy at the end of the day.'

Martin Blunt recounts the band standing by Rob when speaking to the *NME* in 1995. 'There was no questioning our loyalty. It's just standing by your mates. Prison really stripped Rob of his pride. He lost a lot. His wife abandoned him and he doesn't get to see his kid now. A lot of his friends didn't stand by him either. He didn't even know if he was still going to be in the band when he came out. He got what he deserved, and probably could have got a longer stretch.'

Rob going down quite definitely affected the dynamics of the band, and for the first time Tim and Mark started writing songs together. Initially they made every idea they had into a song, banging out five a week. It didn't matter if some of them were rubbish, they just had to get them out. At least some of the tunes were happening, and would be the core of the next Charlatans' record. It opened up a new way for the band to work, and there were now two songwriting teams at work within the group.

Whilst Rob spent the next year in and out of court, and in prison, the band started to write and rehearse the album that was going to save their careers.

That December in the days after Rob's arrest it must have seemed like the band had hit absolute rock bottom, but since they had spent most of the year dodging disaster they found they could cope.

If anything, this latest disaster seemed to spur them harder, pushing the talents of Mark Collins to the fore.

Cometh the hour, cometh the man, and all that!

PORRIDGE

The first six weeks were spent in Shrewsbury Prison, a crumbling red-brick affair in the centre of the antique Midlands town. Here Rob was asked by the prison chaplain to play church organ on Sundays; I guess he was fairly qualified to do that, although the image of him glowering over the top of the keyboards playing psychedelic Hammond runs on the top of those ploddy old hymns takes some beating.

Tim Burgess recounts the bizarre episode of the moody keyboard player playing for the cons. 'When the vicar heard that Rob played keyboards, he got him to play in the church. Mind you, he couldn't play any sort of weird stuff, he had to be pretty careful, you know. The other prisoners worked out who he was pretty fast and were asking if he could supply drugs for them!'

Mark Collins' biggest shock when his band colleague went down was a tad more different. 'We were shocked to find out what his real age was! In the court it was announced how old he was. We didn't know that he had been lying about his age and was a couple of years older!'

For his namesake there was a different sort of shock in store. 'The first week is the worst,' remembers Rob. Straight out of court he was handcuffed and was taken by bus from Stafford to Shrewsbury (he fell asleep en route). When he got to prison he was strip-searched and showered before being told what cell he was in.

'Cell 13, A wing, on the 2s. That didn't mean anything. I just looked and all I could see was these cells going on for days. I was standing there and I watched the tea urn come round and I watched a geezer get a cup of water and throw it all over his cell mate. Next thing, everyone's running and piling in, screws, cons. I'd been there five minutes.'

Collins was finding out fast that jail is a mean and dispiriting place, one where violence is law and where there are more hard drugs than a rock & roll backstage party. The only way through is get your head down and keep quiet, not that there was much chance of that as the organist with his nerves already rattled was quickly due for another nasty shock.

His cell mate, it turned out, was in for 'murdering the wife and putting a knife through my father-in-law', as he casually informed Rob.

The next morning Collins, not used to being locked up with a killer and having nervously not slept at all, asked for a transfer and got it.

His next few days were spent trying to adopt to jail life. Jail itself was unsurprisingly quite a shock to even someone as tough as Rob. Prisons in the UK are antiquated shitholes where offenders are chucked away for a few years and all manner of different criminals are locked together.

'At first I was scared to think or speak to anyone in case I got knifed. The first morning a bloke got into the showers while I was there, and out of the corner of my eye I could see him staring at me. In the end he started humming "The Only One I Know" and came over and said, "Good band, mate." Within two days the whole jail knew. The prisoners were asking me to get Tim to sign things, the screws were asking me to sign stuff for their daughters. I think a lot of them couldn't understand what I was doing in prison rather than serving a suspended sentence. Most people were pretty good about it. You did get a few who'd say, "Big pop star, eh? Well, you ain't a fuckin' pop star in here . . ."'

Not many pop stars have ended up in jail. There have been crimes committed that should have seen them sent down, but a mixture of good briefs and surprisingly lenient courts have seen most get off.

Collins obviously hadn't been so lucky. Not that he was forgotten and left in jail to rot, as being a high-profile person in a well publicised case, his mailbag bulged every day: 'I had to hide it from the others on the screws' advice, otherwise they may have got a bit pissed off.'

The band and Steve Harrison sent him letters every day as did fans. 'I was really made up to get letters. I used to reply straight away, which used to amaze some of the fans. It was something to occupy me.'

At Shrewsbury he worked in the kitchens and afterwards became a vegetarian. 'I don't eat my friends any more,' he joked to Blunt over the phone.

After his kitchen work he would be banged up in his cell, except for a 20-minute slop-out at around seven. He even received a wage for his endeavours of about £5.10 a week, a tad less than he was used to getting in the Charlatans, but enough to spend on phonecalls and tobacco, two items that couldn't be bought with personal cash from outside.

'It wasn't bad. It was better than having a 23-hour bang-up which would have done my head in. At the end of six weeks in Shrewsbury, I was told I could be retained and finish my sentence there working in the kitchens, or be transferred to Hewell Range, an open Prison near Redditch. I thought I might as well stop where I was. But then I was making tea in the officer's mess and one screw took me aside, and said, "You're mad, you know. If you go to Redditch, you can go home every weekend and earn £160 a week. So I said I'd go. First day there, they told me those privileges only exist for people serving more than a year so I was back to square one.'

Redditch was a different regime than what Collins had been used to at Shrewsbury. There he had been living in a nine-by-six cell – 'Imagine living in your bathroom!' he told *Select* – but he now found himself in a dorm with 11 other inmates, and was allowed to come and go relatively freely.

'There was a separate toilet and a TV room and things like that. I only went once, 150 blokes arguing about what to watch. At night, I didn't usually sleep till about 3 am. There was always conversations and arguments about the radio. I used to just switch off and listen to the Walkman which was another thing you weren't allowed in Shrewsbury. But you can see why some prisoners would rather be banged up, just for the privacy.'

Redditch may have been more relaxed but it still had its own set of rules. Inmates were woken at 7.45 and anyone not dressed by 8.15 had seven extra days added to their sentence. Every month, inmates were allowed unsupervised town visits of five hours, but an extra 28 days were added to the sentence for every five minutes late the prisoner was in returning.

'You did get people doing runners, but it wasn't worth it. They'd end up serving an extra month for the sake of one day's freedom.'

On 13 January, with remission for good behaviour, Rob Collins was released after serving four months of an eight-month sentence. The day before he got out he was called to the governor's office and told that his brother had rung up to find out what time he was leaving as he would be picking him up tomorrow. This was weird as Rob didn't have a brother – someone from the press was looking for a story. The prison released him half an hour earlier through the back door, leaving the press hovering outside the jail for hours looking for the keyboard player.

Jail affects people: some go under, some commit suicide, some get deeper into crime, and some like Rob hold it together, but even then there were side effects.

He lost weight and gained bags under his eyes. 'You don't sleep properly. You catnap. That peephole goes once an hour.'

He realised how thin he had got the day he was released. 'On the day you leave, they check whether your clothes still fit you because you lose so much weight in prison. The food is vile. Powdered scrambled eggs and liver that's been on the floor being picked up and used. I worked in the kitchens remember, and I saw what happened, particularly to the food going to C wing.'

Steve Harrison sighs with sadness when he looks back at the jail sentence that he still isn't happy about. 'Jail was the beginning of the end for Rob. It didn't do him any good and after he came out he was a changed person.'

The system had failed again. Hardly a criminal, Collins was carrying the stigma of being jailed on his back. He never got his life properly back together again.

I WAS BORN ON CHRISTMAS DAY

The Christmas single is the ultimate in pop kitsch and like the football song it presents the ultimate challenge to the popsmith to create something with any wit or style to make it rise above the mediocre sentimental tosh that dominates the form.

Great Xmas singles have been stuff like Slade's 'Merry Christmas Everybody', Wizzard's 'I Wish It Could Be Christmas Every Day' or the Pogues' god-like Xmas 1987 number 2 smash 'Fairytale Of New York' duet with Kirsty MacColl; but generally it's a dreaded pit to wallow in and few manage to transcend the form.

That's why Saint Etienne stepped into the breach for the pop project put together by ex-*Melody Maker* writer Bob Stanley and his best mate Pete

Wiggs, with a definite understanding of cheesy pop and how to make it sound classy and timeless. Over the years Saint Etienne have cut some great pop records which have grabbed a lot of praise but, despite several top-20 hits, have never seemed to have grabbed the mainstream like they should have done. Vocalist Sarah Cracknell has the innate charisma and English rose beauty that makes her a perfect pop star; she also has a hard as nails, no bullshit sense of humour and down to earthiness that made her perfect to carry through Bob and Pete's crackpot pop ideas.

Just to team her up with Tim Burgess for a Christmas record seemed like a pop idea that was so perfect that it had to happen. And it did that December.

Of course the press loved the idea, and the *Melody Maker* had the pair photographed during the filming of the video at Chelsea Town Hall in London (which also featured Richard O'Sullivan from 1970s telly sitcom *Man About The House* . . . beat that for tack!) where they were getting married, Tim looking out of place in top hat and tails and Sarah sassy and sexy in all white fake furs.

The song was written three weeks after Sarah had drunkenly bumped into Tim on a Manchester dancefloor where she was hanging out for a few days; they got on famously and decided to do a song together. The song-writing boys, of course, couldn't resist such a delicious pop idea and further tweaked the popness of it all by creating a Christmas record; Bob Stanley being especially keen as his birthday is on 25 December.

Tim Burgess explained the song to the *Melody Maker*. 'The lyric takes the form of two people writing to each other. One of the characters in the story is working in Euro Disney to get some money for presents and his girlfriend is in England pining for him. It's quite a sad song really.'

Maybe it is downbeat, but the song, hooked on to the sort of descending chord sequence that always suckers the pop fan, was the sort of frothy disco pop tat that Saint Etienne were great at trading in, treading that fine line between kitsch and total pop.

And it put Burgess's beaming face back on *Top Of The Pops*, a welcome lightweight break from the shit that was stalking the group.

1994
Getting Out Of Bed

WAKEY! WAKEY! . . . CAN'T GET OUT OF BED

Jesus Kerrist! If 1993 generally had been yet another blip on the band's plans for recovery from their recent malaise, then the tail end of the year jail thing had certainly put a mad blot on that landscape! Again the band had their skinny backs to the wall – a conventional rock & roll career wasn't something that the Charlatans were getting booked for.

The band just wanted now to get on with business, get the great new material that they had quietly been piling up in the last months out on the streets, and to prove that they were a great fucking group. But right now what they mainly had was the air of a bunch of desperadoes. Controversy sells, but it makes the actual mechanics of being in a band damned difficult.

The stench of Rob's incarceration was to hang over their creativity for a while yet (he's not even in the video for 'Can't Get Out Of Bed' because of his jail sentence and misses out on the clip of the band mooching about in pubs and on London rooftops and miming to the song in a rehearsal room); not only were they confused as to what their future could ever be but the pain of the situation was leaking into the songs.

'Can't Get Out Of Bed' was the Charlatans' first single on Beggars Banquet proper and their first in the 18 months since 'Tremelo Song' had disappointed at number 44 in the charts. But the long gap had paid dividends and this was a far more settled band than at the last outing. It was flipped with 'Withdrawn', and 'Out', an instrumental dedicated to the recently released Collins.

The Charlatans celebrated the single's release with a party at a swanky hotel in Kensington and the usual crew of scruffy music biz types hung around in the unlikely environs of the building whilst the upcoming album got a playback. It was an attempt to recreate some sort of 1960s happening and everyone stood stiffly around waiting for it to happen, but the Manc party was over, and apart from getting pissed up there was no sign of the E vibe that had powered along the parties of a couple years back. It was fun but it wasn't a freak out. Those days were gone.

The following night Mark Collins had what he has since described as 'the most drunken night of my life' as they celebrated the release of Rob Collins from jail, and things were definitely starting to look up.

Lyrically 'Can't Get Out Of Bed' is about Collins, and Burgess sneered the vocal line in a far more confident drawl than his whispier vocal outings of the first two albums. 'I was trying to get into Rob's head. I was trying to understand what was going through his head, what he was trying to do, what he was thinking at the time of the incident.'

This peep into the mind of their maverick keyboard player was married to an insistent vocal melody and a delicious bluesy guitar riff that signified the tougher, more rock-based guitar sound that the band were about to explore on the upcoming album. Mark Collins had definitely arrived and brought his guitar with him; the trippy grooves of the past seemed to be getting pushed aside as the Charlatans moved into the business of writing tuffer 6-string pop. Going by the great vibe of this single, the band were about to make that quantum leap from the dead shell of baggy and into the real world of being a great rock & roll band. With a new stronger vocal style and a big jump in the band's sound, the prospect of the upcoming album was mouthwatering.

Rob Collins tasted freedom on 13 January and was thrust straight into a hectic touring and release schedule as the band tried to kickstart their career, perhaps the best way to shake off those jailhouse blues.

Tim Burgess talked to the *NME* about Collins' release a year later. 'He probably could have got a longer stretch, but he did his time for the band, because he believes in us and we believe in him. Anyway, we played *Top Of The Pops* soon after he was released, and that was him back in the fold in style.'

You could just feel the humanity dripping out of the band. Burgess's obvious concern for his mate and the way that the band was like his family, in fact the only family that Collins seemed to have left – the gang would always welcome you back and look after you.

'Can't Get Out Of Bed' had a naggingly incessant chorus and featured some of Burgess's finest vocals to date. It was the Charlatans' best single since 'Only One' and would galvanise the group's career in wonderful style.

WAKE UP CALL

The fightback starts here. Again!

1994 was another fresh start for the band, they had got some hot tracks in the can, and a fab new single for release, they also had a keyboard player back out of jail, this had to be the comeback (part 3)!

An omen for their new year was their *Top Of The Pops* appearance on 24 January. The band was back in business and the main thing that stared you right in the face was that someone had gone out and bought a couple of Bob Dylan songbooks. The Charlatans were now deep into their Dylan period, copping the same sort of influences that the Beatles had years before, giving their music an earthiness and depth.

The Northwich boys were enthralled by Dylan and the lazy kinda drawl that peaktime Bob made his own, enthralled enough to use Dylan's 'Like A Rolling Stone' as a template for 'Can't Get Out Of Bed', enjoying the same sort of rolling groove, keyboard swirls, and chiming guitars that Dylan had utilised years before, coupled with that wistful smoking folksiness of the prime-time troubadour and his edginess. The Charlatans were branching out from their predominantly British influences and allowing some

American ones into their sound.

It is to the credit of the Charlatans that they took this new influence and stamped themselves all over it, some achievement when faced with classic songwriting like Dylan's; you can hear the Dylan flavour in plenty of their songs from this period and when Mark Collins talks about songwriting he tells of taking a pile of classic records out to a country cottage with Tim to get some 'inspiration'.

We were just weeks away from witnessing the astonishing rise of Britpop that April when Oasis released 'Supersonic' and totally changed the map of British pop.

But in those pre-Oasis days 'Can't Get Out Of Bed' managed a fairly respectable 24 in the charts and the usual 3-week run, a sign that the fanbase were still buying their records but the band still wasn't crossing over into the mass market scene. Maybe it wasn't a top 10 hit but the band were back in *Top Of The Pops* land and, more importantly, it was a great single, a sign that the band were about to deliver.

That February the band went out to Europe again, and their tour of bigger-sized clubs were not only packed out but locked out as well.

'LIVING IS EASY WITH EYES CLOSED'

After a long hibernation, a seemingly never-ending period of inactivity and headlines only grabbed by problems, it seemed that in 1994 the band were determined to set the record straight that they really were just a great rock & roll band, full stop.

Hot on the heels of 'Can't Get Out Of Bed' came the next single, released a mere six weeks after that had slipped out of the charts, on 19 March. The band were machine-gunning records at the charts but they still weren't getting further than their hardcore fans; 'Easy Life' snuck in at the bottom end of the top 40, sloping in at number 38 for one week before fucking off again. It was hardly encouraging for the upcoming album and it was starting to look like the band was going to have to settle for cult status, rarely peeping over the pop barricades and into the top ten – in short, getting hits was getting damned difficult.

Nevertheless the vibe in the camp was good and there was a zest about the Burgess interview machine, with him talking everything up with that irrepressible lust for life that's all part of his charm.

'I Never Want An Easy Life', also inspired by Collins' jail sentence, was a Dylan-fused slice of great churning guitar pop, causing the words classic melodies, Bob Dylan and mature to be bounced around – nobody mentioned the Roses. The record was released in a limited edition, an unsuccessful ploy to get a higher chart placing, and the video was clipped together from live footage from their recent European tour.

Radio One's Mark Radcliffe put out their first session for three years and the tracks were 'Jesus Hairdo', 'Autograph', 'I Never Want An Easy Life' and 'Feel Flows'.

In April it was announced that the band's upcoming US tour was in jeopardy. Rob may have been released from jail but PR Jon Best explained to the press that he thought it was likely the band would find it difficult getting visas for the US due to his conviction.

It seemed that the niggling problems were endless, not that the times were completely without humour.

When asked for his least-favourite five people, Burgess had this to say about one of his choices, Phil Collins, 'How can a drummer be a singer? It's impossible because all drummers are stupid. It's not chemically possible for a drummer to sing.'

Wonder what the boy Brookes had to say about that?

BRING IT ALL BACK HOME . . . TRENTHAM GARDENS

After last spring's grand gesture of the Ride gigs had paid off with large dividends, this year needed an equally Big Idea.

Most bands do their glam show bit in the European showbiz capital of London, all the media are there and everyone makes the trip down south; it's like Cup Final day, the big day out . . . storm the capital . . . look like big business.

But with the decidedly northern flavour of mid-1990s pop, the Charlatans took a very different road, and decided to play Stoke On Trent, quite possibly the least fashionable town in the whole of the country. Apart from giving the world the fastest and crudest punk band ever, Discharge, and eventually Robbie Williams, the decade's showbiz king, Stoke On Trent has no discernible pop history at all.

It was an idea that was so Charlatans, so obstinate in the face of music biz convention, that it had a beauty all of its own. They were never ones to go down on their knees to the business, making everything come to them. Also, it was plain common sense too, as this was their backyard and their loyal fanbase lived in the area; it would be a celebration of all things so unhip that they were hip.

This show at Trentham Gardens, a huge faded ballroom, on 2 April was a gesture to reshape their case. The gig was a watershed in the band's career, and the show is now regarded as the band's finest, both by them and their fans.

A big hall of 3,500 capacity, it was sold out. This was down to the Charlatans themselves, and proved that they were still in the big league, one which was getting bigger by the hour, as Oasis were just about to change the very meaning of what an 'indie' band meant.

It was the Charlatans' British comeback show, a glorious resurgence after the difficulties and their perceived slide down the pop league table.

No one of any note had played Trentham Gardens since the Jam had rocked the place in their heyday. This gig was very much the Charlatans' answer to the Stone Roses' mighty Empress Ballroom gig in Blackpool back in 1989, and in pulling it off they proved that they were totally on for the comeback; no wonder Burgess sported a Superman t-shirt over his bony ribs with pride.

It was no mean feat in the pre-Oasis pre-Britpop bonanza to sell out a venue this size, but with a warm buzz of critical acceptance starting to billow around the band, the Charlatans were once more back in favour; in fact, they almost seemed pretty hip. The fans were just happy to have them back, the atmosphere was magical and the moshpit at the front was packed with good-time revelry.

The band were finally back in the groove and played out of their skins. Tim Burgess tonight seemed to step back from the frontman role, just letting his great band throb with their own power. The music now getting so good that it didn't need any charismatic shuffling from him.

After all this time, they had become a tight unit, a group that was playing off itself. The Charlatans had become a machine, that moment when a band clicks into first gear. Mark Collins now was really coming into the fore; a great guitar player, he was the new hidden strength in the band. He was proving to be more than just a simple replacement for Jon Baker, and was taking the band a whole new trip.

The Charlatans had something to prove, and that night they proved it. 'Got to be done, got to be done,' the vocalist muttered as the crowd screamed for an encore.

That was an understatement from Burgess.

Support came from Whiteout, the almost-there denim-clad pure pop band from Greenock in Scotland, managed by the effervescent McD. With their crystalline melodies and pure pop touches, they seemed to be perfect for the current pop climate but for some reason just kept missing out. Their footnote in rock history so far seems to be the fact that Oasis supported them on their breakthrough tour.

The two bands were certainly operating in the same sort of area of pop, something which the NME rather scandalously pointed out when reviewing the Charlatans' 'Can't Get Out Of Bed' and the Whiteout 'No Time' single that January, claiming that the Charlatans had stolen Whiteout's tune because of the similarities between the two tracks. Whiteout were always going to be so close.

Sometimes pop is the hardest game in the world.

The Charlatans themselves were wired, playing old classics and their hot new replacements like 'Jesus Hairdo' and 'I Never Want An Easy Life', and were proving themselves to be a force to reckon with in the Oasis years. Their clutch of great new tunes pointed towards a new direction in their style that was going to be their escape route, instantly updating their sound and proving they were a great band after all. The Charlatans had just returned from a European tour playing Amsterdam, Munich, Cologne, Hamburg and Stockholm, one of their few jaunts to the mainland, where they had never quite reached the same sort of heights that they had done in the UK.

'We've just done eight dates in Europe, and by about the third day it was brilliant. Everything was completely back to normal, we had a brilliant time, and it went down amazingly well. We were only playing relatively small 750-1000 capacity venues, but they all sold out,' they said.

The band's gig at Amsterdam's medium-sized Milky Way venue was their big live comeback, on 12 February. The gig was favourably reviewed in a heap of papers, and it looked like the Charlatans were back in business. Their first live gig for a year was witnessed by the usual barmy coachloads of Britpop fans who were now into football-style following, checking their heroes out across Europe.

The Brit fans loved especially that coach trip to Amsterdam, as the Dutch capital was hallowed ground, where you could walk into bars and get stoned without getting your collar felt, and there was the red-light area to explore and the quaint city to wander around in a daze, feeling psychedelic on spliffs and wobbly buildings. Johnny Cigarettes from the *NME* had drawn a journalistic short straw and was one of the passengers on the coaches, witnessing pissed-off drivers threatening to turn the coach back as smashed kids puked up all over his bus and butty fights.

It was all hi jinx and daft fun, just getting in the mood, a 24-hour trip, 110 quid and the Charlatans thrown in, not counting the booze and the drugs, a great one-day burnout. Burgess impressed with his ridiculously upbeat vibe, grinning and finger-popping his way round the venue like he was stuck permanently on Cloud 9; the man was armed with the sheer joy of being in a rock & roll band, a rare thing in the whinging world of pop. Cigarettes enjoyed the gig, pointing out that the Charlatans were starting to sound like a serious band instead of a lightweight, occasionally good, singles band.

People were noticing that something had changed at the Charlatans camp. And what a change for their recently-released keyboard man, one minute locked up and the next out on the European circuit, where they really know how to look after a band.

Europe had never really taken to the Madchester pop boom and its attendant bands. Maybe they were big in Japan and a cult in the States, Europe just seemed generally disinterested in the clutch of northern groups, and outside the bigger club circuit the bands were finding it difficult to make much space.

The Charlatans held their own in Europe, but the amazing reaction at

Trentham Gardens must have been the best sort of fillip for a band determined to restate their case.

EXIT PLANET DUST . . . ENTER THE CHEMICAL BROTHERS

Acid house had changed a lot since the back end of the 1980s when it had engulfed the whole of the music scene. Its knock-on effect was massive and whole cities were getting redesigned in its image. Manchester city centre was slowly becoming full of cafe bars that looked like rave clubs and handbag house throbbed in all the clubs.

Most of the cutting-edge music of the mid 1990s was getting put together by dudes on the dance scene. Idiosyncratic cut creators like the Chemical Brothers were starting to push music into all sorts of weird shapes, and their activities would hardly be missed by the Charlatans and especially Tim Burgess, who was hanging out in clubs like the Sunday Social in London, checking on the pair's DJing, and getting his mind blown as a result.

The much-mooted indie dance crossover from the late 1980s had become a bunch of 1960s riffs married to a shuffling drumbeat; it was hardly acid house but it was enough for a whole generation to dance around to. The Charlatans, even though certain members like Tim Burgess had been into house music, had never really explored the territory as much as they could have.

But all this was about to change when they hooked up with the Chemical Brothers in 1994.

First it was for the Chemicals' monumental remix of 'Jesus Hairdo', and then Tim returned the favour the next year by singing vocals on the Brothers' 'Life Is Sweet' single, giving the pair their second chart hit following up the summer of 1995's 'Leave Home', crashing in at number 25.

The Chemical Brothers were revolutionary. For the past few years indie bands had been making dance mixes of their records to crossover into the club scene, but this pair were taking things the other way round, by adding rock to their dance. 'It's weird how some people still view dance music and rock music as totally contradictory, we've used vocals on some of our tracks by Noel Gallagher and Tim Burgess and Beth Orton,' said Tom Rowlands.

The vocalists weren't just picked because they looked pretty. 'Tim may be in a guitar band but he's just as knowledgeable about dance music,' pointed out the Brothers.

Things were changing fast and by 1994 most people were crossing over from one scene to another with no problem at all. Indie kids were still digging bands but were also clubbing it, and for the first time since acid house's astonishing rise in the late 1980s and its slump a few years later the music was moving on again. With the addition of lifeblood from the rock scene, a crossover music was being made. It would result in what the

Americans would eventually naffly term Electronic, with the likes of the Prodigy becoming one of the biggest bands in the world.

Riding in the centre of this were the Chemical Brothers. 'I know dance people feel like it doesn't really belong and some people felt it was wrong working with Noel Gallagher or Tim Burgess. Some people have a problem with the fact that our music rocks. With "Dig Your Own Hole" we went after that sort of sound . . . the Chemical beats sound; the acid over the break beats had been done pretty well on the first album.'

The Chemical Brothers live were the perfect combination of this new style, the pair of them poised over their keyboards, shaking their heads in time to the massive beats. They were a rock & roll band without guitars, they had the dynamics of the rock & roll experience and the funk of a dance band. It was the perfect 1990s combination and it was cool that the Charlatans were working with them.

The acid house scene had been intense. It had completely changed a city like Manchester. Before it blew the nightlife culture apart, the city had been slowly sliding into a post-punk malaise, but post acid house the clubs were swinging and the 'youth on drugs' debate had been thrust back on the front of the terrified tabloids. There was a new baggy look that terrified the preceding generation and there was this unfathomable music, all the perfect ingredients for a yoof quake.

It had the city entranced and electrified for years but by the mid 1990s you could sense that the whole thing was going off the boil. Manchester, which had been party central for a couple of years, was feeling the burnout heavily; the gangsters were sniffing money and pressurising clubs, scene makers were getting bored and the clubs were getting lazy.

Most dance music wasn't the leading edge of fashion any more, but more like the dead centre of the mainstream. 'Sharon and Tracey' music some sneered. Fair enough, it was the backing track to weekend copping off at the groin exchanges in town, but it was a genuine people's music and that's okay, but for those that demanded more it wasn't delivering. I mean, everyone wants to go out, get smashed and cop off, but sometimes it's good to do this to a great soundtrack and with some fucking really cool-looking people who can talk great wild shit there as well. Clubs like Most Excellent were making the effort though, based on the London style of clubs set up by the likes of Andy Wetherall and their mates and, concentrating on a heavier, darker sort of dance music with eclectic twists and turns, they attracted a hipster crowd.

The Chemical Brothers were two students, Tom Rowlands and Ed Simmons, who came to Manchester University to study history in the late 1980s, attracted by the Madchester explosion and the vibrant party scene as much as the quality of the course on offer.

Rooted in indie music they had been massive fans of the Jesus & Mary Chain; this was a tuff music that had an edge that the spineless bastards of most 1980s pop disgustingly lacked, and then they had had their minds blown by Public Enemy.

Public Enemy were the kings of hip hop. You listen to their records now and they still sound full-on and inspiring. Crammed with a ridiculous amount of ideas and texture, this was a music of genius. They rode huge fat beats which were scoured with strange noises and spot-on cool samples, and they had a defiant definite image and could play live as well. They instantly revolutionised hip hop and then they went on to tear pop culture apart.

In Chuck D they had an eloquent ball-busting frontman who rapped like no one before or since, with a dark, rich voice bursting with authority he shot the shit across the tracks; his foil was Flavour Flav, a bona fide pop nutter who wore massive clocks around his head just to remind us that there wasn't much time left. Flav would do these mad nasal chants and rhymes that were stuffed with great catchphrases.

For white kids Public Enemy were the dons, they really rocked. Whereas most hip hop before had been really good, it didn't seem to tally with what a white kid wanted from a band; they needed some sort of rock dynamic, some sort of gang thing and some sort of big, big sound that replicated rock without paying any lip-service to it at all.

Public Enemy delivered on all fronts and the fact that they could do this shit live and then some, quickly saw them playing the sort of shows where they quickly picked up a vast audience of people who had never listened to this type of music before. They were the starting point to a whole host of key players in the 1990s UK dance music scene, and the Chemical Brothers were just two of the teens whose minds were knocked sideways by the sheer power and ideas of the group.

Tom Rowlands had played in Balearic dance combo Aerial, who were one of the several bands hanging around on the edges of the Boys Own London scene and who went on to release four singles on Deconstruction.

The Chemical Brothers started by DJing at friends' student parties, throwing on whatever record that came to hand. Getting a taste for the DJ action, they put on their own night, Naked Under Leather, at the Swinging Sporron city centre pub venue that was squashed into a corner of a car park and had been better known as a punk venue, with gigs by the likes of Therapy? and the Ex.

The Two Naked Under Leather nights were a great success, and Rowlands and Simmons went under the moniker the Dust Brothers, in tribute to the West Coast production team who had produced the likes of the Beastie Boys' 'Paul's Boutique'. They were just doing this for fun, they didn't have a clue that they could ever take off, and when they DJed they played dance records and stuff by the Stone Roses, which raised eyebrows in the mutually exclusive dance and rock worlds of the early 1990s. They specialised in the eclectic but also brought in heaps of New York underground hip hop beats to really set the house rocking.

Going to Manc clubs where the Dust Brothers were DJing restored your humble narrator's belief in a brilliant night out in a club with a wicked soundtrack – you just wanted to own all the damned records that they were playing. Brilliant.

When their university course was over they drifted back home to London, and released their self-financed debut single 'Songs Of The Siren' ('it was a record of the Naked Under Leather nights, all fuck off sirens and loud noises') to great acclaim and saw the single picked up by Juniors Boys Own and remixed by Sabres Of Paradise. The buzz intensified and they started on the remix trail, working with the likes of the Manic Street Preachers, getting their name about c/o some heavy-duty rock solid genius remixes of Primal Scream's 'Jailbird' and the Prodigy's 'Voodoo People'.

Their debut album, *Exit Planet Dust*, arrived on the crest of a wave, and getting hip with their DJ sets at Heavenly Records' Sunday Social, their fat beats were the backbone to the sound that they would be using on their debut. They were dragged through court by their heroes the Dust Brothers, who demanded that they should change their name to avoid confusion, and were being courted by mega-bucks records labels. For a couple of guys who were just fucking around things had got very serious.

When they got the call from the Dust Brothers' management in the US, who also looked after Ice T, they realised you just don't fuck with these people. Given 48 hours to change their name, they came up with the Chemical Brothers, naming themselves after one of their best tracks, 'Chemical Beats', which they thought was a terrible name although it now actually sounds perfect.

Exit Planet Dust had been delayed by the naming confusion by some six months before it could be released but it was so far ahead of everything else that when it came out it still turned everyone's heads right round. This was what pop music in the 1990s should sound like!

From the 'brothers can work it out' intro chant on 'Leave Home' to Tim's fuzzbox angelic croon on 'Life Is Sweet' this was some album, a real yardstick by which everyone else should get measured.

'Life Is Sweet' had come together after a few wrecked nights too many down the Sunday Social. The two parties were already aware of each other, as they both shared Heavenly Records' press office.

Heavenly was the record label and press and PR company set up by one of the most enthusiastic people you're ever likely to bump into in the music business, Jeff Barrett. His first foray into the business had been in Plymouth where he was promoter, putting on most of the mid 1980s underground bands and running the town's only cool indie shop, Meat Whiplash (named after the track from the classic Scots outfit Fire Engines). From there he drifted up to London to work for the blossoming Creation Label, doing their press and being the general vibes merchant.

He started to put on bands again and eventually left Creation to set up his own PR company Capersville, doing the publicity for the likes of the Happy Mondays, Flowered Up and Primal Scream. Barrett was totally on the case, the hippest bands in Britain were under his wing, he was the top PR man in the country, and his burning enthusiasm was a key element in his success, as it seemed like this bugger actually liked the bands and he lived their lifestyle as well. Jeff Barrett was the total rock & roll PR.

Capersville eventually blossomed into a record label, putting out the early records by the likes of the Manic Street Preachers, Flowered Up and Saint Etienne, and, moving his operation into the heart of London, he set up shop in Soho. A creaky narrow staircase leads up to offices that are always booming music whilst a load of party-burned 'workers' who walk it like they talk it hustle away, total 24-hour party people – the fact that Heavenly is actually a totally pro set-up is baffling.

These offices were the focal point of much of the hot new talent in the early 1990s, so it was inevitable that he would hook up with the Charlatans, and he started to do their press as well as that of the Chemical Brothers.

Jeff had also managed Andy Weatherall at his peak. So when Heavenly started putting on the Sunday Social, a weekly event on Sunday nights, more of a get together for their mates and pop star pals, they were right on target. In an era of so-called super clubs dedicated to handbag house the spirit of the house scene had all but gone; certainly the crazed party atmosphere and the anything-can-happen vibe had long gone. Heavenly's club was a return to the maverick spirit of the early days of house and was a magnet for wildcard spirits like Tim Burgess.

'We were at the Heavenly Sunday Social one time,' explained Chemical Brother Tom Rowlands, 'and Tim was about, and we were just sat there talking to him. We did that remix of "Patrol" ages ago, and we knew he was really into us so we thought why not get him down to the studio. So he came down and had his cans of Guinness and came up with this surreal lyric about walking the dog and shopping, over this funky weird music that we'd already recorded.'

Typically of a lot of these dance meets indie excursions, it had been as easy as that.

'JESUS HAIRDO' (NO STUPID HEADING REQUIRED – THE SONG'S TITLE IS FAB ENOUGH)

1994 was the year of new flavours in pop desperately looking for a different direction (as ever!). Pop feasted itself on a mod revival (big in Camden but nowhere else), jungle (one of the few true new directions and a brilliantly innovative style of music), the Bristol trip hop sound (finally, a British version of hip hop that worked by changing the very American style into a dope-soaked Brit blunt version, totally reworking the form), and Britpop was lurching over the horizon, a musical scene celebrating British pop culture that would totally dominate the next couple of years, rescuing some careers and kick-starting others.

Pop was moving on and the Charlatans were going to have to find out where they were going to fit in this brave new world. It was a case of sink or swim, and as each successive single had been selling less than the one before it was looking horribly like a case of sink, even if they were starting to release some of the best music of their careers.

Released on 2 July 'Jesus Hairdo' only got to number 48. With a 2-week chart run, it was the band's worst-selling single (apart from the rereleased 'Indian Rope'). It was obvious that the Charlatans had gone a track too far in taking songs off the last album, and not even Tim painting himself in British and American flags for the video could budge the single any higher.

The B side remixes were mixed by the Dust Brothers (soon to be renamed the Chemical Brothers), Van Basten and Manchester-based DJs Luvdup.

With a mellow vibe and a rollicking tune, 'Jesus Hairdo' captured the mid 1990s semi-stoned vibe perfectly in an upbeat slab of pop, chiefly remembered for its insanely catchy 'you shine like a star' hookline. It was a slice of perfect pop, the sort of stuff that the band could knock out in their sleep, and the fact that it wasn't a hit is puzzling.

The single was multi formatted, another unsuccessful ruse to push the record higher into the charts. The second compact disc was a limited edition of 10,000 featuring three live versions of songs from Radio One's *Evening Session*: 'I Never Want An Easy Life If Me And He Were Ever To Get There', 'Another Rider Up In Flames' and 'Up To Our Hips'.

To push 'Jesus Hairdo' the band played a bunch of dates at Manchester Hacienda, Leicester's De Montfort Hall and London's Shepherd's Bush Empire, supported by another upcoming Britpop band, Gene, whose whole career was plagued by Smiths' comparisons. They were always a much more rollicking live act than their records suggested and were another cool choice of support for the Charlatans, who were slowly turning into an A & R department of their own with their choice of supports.

The *Melody Maker* was at the Shepherd's Bush show and was puzzled by the crowd's ecstatic reaction, dragging out the old stick to beat them with that the band were true to their name.

The *NME*'s Dele Fedele was at the Leicester show and was positive about the gig. He had a pretty neat description of Burgess, 'Tim Burgess knows there is only one Mick Jagger, so his stagecraft is that of a scally pretending to be on E – which he is not of course – all upraised hands, Harlem shuffle, frisky microphone technique, pouts and sneers. He's got the audience salivating, this trainee rock god . . .'

Fedele went on to note that he was surprised by the number of Charlatans' songs that were already stuck in his head, and it was only the mid section that he felt dragged on with its blues jams and 'errant psychedelia'.

The Charlatans also played at Glasgow as part of the Sound City week, headlining a bill that would raise eyebrows in the years to come. First on were the Tindersticks with their post-Nick Cave, brilliant dark-heart balladeering; followed by Pulp, who after what seemed like centuries in the doldrums were preparing for the final breakthrough (initially it should have been Hole playing instead of Pulp, Courtney Love was having to look after husband Kurt Cobain who had attempted suicide four days previously).

But all in all it was hardly an encouraging set up for the album. With three under-performing singles and a smattering of dates, yet again the Charlatans seemed to be backed into a tight corner, the only way out would be to deliver a killer new album . . .

Maybe that's why they weren't panicking yet.

UP TO OUR HIPS . . . HOW TO GET INTO THE DEEP SHIT AND OUT AGAIN . . . LESSON 1 IN POP SURVIVAL

'I don't know about being touched by the hand of God. I think we were touched by the hand of Rod with this album with all the Faces and Small Faces influences,' Martin Blunt told *109* zine, nailing the band's new direction but missing out on Dylan, Hendrix and the Beatles, whose fingerprints are all over the record as the band established themselves in the classic line of songwriting.

Martin also added, 'Rob being in jail was a problem, he just went away on a little action. Instead of going to see the Maharishi Mahesh Yogi he went to see Her Majesty's Prison. At that point we thought things can't get any worse, and then Tim did that record with Saint Etienne, ha ha!'

If you look at the Charlatans' career through the cold light that distance and perspective gives, what is really clear is that they were a band growing up in public. Sure, they arrived pretty well formed when they burst into pop consciousness with their debut singles and albums, but all the time they were a young band. Tim had only been in them for a few months and they were swallowed up by Manchester – the scene may have done them some enormous favours, but it also instantly placed a millstone around their necks, as no matter how big they were they were always getting perceived as the runts of the litter, and however individual their Hammond-soaked sound was they were treated as the lepers gatecrashing the party, the Johnny Come Latelys who nicked someone else's sound and got lucky.

The intervening years may have been tough, but each life-threatening blow had seen the band bouncing back stronger than before; there was an indomitable spirit at work.

And this wasn't a band that was existing in a time bubble. Constantly listening and checking out the shit, they knew where the competition was at and instinctively understood that pop was getting looser, more real-sounding. As the decade unfolded, bands were being allowed to make organic records and the stifling studio technology that had suffocated so many groups' sounds in the 1980s was getting pushed aside as bands searched for that live fluidity that is the hallmark of all great guitar band recording.

By 1994 there was no fear of wearing your influences on your sleeve; bands were taking what they needed from pop's past and making their own songs out of it. Maybe as a knock-on effect from the sampling bands, they were reassembling their favourite songs into new material, although it could also be the case that bands could now be more honest than their forbears, who lied through their collective teeth about their influences.

Bands that had broken through in the late 1980s were all going through a similar process of rethinking their muse. New York's white rap trio the Beastie Boys were sounding earthier and freer on their latest album, *Paul's Boutique*, a record Tim Burgess especially had more than a passing interest in. *Paul's Boutique* was a signpost, a marker, a great album that said there's something really special here. It showed a group taking over the reigns of its own creativity and signposting exactly where music was going. The Charlatans picked up on this feel, this looseness and free-wheeling creativity.

Both bands had been at similar points in their career and had been desperate to follow up huge initial success, and had turned to their record collections for inspiration, making the music that they truly loved and to hell with market place. Both records – *Up To Our Hips* and *Paul's Boutique* – were flawed masterpieces but had set the groups up for critical and commercial success. In many ways the records have become over the years lost masterpieces, forgotten in the excitement of future projects but crucial at the time to put both bands on the right track.

Up To Our Hips said that the Charlatans were to be taken seriously; they weren't just good singles and patchy albums but a full-on band. Its success rubbed the slate clean and put the relative failure of *Between 10th*

And 11th behind them. It meant that the band now had a strong sense of their own direction and the confidence gained from that album meant that they approached their eponymous fourth album positively and ready to let the real band flow. In many ways *Up To Our Hips* was the catalyst that spurred the band to the creative peaks to come.

UP TO OUR HIPS . . . BLOOD ON THE TRACKS

Almost two years to the day since the release of *Between 10th And 11th* the Charlatans were back in the frame with their new album, *Up To Our Hips*. This time the reception was going to be far more generous, the two years out had given them time to focus on their sound, gel their line-up and really come up with the goods, and aligned to this was the way the 1990s were drifting.

Stung by the relative failure of *Between 10th And 11th* the band had gone back into the rehearsal room to work on the follow-up – they knew that they could do better. Martin Blunt was back, firing on full cylinders, the main force behind the album. With the man recognised as their backbone once more into the driving seat, the band were in much better fettle for their third album, and it shows.

Up To Our Hips saw the band sounding rawer with a funkier, groovier undertow. The tracks still packed a melodic punch but the added grooviness came from jamming the songs in the rehearsal room. The problems with Rob being in jail during recording were barely noticeable, everyone had rallied round and Collins had done a great job despite the black clouds gathering around his head. Maybe it was because of this that his keyboards weren't really the dominating sound in the band any more rather than a vital colouring of an overall sound.

If *Between 10th And 11th* had been Rob's album, with him being the main creative force behind the band, then his court and eventual jail hassles saw his influence lessening on the group. Blunt had stepped into the breach, the start of a shift in the band politic where the keyboards would be less dominant in their sound as Mark Collins started to find his feet. Mark's self expression meant that his guitar would gradually become the main instrument in the band, superseding the keyboards.

With *Up To Our Hips* they cut an album under bizarre duress, but the extra pressure seemed to coerce the band into making the extra yard. The third album was a mixture of straight pop gems like 'Can't Get Out Of Bed' and 'Another Rider Up In Flames' (in fact both songs have the same sort of melody running through them) to weird shit like 'Easy Life' and 'Feel Flows', a track that showed the Charlatans were still pushing the sound as far as they could.

Not only was it their best album yet, it also had their best sleeve artwork, a striking shot of a cool-looking couple in a stark two-colour shot.

Martin explained to *109* fanzine the concept behind the sleeve art. 'It's based on an idea by a British photographer of the late 1950s, early 1960s, called Louis Morley, who now lives in Australia. He never got the recognition that, for instance, David Bailey got. We nicked the idea from that and just mocked it up. We thought it was better than being retro and using his photo from 1968. So we got a hairdresser friend of ours, Michael, and a model called Giselle to pose for it.'

It was recorded in Wales in Monnow Valley Studios, the legendary neighbour to Rockfield Studios, with bands like the Roses, the Mondays and Lush being in close attendance at other nearby studios, creating a good-time party atmosphere.

Monnow Valley is one of the most beautiful studios in the country, a large white house with a conservatory next to a cold Welsh mountain river and rolling hills. A surge of wild green relief away from the tense cities full of bad memories, Monnow Valley is the perfect place to create a great record, an escape from the hassle and problems from the real world and a place to get lost while making a great album. The Charlatans loved the place so much that they were once conspiring to buy it.

Monnow Valley could be fallen in love with either because of its setting or because its live room was awesome for recording drums, or maybe because of its old Nieve desk in the control room, that had been used for Queen's 'Bohemian Rhapsody' – every microphone, every valve unit that it shared with Rockfield Studios just a mile down the road was dripping in rock history.

With Oasis recording their debut album in the same studio, the Charlatans were running neck and neck with the hottest band of the 1990s, who by then had pre-sales that were already marking them out to be the biggest group in the country. Also down at Monnow Valley recording were Black Grape, whose first London show Mark and Tim were at along with Noel Gallagher, and whose debut album *It's Great When You're Straight . . . Yeah!* the Charlatans copped an earful of and were raving about to anyone within earshot.

Recorded during the stress of Rob Collins' trial and eventual sentencing, and with the media and the pop world looking the other way since the relative flop of *Between 10th And 11th*, maybe the record's title was a reference to being up to their hips in the brown stuff! This was certainly something that Burgess felt. 'We called the album that because we thought that we were up to our hips in shit. But now I think we're up to our hips wading out of that shit.'

Burgess described the album as crucial to the *Manchester Evening News* during its mix-down. 'This is the album that's going to be make or break for us in a way, and we've been working hard writing songs and we're excited about how it's coming out. Obviously we are nervous, but I think people are going to be nicely surprised by the finished result.'

The Charlatans had been working a long time on the record, as Mark Collins points out, 'As soon as we came off tour in 1992 we went straight into a rehearsal room for about four months. We just started playing as a band, as a five-piece, just rehearsing and practising loads, and we were really getting off on what we were doing. I really liked what we were coming up with.'

Mark thought, too, that the album's title was pretty self explanatory. 'With all that was happening last year we could have been up to our necks in shit, but as the year went along we felt we were sort of up to our hips coming out of the water. Even though all that was hanging over Rob, it was probably the most optimistic year for the band ever.'

When asked if the band was particularly disaster prone Mark Collins added, 'What, disaster prone, the Charlatans? I've never felt that. It's usually been a boost for the band – things happen to us. We've found ourselves the most interesting thing to write about on this record, there's a wealth of inspiration musically and lyrically. I suppose these things are sent to try us.'

'Rob's situation was a major influence over everything,' confirmed Burgess, 'the track "Up To Our Hips" was written first when he came out of prison just after he had been arrested. It was a really devastating time. But then as we carried on the mood got lighter and lighter.'

Rob Collins' keyboards, although not swamping the sound like in their dominant prime of the band's early material, are quite superb on the record. It doesn't sound like the work of a man with a personal crisis hanging over his head. Each track is carefully thought out with the keyboard player providing the songs with a different flavour and texture. From the flanged swirl of the near Deep Purple strokes on 'Up To Our Hips' to the Dylan-shimmering Hammond flavour of 'Can't Get Out Of Bed' (with its flavours of the Band's Al Kooper), Collins is ever thoughtful, never just knocking off the organ parts. Some of his playing on this record is utterly inspirational; it makes you want to go out and buy a Hammond and what better recommendation can there be of a musician's playing than that.

Burgess, whilst appreciating the keyboard player's work, felt under the cosh, the cosh that was giving the band the unlikely allure of being a rebel outlaw outfit, a mantle that had previously sat far easier on the shoulders of contemporaries the Happy Mondays. 'It reminded me of the Stones around *Satanic Majesties*, where the whole thing was like a document of them going in and out of court and in and out of drug busts and jail. In a way it inspired me to come up with some really smart lyrics.'

With the court case occurring during the recording, there were other pressures on the band.

'With Rob in jail at the moment, we had to get him to put down all his keyboards in the studio first, and with his court case and sentence hanging over him, there were some days when he was a little distracted,' said Tim.

When the band were recording *Up To Our Hips* and waiting for the verdict on their wayward keyboard player there was a fear that he may go down for a long stretch, and it was difficult to make any plans at all. Tim pointed out to the *Manchester Evening News*, 'Obviously it was a stupid thing to do, and he's paying the price at the moment. Everyone makes mistakes in life, but we don't always have to suffer the consequences.'

Other tracks on *Up To Our Hips* were flavoured too by the strange set of circumstances that the band found themselves in.

'"Inside Looking Out" was my perception of what it'd be like being stuck in a confined area thinking about what your friends are doing on the outside, but it's also a love song as well. I really like it when groups like the Rolling Stones write about themselves like on *Their Satanic Majesties Request*, written about drug busts and going in and out of prison,' said Tim.

The track 'Inside Looking Out' builds from the quietest of beginnings, with a riff similar to Hendrix's 'Crosstown Traffic', slashing switchblade style over a spaced-out emptiness, before reverting to the band's tried and tested slow-burning bass-driven hypnotic groove, and ending on a great cyclical riff, one of those never-ending series of chords that drags you in and leaves you wishing it would never end. It's a superb climax to the album, the band spinning their hypnotic 4-chord workout into a fade out which features a great piece of fractured drumming from Jon Brookes whose playing is spot on throughout the album.

It seemed like the Charlatans were adopting a similar siege mentality to the Stones and their series of drug busts which resulted in Brian Jones's exit from the band and his eventual death.

The single 'Can't Get Out Of Bed' was also touched by the crisis.

'It was supposed to be about all those things that you should get out of bed for. Those lines in "I Never Want An Easy Life If Me And He Were Ever To Get There" was again about Rob and his friend. He came up with those lines,' Tim told the *Melody Maker*.

It didn't end there.

'That line "shoot it up, let's go for a ride" was about the robbery,' Burgess told the *NME*, 'I think I was trying to capture what he was all about with that song.'

Some critics thought that the songtitles hooked the band up with the slacker attitude of the times, but this was something that Tim was having none of as being the up-for-it type, he definitely wasn't the sort of person who was going to loaf around and turn his back on life. '"Patrol" uses the imagery of a police patrol, but it's about getting into somebody's mind. I wanted to get all the juice out of Rob's mind before he went to prison, and inspire more words. The first line is "I want to patrol this innocent mind". Basically if you go through all the evidence against him, he could still have been innocent. There were mysterious circumstances and he wasn't on drugs at the time. He's officially guilty but to us he's innocent.

'We realised that we were in a really privileged position being in a group, and felt that we really had to sort things out and come up with something valid. We felt like every single minute that Rob's here we can write another song. But we didn't know how long we were going to have. At first his sentence was going to be in April, then that was put off until June. Finally it happened in September. We got this phonecall saying that he'd gone to prison and it was almost a relief for us, although it obviously wasn't for Rob.'

'Patrol' rides along some bluesy guitar riffing and a neat chirping harpsichord; grooving incessantly, the band were by now, in their terminology, really 'bouncing'.

Burgess opened his heart to *Melody Maker*. 'I know it sounds like we manipulated Rob before he went to prison, but he completely understood that we had to do things for the good of the record. I really, really think that he was an absolute hero during the recording. Every time it really got to him, he'd just go for a walk for 15 minutes and come back with loads of new ideas. No one, not even himself, is impressed with what happened. But the way he was during it all, the way he dealt with it, I definitely slate him for that. I would have cracked.'

Recorded under the dark shadow of Rob's bust *Up To Our Hips* was the Charlatans' finest album so far. Maybe the pressure of the situation had spurred them on, maybe the band of disparate characters had finally gelled, but there was something that had truly sparked them and they were beginning to show their true potential. Now they were less of a pop band relying on great singles to sustain their career and more of an album band; there are hints here of an impending greatness, that there was something great that would one day finally arrive.

Martin Blunt picked up on the theme. 'You can be 21 or 40 but once in your life you know you've got the chance or ability to do something and be proud of it, and that's what happened to us. It was like a chemical reaction that happened before Rob went away.'

Burgess was wondering at the time just what the banged-up Rob would have thought of the record. 'He did all his parts before he went down, so he's never heard the final thing. But I think he will be amazed by how it sounds. I'm so proud of this record. I can play it to anyone and I don't care what they say. I get so proud of it. I feel I could take on anyone. I've never felt this big.'

These were the very first rumblings of the new Tim, the vocalist who had been through all the shite and pressure, and was reacting in totally the opposite way to what most whinging pop stars would have. He was now cranking into hypa drive, a supa optimistic, buzzing, crazed good-vibes beast, carrying the heavy weight of bullshit on his back and just laughing at it.

UP TO OUR HIPS . . . HOW THEY MADE THE BUGGER

This time around there was much more of a team spirit about the band during the making of the record, which was produced by Steve Hillage. Originally it had been planned to use Flood again as producer but his schedule was too packed, so Hillage got the job.

On paper an odd choice, Steve Hillage had been behind the early 1970s arch hippies Gong (famous track, 'The Flying Teapot Theory', well famous if you were a pothead speed freak back then!) but was getting some critical praise with his current project System 7, but as they were playing an electronic dance music, neither style seemed to be quite what was required for the Charlatans.

But Hillage was keen, so keen he had been bugging Steve Harrison about working with the group and he had the right kind of flavour to his talk, believing that the Charlatans were a great live band and should be recorded thus. This was something that the group believed as well so Hillage looked like the right man.

Being a musician as well as a producer, Hillage made a mental connection with the band, as he understood the recording process from both sides of the control room. 'I'm different from the other producers they have used. I'm a musician producer and Dave [Charles, the engineer] is a musician engineer. I'm like an extra member of the band. All the ideas come from the band; I just master the techniques and help them do it. Every producer is different, and it all comes down to personal chemistry.'

There was an air of urgency surrounding the new album. It was like they were cutting the crap and getting down to what they did best, as Tim Burgess relates, 'I think the album has more of a natural sound than some things we've done before. We tried to play around with a lot of buttons last time, and didn't know what we were pressing. All the songs that are on the LP are the ones that come the quickest. The ones we really had to struggle with we ended up leaving out. We learned that it only takes a minute to get something good.'

Martin Blunt explained to the *Melody Maker* the Steve Hillage choice, 'We were worried initially by the idea of Steve Hillage. We loved what he did with System 7, but he was so much older than us. Some people have so much of a past that they can't see the future. But Steve did wonders because he lets stuff breathe . . .'

Mark Collins added his bit on the off-the-wall producer choice, 'We really wanted to capture the sound of a 5-piece in a room, having a brilliant time. That's one of the reasons why we picked Steve Hillage to produce it.'

Not the most obvious choice? 'We had a few preconceptions about him, but they were all totally blown out of the water when we met him, all this stuff we'd heard through Gong and the Steve Hillage Band. But he's always been one for moving forward, he's not always had his head stuck in the past. When we met him we thought "Yeah, brilliant". We met a few other producers, and Steve came back to us and said, "Listen, I wanna make you sound like your demos, except better."'

There had been plans to use Hugo Nicolson (a dance producer who had worked with Primal Scream and Jah Wobble) and even Andy Weatherall (then one of the hottest names on the indie dance crossover scene, his reputation reaching boiling point after Primal Scream's *Screamadelica*; Weatherall was indeed a great person to have on board, his eclectic music taste and sense of maverick adventure had resulted in some great remixes, and his understated influence can be felt across the whole scene today, from the Chemical Brothers to the Prodigy to David Holmes and onwards – in reality he is the granddaddy of the whole cutting-edge electronic pop scene and he deserves far more credit than history seems to have given him).

Burgess said, 'We were really up for Hugo because of his track record, but then Steve Hillage came into the room and he was brilliant, he knows loads of stuff about modern music.'

Mark Collins liked the way the producer worked. 'He recorded us live, or as live as possible in the studio. There was no reliance on click tracks or anything. If a song didn't need one, we didn't use one. The way Steve worked was "let's go with a good feel". His role was really to keep us in check and make sure that we didn't disappear up our own arses. He just kept coming back to our demos and saying, "Listen, you may be losing a bit of the feel here, why don't we go back to doing it this way."'

This obsession with 'feel' is a musician's curse, especially in a tight-knit band. The beauty of rock & roll is when you have several disparate characters playing in a room and it all gels together – you can just feel that magic moment when it all clicks – but to recreate this in the studio can be very difficult, as many have found out over the years.

Although Hillage understood the dynamics of a band playing together, bizarrely enough before he got the job he advised the Charlatans against using a big-time American producer because the said producer 'had never understood punk' – this coming from someone whose whole career had been in hippie bands like Gong and the Steve Hillage Band, whom punk had set out to destroy. It was either total bullshit or a stark statement of truth; the band obviously thought the latter and Hillage was hired. He certainly added something to the band sound, a certain rawness and liveness that made the band sound far more 1990s.

Right then there had been a real return to the raw and analogue rootsy sound on records, where the sound was mixed in with the drums instead of just being reverb slapped on everything; valve guitar amps and analogue decks were making big comebacks, and the squeaky-clean 1980s feel was getting pushed aside.

The Charlatans captured this rawness on *Up To Our Hips*, where they sounded like a band playing live. It was just the way that everyone wanted to hear them, a timely move.

Burgess spoke of Can and the Beastie Boys being especial influences on the record, and although it's not immediately obvious from listening to it where these influences fit in, they are there, from that looseness of playing that the German 1970s avant rock kings Can specialised in, to the loose sense of pop reassembling that the Beasties were messing with.

After the disappointment of *Between 10th And 11th* the group needed to get back on some sort of even keel, and Mark Collins, already a guitar player of some renown, was required to help this revival.

For Tim it meant that there was going to be a difference in the way that he contributed to the writing process. 'Before, I'd always written the lyrics to Martin, Jon and Rob's music, but I'd never actually written any music until "Another Rider Up In Flames,"' (once called 'Set Your Hair On Fire') which was Tim and Mark's first song.

'Can't Get Out Of Bed' was a great lazy laconic track, the music capturing the stoned vibe of the vocal perfectly with the same sort of effectiveness that the Beatles had managed on *Revolver*'s 'I'm Only Sleeping'. The fact that both songs captured that hazy lazy drug-induced laid-back ooze was very apparent, something Burgess had definitely intended.

In fact the whole album, like the Beatles when they cut *Rubber Soul* back in 1965, stank of drugs, especially the warm drift of dope smoke that seemed to seep from every pore. Its modern equivalent was the Beastie Boys who in many ways had a similar career span to that of the Charlatans, massive from the start, then slagged off when they started going all weird round the edges and welcomed back again with their third album.

The key track on *Up To Our Hips* was 'Can't Get Out Of Bed', a moment when the Charlatans rediscovered the key to writing truly classic pop. It also captured the semi-stoned zeitgeist of the times although it also had a certain depth to it, as Burgess told *Select*, '"Can't Get Out Of Bed" got us taken for real. At the time, me and Mark were living in Salford, banging down loads of Es.'

It was the sort of sentiment that most rock & roll fans could easily identify with, living in that twilight world of smoking dope, cool records and trash TV; their closest friend was the grubby duvet and bed was their eternal home.

'Feel Flows' started off as a normal song; Burgess had wrestled with the track's lyrics, and in the end left it as a bare instrumental. Modest and a team player to the last, he talked the track up to the *Melody Maker*. '"Feel Flows" is my favourite track . . . and it doesn't have any singing on it. I piled loads and loads of words on it, then decided that the singing was bollocks. It was my idea to take the singing off it. It does flow. It's amazing, a real eye-opener.'

Mark Collins remembers how they wrote the track. 'We were in this studio and Martin and Jon just started jamming together while the rest of us were in the control room. Jon was doing this amazing drum pattern and with the sound of the room as it was [amazing – take it from someone who had produced a record in the same room; the drum sound, if you get the ambient mics in the right places, is superb!] it sounded brilliant. We just said, "Hit the record button when they're doing this." We recorded ten minutes of it and we said, "We're gonna jam on this and do something amazing." That's how it started, it was really spontaneous. We started playing riffs on top of it and getting this real feel thing going. We thought it definitely had to go on the album. We fell in love with it immediately.'

'Feel Flows' is one of the fans' favourites; a massively compressed stomping drum loop runs through the song, underpinning its smouldering growing power. It's the sound of a band totally at ease with itself, enjoying the sheer power of people who can play together well.

This sort of off-the-cuff, keeping the feel edge to songwriting is something that the Charlatans have specialised in.

The album opens with 'Come In Number 21', which could be a lament to their average chart position! It's a case of the band being wilfully perverse, as instead of kicking in with 'Easy Life's crashing chords it sneaks in on a Hammond-driven keyboard chop that is primetime Stranglers in flavour; the song has a nagging chord structure that is pure 1960s.

The album's title track kicks off with a classic splodge of distorted keyboard that reminds one of Deep Purple before slipping into a funky guitar figure from Mark that almost hints at Santana, and a bass that drives along in the same way that dominated the Beatles' 'Come Together'. It's anthemic and again it showcases a band with the imagination to take a simple idea and really make it sweat.

Lyrics were something that Burgess just did, and were never intended to be poetry torn from the heart. 'I always think that our audience writes our lyrics for us. It's like I've got an aerial on my head and I wake up in bed and I'm picking up on all of these words and I just write it down on paper,' he once claimed.

Even if most of the words sounded like free associations, the songtitles were spot-on on this album, perhaps the best title that Burgess had come up with yet, rock & roll beat poetry processed through a chemical-stained northern pop mind.

Burgess was examining celebrity on 'Autograph', the album's spooked acoustic ballad hooked around a clapping hand backbeat. Featuring a strong vocal from Burgess, the song was an introspective workout that preceded the sort of thing that the Stone Roses would be doing on some tracks of their still to be released *Second Coming*.

Burgess explained the track to the music press. 'Then there's a track called "Autograph", which is about sitting on the wall with your hero. It's kind of like that book *Wonderland Avenue* by Danny Sugarman. There's this line from the book, "Can I have your autograph? It's not for what you are, it's only for what you're not." I love that. We've tended to avoid our heroes, so as not to be disappointed. Mick Jagger and Mick Jones have come to our shows, but I never met them. But Ian McLagan, the old keyboard player from the Small Faces, sent Rob an Ogden's Nut Gone Flake beer mat with an autograph saying "keep on keeping on" while he was in prison. That did a lot to keep the spirits up.'

What a cool thing to do, a bit of keyboard camaraderie across the generations and from the Small Faces too, the bands' band, the group that most Britpop bands have mentioned in passing. It must have meant a lot to the then imprisoned keyboard man.

The peculiarly titled 'Jesus Hairdo', which had a flavour of the Fall's lyrical obtuseness about it, could also have been a description of the man Burgess's luxuriant haircut, which had now blossomed into a thick-set popstar mane, described by some as one of the greatest pop star hair cuts of the time.

Dave Simpson from *Melody Maker* remembers standing backstage at the Paradiso in Amsterdam watching the vocalist in front of the mirror. 'He was stood there moaning about his hair and how he just couldn't get it quite right, running his fingers through it, shaping it up, and I was thinking, "Jesus, you've got the best hair of any band in the country."'

Burgess himself explained 'Jesus Hairdo'. 'It's inspired by a book called *Shampoo Planet* by Douglas Coupland, who wrote *Generation X*. There's just so much shit on there that you just don't focus on the great things you can get from TV. There's a line I'm really proud of: "We all live in America, And if everything you say is true, it's just bad TV."'

UP TO OUR HIPS . . . WHAT THE PAPERS SAY

If *Up To Our Hips* is generally recognised now as the great Charlatans come-back record, or at least the turning of the corner from a band that was starting to look at some serious shit ahead, then the press was having none of it.

The band had been sitting there quietly confident that this was their great comeback classic record and would be warmly received by the press.

They were wrong.

Vox's Craig McLean gave the record 4 out of 10 and stuck the boot in, 'Tim Burgess and his fellow dullards mooch through an album that is almost totally bereft of colour and spirit.' He went on to describe the music as 'lost in a sludge of muted guitars and wobbling bass and organ doodles' and signed off with 'it's not just their keyboard player that is criminal'. He found the record saggy more than baggy and dismissed it.

Sian Pattenden from *Select* gave the album 3 stars out of 5, deciding that the band were picking up from where they had left off: 'cheesy guitar embellishment, guitar solos, alternately on flange and wah wah, whiny vocals etc . . . and it's actually not half bad,' she grudgingly admitted.

Jon Harris, reviewing for the *NME*, gave the band six out of ten and felt let down by the record, 'That almost there but not quite sensation is *Up To Our Hips* all over. Maybe we were slyly holding out for the Charlatans' *All Mod Cons* [the Jam] or *Pills 'N' Thrills And Bellyaches* [Happy Mondays] a record that would suddenly come all over incisive and commercial and confident and finally accord them some kind of immortality.'

He felt that the 'blissful lethargy' which made the record so appealing was probably the reason that stopped it truly delivering. Harris would have to wait for another year, his feeling that the band were close but not close enough was something that the Charlatans in their heart of hearts knew too.

Although the band felt that this record was a good comeback record, within weeks of release they were back songwriting again, a combination of a rush of confidence from scoring a hit record and knowing that they had much more potential with which to make an even better album sent them racing back to the rehearsal room.

Melody Maker was very pro the album but was still baffled by some of the odder tracks that they felt spoilt a potentially great album; they called it 'the riddle of the Charlatans', questioning slower moments like 'Autograph' and 'Up To Our Hips'. 'These tracks deliver sluggish boredom,' they claimed after championing some of the record's great pop moments.

At the time, in one of a series of ebullient interviews, Burgess spoke to yours truly, who was writing for the *Melody Maker* at the time. 'Everything that happens to us is a great story. On each record you get to find out what ridiculous things had been happening to the band. It would make a great book!'

!!!!!!!!!!!

UP TO OUR HIPS IN NEW LAD CULTURE

If the first album had come out in a post baggy climate where the new mass rock audience was drifting away back into football and clubbing, by 1994 the lad phenomenon was on a rush, and suddenly the Charlatans seemed to be in the right place at the right time. The new *loaded*-reading lad was looking for 1960s-tinged pop made by post Stone Roses bands with bowl cuts and casual clobber. The Charlatans may have been pioneers but by the time they released their third album they may as well have been a new band for most of the new lager-swilling football-chattering classes that were chewing up their take on pop & roll.

The result was a top 10 album, with *Up To Our Hips* hitting number 8 on a 3-week chart stretch. It was hardly spectacular for a big band but it certainly put them back in the frame, and with Oasis lurking around the corner just about to happen, the situation in the UK for Manc-associated bands was going to change irrevocably. Couple this with the fact that the Charlatans were showing signs that they hadn't reached their peak, and many pundits were excited. It was felt that after years of dithering around the band were on the threshold of delivering a major work instead of the good pop they had been dishing out so far.

If 1993 was the low-water mark for many of the Charlatans' contemporaries, 1994 was the year that Oasis burst through and totally changed the pop climate in Blighty. Before the Burnage crew, it was generally accepted that Manchester was going to be a scene of diminishing returns; it looked like the Stone Roses were never going to get their new album out, the Happy Mondays had fallen apart since 1992's *Yes Please* and left the rumour mill to crank into overtime churning out stories about their whereabouts and behaviour before they had miraculously returned as Black Grape, Inspiral Carpets' last album *Devil Hopping* had been a surprise top 10 that March but they were very much on the fringes of fashion and were soon to fall apart.

Oasis had taken the Madchester theme and made it supernova, grabbing all the traits of northern pop, like the melodic nous, belligerent attitude and post-baggy style, before making it into a super distilled version. Guitar man and songwriter Noel Gallagher had learned a lot during his years on the road with the Inspiral Carpets, and with a keen talent for a tune and Liam's X factor, had taken the blueprint and delivered. They had done everything the Stone Roses had threatened but never delivered, and although they were more than mainstream they were on their way to being bigger than the Beatles.

Despite the fact that no one was expecting a band to break out of Manchester, there was a shock takeover of the music scene. Sometimes great tunes, a great attitude and a great frontman will explode on the UK scene.

Where did this leave the Charlatans, a band who had looked little more than outsiders after *Between 10th And 11th*'s modest chart placing?

'Even during that period we didn't panic,' points out Steve Harrison. 'We always sold out gigs, the fans were always with us and we felt confident that we could get things going with the band again.'

It was an optimistic statement but one that the band could easily justify. By never letting their fans down live and building up a great relationship with a loyal and hungry fanbase they were still contenders. Now they just had to get a truly great album together to justify everything.

There was certainly a much more positive team feeling around the band at this time, as Tim remembers, 'When we were recording *Between 10th And 11th*, we were all sitting in different corners of the room, we weren't communicating particularly well.'

1995
Life is Sweet

JUST LOOKIN'/BULLET COMES

Classic pop is about singles, it's about a machine-gun attack of great tunes thundering out every couple of months, it's about great groups twisting and turning their way through their shtick. 'Bullet Comes' gallantly rode in that May on a choppy energy-fused cascade of sound, a euphoric pop rush and a sign that the band were hitting first gear.

The B side was 'Floor Mine', a near instrumental of the type that the band seemed totally adept at knocking out when one was called for.

By the time 'Bullet Comes' was released frontman Burgess was on a total good vibes grinathon – marked down as 'the happiest man in pop', his one-man crusade to pump some good vibes back into the Brit music scene could almost be seen as a reflection of the pain and bullshit his own band had faced, and its eventual triumph. If the last year he had been buzzing in the middle of a crisis, this year he was buzzing like a maniac in the middle of the long-dreamt of golden period for the band; last year may have seen him a happy man despite the odds, this year he had gone through the roof.

The Charlatans themselves were enjoying a renaissance, they were getting the hits, get the critical thumbs and finally hitting the groove that they had promised for so long. No wonder Tim was one happy fucker.

That spring he was totally buzzing, because although the swaggering new double-A side 'Just Lookin' and 'Bullet Comes' only reached number 32 in the charts, the band had a new eponymous album to grin about. It was a truly brilliant record and something that was bound to make even Martin Blunt, a man whose demeanour never wandered far away from the word 'stoic' in most press clippings, grin with pride.

'Just Lookin' sounds like a band that have discovered all their strengths all at once, yet another class single, a celebratory rush of garage pop.

'Bullet Comes' was inspired by New Orleans piano-playing legend Dr John, as Burgess explained to the *Melody Maker*, 'This was inspired by Dr John's *Gumbo* LP. I love the lyrics because I've really been trying to simplify them and this is like nursery rhyme stuff. It's got the line "live it like you love it", which was gonna be the title of the LP and, in a way, it's our surf song. I saw a surfer the other day and he had a t-shirt that read "Life's too short and you're a long time dead". That's the sort of idea.'

By now Burgess's sheer joy and lust for life was marking him out from the usual negative pop stars; it was a euphoric babble that had initially confused Johnny Cigarettes at the *NME*, who asked Tim if the singer had a slight serotonin imbalance.

Burgess wasn't sure what he meant but when Cigarettes asked if he downed a few too many Es he instantly understood. 'Well I did a lot of that in 1991 and 1992, I probably took it every day for a couple of months. We knew this chemist who could get us pure MDMA when we were in America, you gotta have a bit of that, but I don't do much any more. I did speed and coke for a while, but somehow that just neutralises my energy and makes me like everyone else when they are sober.'

'You should see that bastard on E,' added Mark Collins. 'He's impossible to shut up. He'd be there at the stereo, putting on 1000 records a minute.'

REVAMPED, REVIVED . . . MAYBE THIS TIME THE CHARLATANS ARE GOING TO BE A NORMAL BAND

Building, building, building upwards and onwards, with the new album a couple of months away the Charlatans hit the live circuit. Headlining venues like the Manchester Academy, several universities and places such as Nottingham's Rock City, it was a big-level tour but not the super stadiums. It was their first full-on national tour for three years; the year before they had only played four dates when supporting *Up To Our Hips*.

NME's Johnny Cigarettes interviewed the band on the road and had hung out with them, bumping into Tim who was living in London with his girlfriend Chloe, who worked at Heavenly at the time. 'Whenever I met Tim, I was always really struck by the way he was so fucking wired and up for it all the time. In fact he was the only person you could say was really "mad for it" whereas you can't quite imagine Liam Gallagher being like that. I interviewed them when they were doing the "Just Lookin'" video and even though Tim had been up since five in the morning and it was nearly one the next morning he was still on one and he wasn't doing any drugs. When you saw him with Chloe he was so affectionate, he was like a little teddy bear or like a big kid and you couldn't help warming to him. He's one of those people that doesn't give a shit what people think of him, he's a genuinely up person, which is pretty rare in a band.'

Cigarettes spent a few wild nights out in London with Burgess, once hooking up with him and Matthew Priest (the drummer from Dodgy who came up with the amusing 'King Monkey' nickname for Ian Brown when he hoodwinked the gullible *Guardian* with a story about Brown only answering to that name). 'We went to the Electric Ballroom and squeezed into a cubicle doing whatever you do in a cubicle and I remember a bouncer came over and threw everyone out.'

They went back to Tim's where the singer insisted on watching his current pet love, the film *Once Upon A Time In America*. 'The film is four hours long and he had already watched it, like, four times that day. We sat there and he put it on and promptly fell asleep and I was left there like a fool on my own watching the film. He seemed really into all that Italian gangster film nonsense,' laughs Cigarettes.

On the road he noticed that the band kept their distance from Rob. 'Rob sat there like drinking to himself, like the old man in the pub. He seemed fairly taciturn, he was a dark horse to say the least, and everyone kept away from him.'

Of the other members Cigarettes remembers Martin being 'very intense' and Mark and Tim being the most affable.

The tour support came from the Rainkings and the Bluetones, whose Stone Roses-influenced guitar pop was about to explode big-time for them. The Bluetones would eventually occupy the same sort of space as the Charlatans, one of those bands that sells a lot of records but no one really knows how big they are, a curiously dissatisfying position.

All the press clippings from the time are talking about the 'baggy revival', and the Charlatans, on the verge of their fourth album, are described as 'Madchester survivors'. They were still getting talked about as the 'bridesmaids of the Manchester scene' and yet here they were selling out venues on their first tour for years, still surviving, still out there. It was a frustrating scenario, but one the band were about to break out of.

The whole tour was a triumph. The band, maybe galvanised by the success of Oasis and maybe after slugging it through the lean years, were feeling that they were now contemporaries of their fellow bands instead of the young band on the coattails of other hot outfits.

The debut show of the tour was at the Bristol Anson rooms on 6 May. They hit the stage with 'I Never Want An Easy Life' and the place went spare; again the band/audience relationship was moulded in the heat and lust of the primal gig atmosphere.

Typically the rest of the tour didn't pass without incident, and typically it was down to Rob Collins to cause problems. After an altercation in a club the keyboard player broke a finger, and the band were reported to be very pissed off with him for nearly throwing the series of gigs into jeopardy.

Gigs like Glasgow's Plaza were so oversubscribed that they had to switch venues to the far bigger Barrowlands; they may have still played 'The Only One I Know' and left the stage to 'Sproston Green', but it was the new songs that were whipping the crowds up. The Charlatans were now touring with an extensive back catalogue and it was hit after hit (even if most of them were smallish hits). If only they could find an album that would truly deliver their whole potential.

In many ways they were like their idols the Rolling Stones, who took years to make the definitive great all-encompassing album, *Beggar's Banquet*, only then that was the 1960s and bands were allowed to be crapper for longer than in the easy come, easy go 1990s. The band did have a slight Stones obsession, from Tim's Jaggeresque moves to Mark's Keefisms, and on the 4-date tour they did the year before, they were very excited about playing the Shepherd's Bush Empire, which had been closed for years – the

Rolling Stones had played there in the venue's glorious past.

A combination of great singles and changing times was seeing the Charlatans at last break out away from their loyal fanbase. Word of mouth was on the streets and there was talk of the band turning into something quite special. The Charlatans were starting to come back into fashion; *Up To Our Hips* had sparked off some interest, and Noel Gallagher and Paul Weller were dropping their name. They seemed to be arriving fully formed into the mid-1990s pop scene, one that in many ways they had helped to pioneer years before. Madchester had given way to Britpop, and the Charlatans were, for the second time in their careers, finding themselves in exactly the right place at the right time.

After their time off the road, the tour gave the pundit the chance to sit back and realise just why this band was so popular; their bond with their fans was so strong, but it wasn't just the songs and the performance, it was the way they captured a feeling, a euphoric rush.

The Charlatans were that rarest of things, just like Noel's Oasis, a people's band.

FESTIVAL FEVER

For years festivals had been much maligned, sneered at in the press, with an image of being all beer, chips and stale rock riff, but by then they had become high fashion. Better organised and with cooler groups, festivals were getting hip; combine this with the new drug-taking post-rave generation, and you've got the perfect combination of factors for festivals to emerge as the key events in the rock calender in the 1990s.

In June 1995 the Charlatans played at Glastonbury. This was the Glastonbury where the Stone Roses didn't show because John Squire had broken his arm in a cycling accident, and Pulp stepped into the breach, becoming one of the biggest bands in the UK overnight. No such luck for the Charlatans though – they just played a great show and kept their fans happy.

The band also appeared at the Phoenix festival, the lesser attended of the big festivals in Britain, but the one that always came armed with the biggest and most eclectic bill of cool bands.

The sets they played were smash and grab raids of the band's classic tunes, proper festival fare, nothing too weird – just get in for 45 minutes, keep the place rocking and then fuck off. The Charlatans were a perfect festival band, a set stuffed full of hits and a commitment to an exuberant professional show . . . just check the set list if you want proof of how hot they were at these gigs: 'Easy Life', 'Can't Get Out Of Bed', 'The Only One I Know', 'Hear Comes A Soul Saver', 'Weirdo', 'Just Lookin', 'Crashin' In', 'Jesus Hairdo', 'Just When You're Thinkin' Things Over', 'Then', and of course 'Sproston Green' to exit with, a non-stop rush of cracking tunes.

No wonder they were rocking the festivals.

Also, they had the right crew behind them; supplying the PA and behind the mixing desk was Manc sound legend Oz, a man who had mixed all the northern legends and always did a killer job.

On the other end of the live scale, Tim and Mark also popped up in London to play an acoustic session for Heavenly Records in the upstairs room of the tiny Soho pub, the Crown And Cushion. They gave it their all, scrubbing their no-electric no-frills way through 'The Skies Are Mine', 'Just When You're Thinkin' Things Over', the Sly Stone cover 'Time For Livin' Time For Givin' ', then a cover of East Village's (the band which Martin from Heavenly Records was once in, a pretty damn fine band who unfortunately never had to give up their day jobs) 'Silver Train', Tim reading the lyrics off a crumpled sheet of paper; they finished with 'Here Comes A Soul Saver'.

'JUST WHEN YOU'RE THINKIN' THINGS OVER' . . . THE CHARLATANS PUT OUT ANOTHER GREAT SINGLE

Hits, hits, hits. What the band needed now was an anthem, something that would hang in the air in a million indie clubs across the land, a rumbling, tumbling tune that spilled out of the grooves oozing a warm good-time spirit. Riding on a great bouncing piano shape, 'Just When You're Thinkin' Things Over' was a massive warm gust of pop, fanning the flames of their career redemption.

Released on 26 August the single hit number 12 on a 3-week run. Late August is usually a quiet time to lob a record out and it's notoriously difficult to get good sales as the students aren't back at the universities yet and everyone is in a mid-summer slumber.

This year, though, things were very different.

The very same week that the Charlatans released their new single was the week that the indie civil war broke out – it was Oasis v. Blur, both bands having their singles released on the same day, a move initiated by Blur moving their 'Country House' jaunt along to collide with Oasis's 'Roll With It' release date. In chart terms Blur won the battle, grabbing the number 1, but Oasis won the war with the sheer volume of their album sales and Britpop mentioned on the national news.

The Charlatans just got on with business. They had just released another great cut and were quietly creeping up the league table.

'Just When You're Thinkin' Things Over', is an understated anthem, a classy catchy song that worms its way into your consciousness and won't budge, and it's a song you want lodged there, unlike the Blur tune that was annoyingly catchy but which didn't have the same sort of class.

The video had the band doing their pastiche of the classic Nicolas Roeg early 1970s film *Performance*, the one where Mick Jagger drags a tuff East

End gangster into a bizarre world of sex and masochism; its end sees the dandy pop star and the villain blurred, when the gangster James Fox dresses Mick Jagger in his Kray Twin duds – the Charlatans dressed likewise, Tim, with his hair scraped back a la Jagger in that final defining scene from the film.

As another taster to the forthcoming album, Mark Radcliffe's evening show on Radio One put out another session for the group; the four tracks were 'Crashin' In', 'Just When You're Thinkin' Things Over', 'Just Lookin'' and 'Here Comes A Soul Saver'. If this session didn't make the fans hungry for the album, then nothing would.

AND AT LAST . . . THE ALBUM

Calling a record after yourselves is a sign of one of two things: you've either got no imagination, or you're looking for a blunt statement of intent, a proud shout of 'this is exactly what we are and we're not hiding anything'. For the Charlatans' eponymous fourth album the latter was applicable.

When you know you've got something hot, then releasing it is pretty damned exciting. With *The Charlatans* so titled to underline the fact that this was the album that they finally felt represented them properly, the band was ready to become a big-league outfit. No longer existing in the shadows of the other Manc bands, they had already proved they could sell records, and now they also had an album that was brilliant all the way through.

This time there would be none of the occasional flashes of pop cool and frustrating near misses; this wasn't going to be a Man City of an album, no last-minute let down, but a sleek whole. This was the Charlatans – perhaps the first Manchester band to keep their act going long enough – ready to deliver a whole mature record.

This time the band had had a special urgency about them during its recording. They went straight into the studio and there was no fannying around with demos; they just wrote ten songs and headed off down to Monnow Valley to get them down on tape. They knew they had their stuff together and there was no point in fucking around with the tunes, they just knew that this stuff was the shit.

Album engineer Dave Charles wasn't keen anyway on the band making demos, as he explained to *109*, 'I think they should go straight into the rehearsal room, put the songs on to a ghettoblaster and then come down here and record it, rather than demo it.'

They followed his advice. Songs this good didn't need tinkering with and they were ready virtually from the off.

Released on 9 September 1995 *The Charlatans* was a vindication for the band. It was their first number 1 since their debut *Some Friendly*, going gold in the process. The slow build-up of singles and the new climate of Britpop guitar band culture was suiting them perfectly, and the fact that they had released a great album as well was hardly hindering them! The pain and the turmoil, the uncertainty and the bullshit was all swept away when the band finally managed to score the top spot again after five years, a remarkable comeback in pop where the ground is littered with the corpses of those that never made the grade. The album stayed in the top 75 for nine weeks; the band had by now well and truly crossed over, and were holding their own in the middle of Oasis mania.

If the last album was an attempt to make the classic drop-dead Charlatans album with the optimistic rush for life the vocalist wanted, there had been too many problems bogging them down; *Up To Our Hips* was considered a flawed return to form. There would be no problems with consistency during making *The Charlatans*. This time, with the decks cleared, they could sit back and make the record they had been threatening for so long.

If *Up To Our Hips* had been a great pop record that had worn its influences on its sleeve, this time the band had come up with a record that was totally their own. There was no trainspotting riffs this time and every song sounded wholly like the band, who had discovered a real solid power and confidence. This record was overflowing with the stuff and in many ways is their first real record, the album where they dropped all the disguises and came out as themselves, setting the blueprint for their own totally individual sound.

Or, as Burgess pointed out to the *Melody Maker*, 'We always felt that because the Roses and the Mondays were seen as the main bands from the Manchester thing that we had more to prove.'

And now, finally, they were able to do so.

As 'Who do you prefer, Blur or Oasis?' rang out across the country and even on the nine o'clock news, for many the smart money was on the Charlatans.

Burgess was buzzing about his guitar-playing soulmate. 'As soon as we started that album I knew it was a potential number 1,' he told Manchester's *City Life* magazine. 'But for me things really started to come together when Mark joined the band. Over the past three LPs I've been able to have a laugh with someone on a day and night basis, going out, talking about what you're going to do the next day, all that kind of stuff.'

Jon Brookes felt too that this time at last the band had got it right – and how! – as he told the *Melody Maker*. 'I think we've made the album. We've really gone and done it. That's because we've just steeled into it and made the record we wanted to. There's no point chasing success. It's like chasing your tail. All I want out of it now is to play live in some mad places and maybe get invited to the Brits, refuse to go and therefore not get nominated. That would be in true Charlatans' style.'

There was the crucial gelling of the band that really come together with this album. In some senses the Charlatans were a very glued-together band; they started off being Baz Ketley's project, with Martin Blunt bringing a whole different history along with him, then with the rest of the band building up with a sturdy Midland's band background between them. The addition of Tim had been another twist, and if that wasn't enough the Madchester thing knocked them askew and they had reacted to it brilliantly. They had released a couple of albums that were attempts to fuse this disparate bunch into a whole; there was enough of a strong personality and identity to make some great pop, but when Jon Baker left and Mark Collins joined the band seemed to suddenly lurch into a far more classic pop mode, fitting into a 6-string tradition that goes back to the 1960s. They seemed to at last have some sense of direction and also of the fact that they were a big-time rock & roll band. They had now made a brilliant album that was critically admired and, more importantly, was capturing them a whole swathe of new fans.

Back at number 1, what a buzz!

'It felt like the first one didn't count,' claimed Tim, 'I don't think that we treasured that one enough or celebrated it, thought about it or even cared about it the first time around.'

Some Friendly's success had almost seemed too easy. Now, with a taste of struggle and a couple of tough years behind them, the return to the big time that *Up To Our Hips* had hinted at, had been delivered.

With *The Charlatans* they were ready and bustin' loose, and Tim was making no apologies: 'I'm hungry for it, I want us to be massive, I really do.'

GETTING THEIR SHIT TOGETHER . . . RECORDING THE DAMN THING!

The Charlatans was initially produced by Steve Hillage, who spent a bunch of time with the band in the studio (ending up with a full production credit for 'Crashin' In' and a shared production credit with the band and Dave Charles for the rest of the songs). But overall it wasn't working out, and there had been a *Melody Maker* interview where Tim Burgess had said that *Up To Our Hips* was bollocks – he hadn't intended it in the way that it had come out, he had meant that it was bollocks compared to what was coming up, but it had understandably hurt Hillage's feelings.

Tim didn't mean no harm as he explained to *109*, 'I just said that compared with what we are doing now, some of it I'm not happy with. Stuff like "Feel Flows" and "Can't Get Out Of Bed" are great though.'

But Hillage was miffed, and added to the fact that during the elongated recording period Hillage was double-booked, with other jobs breaking the flow of recording, then you've got a difficult situation.

The band wanted total commitment and they had no idea when they were going to finish the record, so this put the sealer on it. They felt that Hillage was trying to rush them through the recording, pushing them so they could meet his deadline. This wasn't the way that they wanted to work, so they sacked him and carried on working just with the record's engineer Dave Charles.

Dave Charles was a man who understood how to record a live band as he had worked on a whole heap of stuff, from Elvis Costello in the 1970s to the La's' 'There She Goes'.

With Charles in the hot seat the band were, in reality, co-producers of the project. It's a move that most bands should make; once you've got the idea of how a studio works and a solid idea of how you should sound, then just work with a good engineer . . . take over the controls, have some independence!

Mark Collins raved about Dave Charles to the press. 'He's one of the best engineers in Britain, he's old-school. He knows what a live feel is all about. Hillage had a bit of a techno head on him which wasn't a bad thing, cos now we've got a bit of both. It was the best time I've ever had making a record . . . no one was in hospital or jail!' he explained and then remembering the beauty of Monnow Valley, its amazing surroundings and superb live room, he added, 'I love Monnow Valley to death. All I need to do is raise half a million quid and I could buy the place!'

The move to working with Dave Charles would pay quick dividends, as where Hillage had managed to make a record with *Up To Our Hips* that showcased the Charlatans as a raw yet polished live band, the new album was the band taking over the ship, as armed with the knowledge picked up from years of sitting around in studios they were now ready to make their own records.

Spending six months in their beloved Monnow Valley they worked as they wanted. This time the black clouds had quite definitely fucked off and there was none of the pressure and listlessness that had marred the second album or the desperate rear-guard action that had salvaged the third. They were working at their own sweet pace, partying and getting the vibe just right, with drugs and plenty of good times. They were cocooned in their own weird studio world, and the rest of the planet receded into the distance while they became a tight unit.

'Toothache' was driven along by filthy blues supplied by the hot, wired Collins, crashing the songs with powerful riffing alternated with catchy as fuck guitar licks. For years rated in Manchester as a great guitar player, the raggy-mop-topped Keef-lookalike guitarman was by now in his element.

'Toothache', along with 'Nine Acre Court', were two tracks that were eventually remixed by the Chemical Brothers for singles. 'Nine Acre Court' was inspired after the band took a jaunt down to nearby Bristol and had a great night in a club, and returning to the studio they decided to put together their own dance track. Burgess wasn't on the song because he 'had to entertain an A & R man that everyone was trying to avoid'. The initial riff had been put together by Mark at his girlfriend's flat at Nine Acre Court, hence the title (originally called 'Acre Court Salford'). Tim Burgess explained the weird germination of the song to *Melody Maker*, 'Mark put it together with Jon doing his first-ever vocal, backed by Rob and Dave Charles the engineer. When I first heard it I was dead jealous, but at the time I had my own little duty to do.'

Underrated as a drummer, Brookes had taken his initially Reni-influenced funky drumming and made it into his own style.

Burgess also explained 'Feeling Holy', the ambient noise that opens the album segueing into 'Nine Acre Court', to the *Melody Maker*. 'This fits in with the intro to the album which is a sample of the Jesus Army. Jon had gone down to Oxford Circus to get himself a Sony Discman, and suddenly he saw the Jesus Army approaching, chanting and stuff. He thought, "Oh brilliant, I'll tape this", and just as they came closer, a bus pulled up. That's the sample. The song is about feeling brilliant, dead good, which is how I feel whenever the band's involved.'

Mark's favourite track on the album was the eventual single 'Just Lookin''. Burgess claimed that he wanted the track to be 'about getting people off their arses, I really think there's a lack of youth spirit in this country', letting a little bit of the spiky teen punk in him leak out in the apolitical couldn't-give-a-fuck late nineties, and added, 'The youth spirit has been drained away by the Tories.'

This kind of hypa enthusiasm is riven through Tim Burgess; his genuine feel-good vibe was something he was trying to pass on to his fans.

Tim was taking this sort of rabble rousing more and more on himself as the band's career continued, and the fact that he hadn't started doing it at the beginning was something that he regretted. 'Here Comes A Soul Saver' was typical: 'It makes me think of "I Wanna Be Adored" [the Stone Roses], though the sentiment is completely different. I do wanna be loved, but only for the right reasons, and I want people to feel that way about themselves.'

'Just Lookin'' was one of several songs that Tim and Mark had written together, along with 'Tell Everyone', 'Bullet Comes' and 'Nine Acre Court'.

Another single, 'Crashin' In', was about Tim moving down to London and 'trying to get people to come out when they weren't having any of it'. That track was one of the last things that Steve Hillage had worked on; the producer wasn't turning up that much and one night Burgess himself assumed the production controls. 'I was a little worried at first because I've only mixed cocktails before, but I had a vision and it turned out brilliant.' Not that he should have worried as the main thing a producer needs is a massive pop knowledge and a pretty firm idea of what a track should sound like – two credentials that the vocalist had been fostering all his life. The track would soon become a live favourite, battling it out with 'Sproston Green'.

The single that preceded the album, 'Just When You're Thinkin' Things Over', was recorded without Jon Brookes' drums – another small slice of the Charlatans' curse had seen the drummer breaking his foot in a football match when he was tackled by Laurence from the band Levitation. He had to content himself with percussion stuff and the drums had to be built up from a loop.

The album wasn't all about firing up the people and not every song was a rabble-rouser. 'Tell Everyone' was maybe the 'soppiest song' they had ever recorded, and was a crisp, acoustic guitar-driven ballad about 'not faking it and staying loyal', a song of commitment to Tim's girlfriend. For a rock star Burgess was sweetly faithful to the people close to him, 'I think everyone's got their own reason for being unfaithful but it still pisses me off a bit when I see it – I don't like shagabouts. Stay true to yourself, stay true to your girlfriend and one day it'll get better.' Burgess singing 'I don't take no shit from anyone' could have been about everything the band had had to deal with, as well as the love angle.

'Toothache' nearly didn't make the album because Mark thought that the guitar playing showed up his playing inadequacies, but Burgess raved about it, claiming that it was one of those weird little guitar sounds that you would have to spend hours looking for. In fact the dirty fucked-up bluesy slide makes the track; it's a superb stinking ache of a riff that nags like worst toothache – the song could be Led Zep with Brookes' slow stomping drum beat hooking up with that mean guitar shape. Tim's vocal is a great compressed thing, again this crushing of his voice into a tin-can telephone sound really suits him, especially on these weirder tracks. Burgess, typically, has his own slant on the song, 'It was from our voodoo period. I'd given up smoking and got on a health kick, jogging and stuff. But I always had a bagful of speed, so I was going off like Linford Christie. In the meantime Mark and Jon were bonging up all the time and the whole thing became very swampy, so we did a song to capture the mood.'

'No Fiction' was kicked off by Mark cutting loose with a riff, Martin hammering down a bassline and Tim putting down a vocal, one that hooks a great tune in a belligerent northern whine. . . the song oozes out on a swirling outro of discordant guitars and great rolling drums, Jon Brookes an unsung hero on the kit. Apparently it took four months to persuade Blunt to put the track on the album because he was typically worried about it. The track was about parents who demanded too much from their kids.

Burgess explained 'See It Through' as, 'This brilliant explanation the other day about how the group evolved. It's like we put a rucksack on at 22, spent all the time putting things in it that we really liked and we're emptying it out now.' The song was the first one written for the album and was trad Charlatans, swirling keyboards and upbeat melodies.

Finally, 'Thank You', was an instrumental written by Martin as a thank you for all the people that had supported the band, the sort of cool gesture that the people's band were wont to make, helping to explain the strong bond between that band and their audience.

Tim Burgess told the ever faithful Stud Brothers in *Melody Maker*, 'It was only when we were making this album that we finally realised how complex it all was, how completely different we all were as people. There was Rob, the E man, and Martin who really, really worries about keeping it all together. Then there was Mark, who's quite sensible sometimes, and Jon, who broke his leg playing football during recording [Christ, when would this band ever avoid the bullshit!] and ended up playing congas and shakers. And then there's me being a bit hyperactive, getting up at 11 and trying to get things rolling, even though the others tried to bug me and wouldn't do anything till half past three.'

Not only were the last two tracks fucked up by Brookes' broken ankle, Rob Collins managed to break his hand dragging his keyboard roadie through a nightclub door, typical of the wild man and typical of the band who just didn't seem to be able to do anything in a smooth manner.

At last the Charlatans had finally put together a definitive record, one that would hold them in good stead for years and one that made the leap between being a young pop band and a proper grown up rock & roll band. A difficult transition had occurred, and the Charlatans were now a serious band about to get taken seriously.

LIFE IS SWEET, OH SO SWEET . . . BACK IN THE CHARTS WITH THE CHEMICAL BROTHERS

'Life Is Sweet', culled from the Chemical Brothers' album, saw the two bands' love affair charting once again. The Brothers' remix of their 'Life Is Sweet' was one of the great pop moments of 1995, a true marriage of indie rock and dance, and it made the Charlatans sound modern in a way that they had never sounded before.

A slightly less heavy breakbeat than usual dominated the song but it still kicked a rock dynamic with a funk feel and an electronic texture. With 'Life Is Sweet' Burgess was asked to sing over a typically frenzied monster breakbeat. His vocals were heavily distorted and sounded more powerful than they'd ever had before – in fact it could be argued that this is one of Burgess' best vocals and certainly it's one of his best produced vocals, an avenue that disappointingly he has never pursued again. There are definitely some Charlatans' songs which would suit this fucking around with the vocal, giving them a stranger and edgier feel.

'Life Is Sweet' was released on 9 September and hit number 25 in a 3-week chart run. The accompanying video was fab as well, with Tim all lost in a mad world of computer wires and leads – it caught the mood of the record perfectly.

A couple of days before, the band had returned to the Boardwalk in Manchester for a steamy homecoming, the first time that they had played there since the early days. The 5 September gig was so fucking full it was pretty damned difficult to see if the band were playing or not, but as usual the atmosphere was amazing. This was a band that knew how to put on a party and the show was the best of that year's In The City gigs, of which it was a part.

BRIXTON ACADEMY

The comeback kids were at it again – back in the ring more times than Mohammed Ali. After being officially announced finished, the Charlatans were back, and how.

The band were playing in Nottingham the night that *The Charlatans* hit the number 1 spot, so they went to the pub and got pissed.

It seemed the sensible thing to do at the time.

Being number 1 after all the hassles and the bullshit was an incredibly satisfying feeling for the group. If the first album had been a rush getting to number 1, then this last album clambering back to the pinnacle was a major victory; this time there could be no speculation about bandwagons as it was now clear to all that they had got there through sheer gritty talent. A fully sold-out UK tour was testament to the tremendous loyalty of their fans but it was the way that there was a buzz about the new album, the way the whispers were getting louder, which meant that the eponymous fourth album was going to take the Charlatans from being those lovable survivors of the baggy war and put them right up there with the new Oasis breed of hungry, snarling super-bands.

The Gallaghers hadn't only shifted the goal posts, they had stolen, vandalised and desecrated them, and how large a band could get was now a whole new question. 1995 was no time for idle boasts about your band being capable of being bigger than the Beatles, that year your band *could* be bigger than the fab four, and it had taken a couple of scruffy brothers from Burnage and their lucky mates to make this clear.

The new Charlatans album was a case of put up or shut up, and the band didn't look like they were going to be shutting up just yet.

Prior to the UK jaunt they made another of their annual attempts to consolidate on their initial success in the US. Since their debut had grabbed the crown of being *the* Manchester album in 1990, Stateside they had been on a slide, not a disastrous one but their fanbase had been slipping and by

1995 they were dealing with a purely committed ragbag audience of total fans and anglophiles who, going against the mainstream US tastes, found all things quirky and British the height of good taste.

Joining them as support on the tour were the much maligned Menswe@r, who had talked themselves into a cool big-money deal on the account of some good connections wrung from some hard partying in what was considered then the centre of the rock & roll universe, Camden Town. The besuited Menswe@r had set themselves up for a fall; most people considered them a lucky bunch of chancers and overlooked the fact that despite their heavy-duty ligging they had found the time to cut some pretty good singles. On the US tour the unlikely coupling of the non-mainstream-courting Charlatans and their grab-every-opportunity-whilst-you-can London-based cronies was going off like a crazed fire.

The tour was rock & roll madness, with chemical good times and excellently daft behaviour which saw pranks like Tim Burgess wandering round dressed as a woman reporter in the *NME*. It was the sort of ridiculous bonhomie and japery that dominates the life of any travelling party cramped into a small space for a long time; from armies to sports teams, to secondhand car salesman conventions, lewd and schoolboyish humour coupled with heavy excess is the norm, but in the case of bands it's worshipped as some sort of five-star lifestyle grossery. The rock & roll lifestyle, hugely mythologised and much loved by the punter in rainswept Blighty, is nothing more than the sort of good-time jape that anyone would get up to given half the chance.

The tour had got off to the sort of rock & roll bad ass behaviour that had made the Sex Pistols and the Rolling Stones such great role models.

8 MILES HIGH – SOME CLASSIC ROCK & ROLL

Sure the Charlatans are a rock & roll band, but they were never a band that indulged in the sort of yobbish behaviour that often comes with the territory. Okay, they had a keyboard player who had been in jail and there was the odd lightweight incident, but these are not real rock & roll yobs; this is a band that doesn't really go for the, let's say, Happy Mondays' style of supa yob performance.

So it came as a big surprise to find that in September 1995 the band had been arrested after a transatlantic flight and got into a spot of bovva with the FBI at New York airport.

The truth of course was far more mundane, if not more hilarious in its very pettiness. They were flying out to the States to headline a tour and on the long and boring flight the band, like all bands, were passing the time in giggly beery tomfoolery when the grumpy fucker in the seat in front of them, like all grumpy fuckers on planes, objected by, bizarrely, putting his hands over his seat to cover Tim's in-built TV screen in the back of the seat.

Tim and fellow troublemaker Mark started to tickle his fingers, and 'he went berserk', slamming Tim's seat, and made a formal complaint.

The band didn't really expect anything to come of this, as after all it was a bit trivial. But, 'When we landed in New York there was a Tannoy announcement saying the plane would be delayed whilst they waited for the police,' said Tim. 'They moved everyone out except for us and the police came on and cuffed us all up. We got taken to the Port Authority cells. There'd been these Chinese whispers that we were all swearing and spitting and smoking on a no-smoking flight, which was all lies. I was a bit scared, the guns and being cuffed, and they're massive on planting stuff on you. They read us our rights, all this knobhead stuff. Got the FBI in. Took our passports off us and took our shoelaces off us – don't know what that was for. I thought, maybe it's just because they think we'll hang ourselves! I wouldn't hang myself, I'm loving it at the moment, you can't put a downer on me!'

Martin Blunt saw as usual the whole incident in slightly less romanticised outlaw tones. 'The only thing I saw was when it was all going off in mid air and Rob Collins was strangling Johnny the keyboard technician because he'd forgotten to bring some valves for the organ. I just saw him with his hands around his neck and Johnny's face going purple.'

It sounded like it was quite a flight!

On the tour the band were joined by the ever effervescent and by now almost as crazy as the band he was interviewing, Paul Moody from the *NME*. Moody had cut his teeth in the mod fanzines that used to detail the adventures of Makin' Time and had moved on to the music press via the much-missed *Sounds*, where he was the quiet boy in the office. He hit his ascendancy at the *NME*.

Moody was buzzing about the Charlatans' success. 'Honestly, who would have believed we'd be here a year ago? Just when you were thinking that you'd got the whole Britpop world sorted out into a Woolworths pick 'n' mix of misshapes and pisstakes, back come those lippy scuzzed-up Charlatans with a surprise return ticket from the wilderness and an attitude to match, intent on reminding us that Oasis aren't the only ones with a handy line in tour-mania, that the baggy revival wasn't just a two-horse race after all.'

Oasis's mass success was definitely benefiting anyone who was still compos mentis from the old days. Shaun Ryder was again about to pillage the charts with Black Grape, and once again the Madchester mad-for-it scene was back at the peak of pop fashion. For the Charlatans this meant that there was a whole brand-new pop generation hungry for kicks – all the Charlatans had to do was be hip, smart and cool, and keep the great albums coming.

Easy, eh!

As Moody pointed out, if it was that easy for an indie-related band to score a number 1 hit in the post-Oasis climate then why the hell were Echobelly languishing at number 30? Nope, the Charlatans had what it took to make the major-league breakthrough for the second time in their career. It looked like the jail/breakdowns/split-up series of disasters definitely wasn't going to fuck with them, especially as they had now grown up into being a shit hot rock & roll band, leaving the unsure flavour of their indie youth behind them.

Speaking to Moody after the show in Montreal about the band's loyal coterie of fans on the US side of the Atlantic, Burgess hit upon one reason why the band had managed to hold its big fanbase despite all their hassles. 'I think the reason people keep coming back to us is because they trust us. They know we're not going to let them down no matter what. That's a really important thing about the group. We've been through a hell of a lot and people know about that and respect it. We've been through miles more than most bands!'

Back home again the tour was the usual sell out, even if a reviewer in Nottingham said, 'Tell my friends I'm going to a gig by the Stone Roses or Black Grape, you can guarantee an opinion at least, but the Charlatans only generate indifference.'

The tour was also the band's first in the UK with their new rock & roll edge to their sound; they may have still been hooked in with Britpop but their music had a far more sexy strut about it than their Kinks-pilfering contemporaries. It made for a far more exciting live show even if the man from Nottingham thought, 'They are not going down in history – there is half an hour of great stuff here but the rest of it sounds like B sides.'

After all the ups and downs of the year the Charlatans were spending November selling out Brixton Academy, supported by Chester's Mansun (who were in the throes of changing their name from the rather more contentious Manson) and who were just about to release 'Skin Up Pin Up', start bursting out of the ranks as the leaders of the fourth or fifth wave or whatever the post-Manchester fallout was now up to. Mansun seemed to change pop style with every song and were being sneered at by the Liverpool scene that they had tentatively dipped a toe into; the still Beatles-scally-pop-obsessed city was never going to see eye to eye with a band that had such a breadth of ideas in its music.

1995 was the high-water mark for Britpop in terms of sales and creativity, and every week a new band appeared on the front covers of the music press on the way to the top 5 clutching guitars and looking hopeful under their moptops. It was a boom time for rock & roll, and getting the support of daytime radio, guitar music was proving its eternal appeal.

When the money is pouring in minds turn to charity. Go Discs, a label that always had a good socialist edge to their proceedings, was where the bubbling ideas man Tony Crean worked. Inspired by John Lennon's 7-day schedule for the release of 'Instant Karma' (record on Monday, press up on Tuesday, sleeve on Wednesday, etc – it usually takes four weeks to make a record but Lennon wanted the song written, recorded and released in one week) the same timescale was decided on for a compilation album which would provide money for the starving Bosnian refugees that Crean had seen on his telly.

Named after the Beatles song, the *Help* album was on paper a total nightmare – getting the biggest bands in the country to record exclusive tracks and hand them over in a matter of days was pretty damned difficult, but that he even managed to get the Stone Roses to hand over a track at all was testament to the burning enthusiasm of Crean. He did it from idea to hitting the shops in six days.

The plan would have been perfect, creating a number 1 charity album if the stupid chart rules hadn't intervened, meaning the best selling album in the country that week wasn't allowed to chart at all, allowing ironically *The Charlatans* the top slot.

The band felt confident enough to record a cover of Sly And The Family Stone's 'Time For Livin' (genius tune, genius band, no messing) for Tony Crean. 'It's the best track we've ever done,' glowed Burgess positively.

1996
We Are Rock

'Here lies Rob Collins – he just ran out of time,' – Rob, when asked what he would like on his tombstone.

1996 arrived with the band on the fast track. A combination of fashion and some top song writing had returned them to the path they had wandered off a couple of years previously. The workaholic band were already back in the studio working on the next album, they knew that there was more to deliver and that they could better their much-loved *The Charlatans*. They hadn't stopped working for years but they knew that they were burning; it was the same sort of hothouse environment that had seen Dylan produce his classic trio of mid 1960s albums that had set him up for life.

That summer they were back in their favourite studio, Monnow Valley, working on tracks that already sounded like they were going to blow everyone's minds. There was a real buzz around this album – if everyone thought that the last record had delivered, then just check some of this new shit out!

They believed that the bullshit was behind them, nothing could go wrong now; the past was fucked up, but they had got everything together at last. Now they could concentrate on being a proper pop band.

In the end 1996 was a year of ridiculous extremes.

INTO THE HEART OF DARKNESS . . .

The Charlatans were just meant to be a pop band, nothing heavy; sure they played their pop with a damn sight more intensity than most, sure they were riding the rock & roll dream like most bands do, and yeah, they had flirted with the outlaw side now and then, but they were meant to be a bright shiny pop group, playing classic British pop, something celebratory, making people feel good about their lives. There wasn't meant to be anything heavy going down here.

Somehow, though, there was a darkness at their heart and pain at their core, and most of that came from Rob Collins, a man who seemed at perpetual brooding war with the rest of the world. It gave the band their edge but it also caused most of their disruptions. But this was a price worth paying as Collins had been both a major creative force in the group and a glowering edgy presence, preventing the band from tipping into the tweedom that many other groups in their position had found all too easy to slide into.

This tale has seen the band have their ups and downs but it wasn't meant to relate something as shit as the death of one of them.

Just as the band was peaking and it looked like things were more than ever on an even keel, disaster dealt the cruellest blow that any band can ever have to deal with.

With *The Charlatans* universally recognised as their greatest album and the band ensconced in Monnow Valley Studios looking more than equipped to produce an equally successful follow up, Rob was killed.

It was a dismal and depressing turn of events that would have finished a lesser band stone dead.

As the sessions were going well and three quarters of the necessary work had been done, the band were planning to record their next but one single, putting the final touches to their campaign. With a break in the recording schedule they and some friends popped into town to go to the pub.

The local hostelries were used to seeing rock stars hanging out and were convivial places; Monmouth is dotted with relaxing pubs full of local kids waiting to spot Liam Gallagher or Ian Brown mooching about. It is a 10-minute drive from the studio down narrow country lanes with steep hedges overgrown in summer, the sort of roads that only yokels seem able to navigate safely; it takes great care to drive these roads.

Tim remembers Rob arriving at Monnow Valley at six o'clock that fateful evening. 'He was miserable as ever, no more or less than any other time. He was just Rob, you know, slagging everything off, taking the piss. He was ready for work as far as I was concerned. The thing is, it was this mate of ours' birthday, so we decided to go and celebrate. It's like this guy had waited all day for Rob to turn up so we could all have a drink together. By about nine, it was fucking magic in the pub, man, you know what I'm saying? We were all just mad for it. Everyone was having a great time. Even Rob was more fucking social than usual. He was happy as fuck cos he'd just won 60 quid on the fruit machine. I mean he was off his fucking head, having a top night out, and he won all this fucking money. See, when Rob went down the pub, he wasn't exactly social, he was quiet. His thing was stuffing money into machines. He'd stand there, with his pint on top of the machine, staring at the fruit. But that night, he was jumping about all over the place. He was dead fucking happy. So anyway around ten o'clock, I've got to get back and put some vocals down. Rob tells me to take his car back to the studio and order him a cab to come back and pick him up. I got into his car and . . . Ah fuck it, the handbrake went off, didn't it? I ended up bumping this fucking car in front. So I thought, I'm not fucking driving this, man. I mean, I haven't driven for five years and after that fucking handbrake going off, I just didn't trust myself behind the wheel. So I took the keys back and said, "I can't fucking drive this, man." I get into someone else's car, get back to the studio and get on with me singing and that.'

An hour later at closing time Mark Collins and Rob and the rest of the crew in the pub headed back to the studio. Mark nearly got into Rob's car but decided to ride back with his friend's car because it would be, ironically, more exciting. Mark remembers, 'A friend of ours had this old Granada. It was a really cool one, like you see in old telly programmes like *The Sweeney*. We'd been watching that GTI advert where you get the two blokes taking the piss out of *The Professionals*, so we just spent the weekend racing around these little lanes doing handbrake turns and stuff.'

Rob and his passenger, a 31-year-old sound engineer, were in his red BMW whilst everyone else piled into the Granada.

The Granada left first as Rob was jammed in between two other cars, which he slammed out of the way, starting off their car alarms. This did his head in and, pissed off, he sped off down the road and caught up with the other car pretty quickly. They thought that he was playing their daft car race game as he zoomed past and his headlights disappeared into the distance. They thought that Rob had grabbed a quick shortcut or stopped for fags.

But the truth was far more chilling than that or any of the mad jokes that Rob had played over the years, wind-up games of pretending to be dead.

At 23.53 pm on that fateful Monday night the car slew off Rockfield Road – after hitting several parked cars, it flew 50 yards through the air and ended up in a cornfield. Rob wasn't killed instantly; he wasn't wearing a seatbelt and was thrown through the window. He got up and staggered around before collapsing, and it was this image of the tough keyboard player fighting to the bitter end that helped inspire the Charlatans to continue.

Qualified first-aider Linda Williams, a local resident, gave Rob mouth-to-mouth resuscitation and said that he was still alive when he was put inside the ambulance and sent to the local hospital.

It was the last journey that Rob would ever make. He died in the ambulance moments later and was pronounced dead on arrival at Nevil Hall Hospital, Abergavenny. His passenger was uninjured.

Tim was back at the studio and completely unaware that there was anything wrong. 'Mark gets back to the studio and Rob ain't there, so now we're all positive he's stopped off on the way back. He might've popped into Rockfield cos he had a lot of mates there, or he might have gone on some mad country drive, which he used to do occasionally. At any rate, we just assumed he was going to turn up later and get on with the stuff he'd come to do.'

Jon Brookes was starting to get worried though. 'I'm not a religious person but I felt compelled to pray. I did, man,' he told the *Melody Maker*, 'I swear to God I just fucking knew something fucking terrible had happened. I mean, I've seen Rob do a lot of crazy stuff. I've seen him have fights. I've seen him in a lot of scrapes. I've seen him in violent arguments. I've seen him kick stuff about and smash things up and chuck shit out of windows. I've seen him doing all sorts of mad stuff, but never once did I think he would wind up dead. This time it was different. I just sat there on the couch with the phone in my hand and heard myself praying for his soul. I envisioned him on a stretcher, a bit cut up, a bit fucked up and I thought, "Rob, if you're still there, hang in, fight it, you'll be okay. The doctors will sort you out, just fight it" . . . 20 minutes later, I'm pacing about the fucking house and the phone goes. Steve tells me he's dead.'

Tim remembers the dreadful moment when he found out the truth. 'What happens is that we get a phone call saying that Rob's been in a car crash. It was a mate of ours that called. I think he'd actually gone looking for him. He calls up around midnight. He'd seen the car wreck and the ambulances, and he clocked what had happened. So he rushed into Rockfield to ring me and Mark. All we knew then was that he'd been taken to hospital. Shortly after that we got a visit from the police.'

The cops went round to the studio and broke the news in their weird clumsy sort of way, as Tim told Ben Stud in the *Melody Maker*. 'The first thing I remember them saying to me was "How old is he?" and I hear "How bald is he?" I'm thinking, what the fuck is going on? What the fuck are they on about? You know, I'm pissed and a little dazed, and I just don't know what the fuck is going on. But I'm still not thinking the worst. The police are just asking a load of questions. Mark's doing his usual bit, walking around casual as fuck, trying to bully the police and take the piss out of them and that. I'm just fucking dazed. But I did get an inkling. I remember them saying, "What instrument did he play?" And I thought they're using the past tense. So I go, "He fucking plays keyboards." But it was only fleeting. It came at me, but I didn't realise what they meant. I did, but I didn't. I don't remember dwelling on it.'

The cops then oafishly told the band what was going on. 'The two coppers tell me and Mark that Rob's been a bit of a naughty boy – those were their words, "naughty boy". They tell us that we should go and visit him. It took us about an hour to get to hospital. We were driving like madheads. I'm sitting in the car singing "One To Another" to myself. Just singing it in my head. You know, like trying to stop myself from thinking too much. But I've got this nagging little fucking voice that keeps jumping in and saying, "He's fucking dead, he's fucking dead." And I'm saying to myself, "Bollocks, is he." By the time we get to the hospital, I've virtually convinced myself he's fine.'

They arrived and parked up, Mark went into the hospital first and like Tim he was thinking that Rob must be okay. I mean no one ever dies like this in the never-never land of rock & roll; things may fuck up but nothing could ever go this wrong, could it? When they got into the hospital it started to dawn on Mark and Tim that things were a lot more serious when a nurse showed them into a room, not a waiting room but a bad news sort of room; she broke the news to Mark and he told Tim, who couldn't believe it, repeating it over and over in his head until it sank in.

It was another pointless rock death, another young musician taken out way before his prime. Rob Collins died at the point that the Charlatans made their comeback; the total victory that seemed so elusive now clearly within their grasp, their music had a new maturity and confidence, and they sounded like a band that was going to make a mark in the new Oasis Britpop era of UK pop. The Charlatans now had the chance to be one of the few survivors from the scene's early days, elder statesmen with all the respect that that brings.

Rob's death was a bitter, bitter blow. A spokesman for Beggars Banquet commented, 'He was a whirlwind type of person, he had the capacity for causing trouble and general anarchy. He was never going to die in his bed at the age of 87.'

Sandra Ward, the joint owner of Monnow Valley Studios, said that the band was turned by the accident. 'The atmosphere here today is one of almost complete disbelief. The band knows what happened but it's as though they can't believe that it is real.'

The band recoiled in shock and disbelief as the news of Rob's death started to spread.

Jon Brookes had gone to bed early that night but he couldn't sleep. 'I was lying there with my girlfriend and it was really hot,' he told *Melody Maker*'s Ben Stud. 'I was looking at my clock and getting more and more restless. At about 11.30 I think, fuck this, so I pick up my book, go downstairs, put the TV on, put the kettle on and plonk myself down next to the phone. At around midnight I turn the TV off and the phone goes. Now I think it's Rob cos he always used to ring me at daft hours of the day and night to talk gibberish, especially when he had a drink. Anyway I pick up the phone and it's Steve Harrison, our manager. So I'm like, "All right, man, what's up?" He tells me there has been an accident. Immediately I say, "Yeah, Rob." Steve says, "I've spoke to the police. The guy in the car with Rob is fine, but Rob's in a bit of a state." Steve said he'd call me back when he had some information.'

Jon Brookes described his last talk with Rob, 'Every conversation I'd ever had with Rob would begin with a discussion about the music. Rob was utterly obsessed with the band. He wanted to know every tiny detail. That day, though, he sounded a little odd, like he was in a semi coma or something, which was sort of weird because he always had to be on top of things. So he rings me up and tells me he's still at home and getting ready to come up to the studio. He wants to talk about some of the ideas he's got for some of the songs, so we chat about that for a while, and I'm saying that some of the keyboard stuff that he's put down sounds a little bit wishy-washy. And he gets a little uppity about that. He didn't take criticism too well, did Rob. Then he starts kind of agreeing with me and the conversation ends with me telling him to get stuck in. I told him I'd be there in a while. I wished him luck and that. But there was something odd. He sounded so slow and quiet, like it was one heartbeat an hour. That was the last time I ever spoke to him.'

Although shellshocked by the death of Rob, everyone still had great stories about him: the band's wildman, the crazed all-night partying and banging on hotel doors at all hours looking for partners in crime, covering the driver's eyes on the way to gigs and general looning around . . . the burning spirit of the keyboard player would be sadly missed.

The *NME*'s Johnny Cigarettes was most impressed by the band's drive in the face of this latest disaster. 'It's what really made them. Rob's death, if anything seemed to fire them up even more, it's what makes them great, their determination, you can hear it in the more recent tunes like "One To Another", that grating, grinding riff, it sounds like a band of people that just don't give in.'

AFTERMATH . . . A STUNNED BAND ATTEMPTS TO PICK UP THE PIECES

Tim and Mark went back to the studio in total shock: 'We were all over the place. We couldn't string sentences together half the time. We were probably close to calling it a day.'

The loss of a friend is bad enough, but the death of a key band member in a tightly knit group that prided itself as being family was far more difficult. The days that followed Rob's death were touch and go for the band, and it took a call from Rob's dad to Steve Harrison the following week to strengthen their resolve. In the course of the discussion he told the manager that Rob would have wanted the band to continue.

The Friday following the crash they went round to Steve's house for an emergency meeting. The upcoming support with Oasis on tour had already been cancelled but the Knebworth show was still there if they wanted it; Martin Duffy from Primal Scream said that he was prepared to come in and learn the keyboard parts.

Rob's Hammond was a key constituent of the band's sound; it was its sheer classiness that gave them an authenticity, an authenticity that was crucial in crushing detractors of the band that they were too lightweight. At times Rob's Hammond had been out of this world – the slash and burn riff he employed for 'Weirdo' was one of the greatest moments of the Charlatans' recording career – and the powerful driving keyboards had been one of the hallmarks of their sound. When Rob had served his prison sentence there had been some serious talk of folding the band; now this question was thrown back in the ring again. To many it seemed like this was the conclusion of the Charlatans' recording career, and as the flowers and the wreaths started to pile up on the doorstep of Omega Music there were some decisions to be made.

Gigs lined up already were cancelled immediately, and their appearance at V96 in Chelmsford was in jeopardy, as a spokesman for their record company pointed out, 'It's not a decision which is very easy for them to make. The last thing I have heard is that they want to carry on being the Charlatans as far as that is feasible. But it will be very difficult to find someone who could play keyboards as well as Rob could. He also wrote a lot of their songs. They realise that the festival at Chelmsford is just one of several that they have been booked to play and they know that they have to come to a decision quickly.'

Chris Sharpe, speaking for Beggars Banquet, told the press, 'The band still haven't decided what they are going to do. But it's unlikely they will be able to find a replacement within a week. Rob wasn't just a keyboard player, he wrote the songs and knew them inside out. Musicians like Rob don't grow on trees.'

This discussion over whether to carry on or not had, of course, taken place before, when Rob was staring a long jail stretch in the face. At the time Tim commented, 'If he had gone down for four years there's no way we would have carried on without him.' But now circumstances were different; Rob's keyboards, which had been the band's initial calling card, had been less to the fore since the jailing, and Mark Collins' guitar was fast becoming the most important instrument in the band. Creatively they could carry on without Rob to a certain extent, but emotionally it was going to be far more difficult. It's not the sort of problem that any band ever thinks it's going to face, after all the pop world is never-never land, and when the real world comes and slaps you in the face, hard, it's a deadening blow.

After much deliberating a spokesman for the group announced, 'The band, their management and associates are naturally devastated with the loss of not only an influential member of a brilliant rock & roll band but more so a great and loyal friend. The decision to carry on has been made because we have to continue in his memory. It is what he would have wanted. He lived it like he loved it and he ran out of time.'

Although close to calling it quits eventually they decided to go on; it didn't feel right continuing, but it was the best of a bad lot of options.

The band then sent a statement to the press. It was short, it was succinct and it was powerful, and it could stand for anyone who believes in anything in this shitty old scene: 'THERE WILL BE NO CHANGE. WE ARE FUCKING ROCK. WE'VE LOST OUR MATE.'

BRITPOP HITS THE HIGH-WATER MARK . . . KNEBWORTH

Knebworth was incredible, a definitive movement in British pop history, or 'this is history', as Noel Gallagher announced from the stage as he surveyed the 125,000 punters at the show, one of the biggest crowds ever gathered for a gig.

Oasis's remarkable rise had gone through the roof. No pop group in Britain had ever got so big so fast and against impossible odds (remember, they appeared in a year when most pundits sneered at Manchester bands and baggy had been officially pronounced dead). So what the Gallaghers did was to totally upturn the pop applecart. That evening Oasis were untouchable, but the support bill they brought along with them was hardly padding, with Liverpool's Cast, and the brilliant Prodigy with their own avant garde music of clattering, dislocated rhythm and mad jester shouting. Prodigy were something that would have been on the sidelines ten years previously but as a marker of how freaky pop was becoming they were on the verge of massive success themselves.

Also on the bill were the Manic Street Preachers, another band recently touched by tragedy after the disappearance and probable suicide of their guitarist Richey Edwards; the Manics were crossing over from their glam punk phase and were reaching deep into the Oasis heartlands with their most commercial album and a wardrobe that was far removed from their vicious new art riot clothes of the past.

Oasis and the Charlatans had been close before, the two bands giving each other mutual plugs in the press, good northern solidarity and all that. Noel Gallagher eventually even went as far as turning down one of his Brat awards and dedicating it to Rob Collins in one of those touching asides from Noel that show that behind the press-hyped bad-lad image he's a very sentimental person.

The day, although belonging to Oasis, was so close to being a victory for the Charlatans, as the other bands flailed away in the murky distance getting largely ignored by the crowd, but they were given a massively warm welcome. Maybe it was a sympathy vote, as after all you'd have to have a heart of stone not to appreciate the fact that despite all the traumas of the past days the band were still prepared to get up and play. It was just three weeks after the death of Rob Collins.

Rock & roll doesn't get much more raw and emotional than this. It must have been a hell of a difficult gig to get through. The Charlatans were set up to be a pop band running the usual gamut of pop emotions, and those didn't include death. It was all a bit too much.

Mark Collins looked back on the gig less than favourably. 'I hated every second of Knebworth. Turning round and not seeing Rob there was incredibly hard. When we came off it was the first realisation that one of our mates was dead. We just sat there for two hours saying nothing. But it was useful for us to be there, because if we hadn't gone through with it we might never have got going with the album again.'

Burgess, as well, felt strange at the gig. 'Walking off that stage at Knebworth I just felt gutted. It was the first realisation of how the band had changed. We didn't have time to catch our breath really, but I think that was a good thing, it meant that we had to do something.'

Martin Duffy stepped into the dead keyboard player's shoes at incredibly short notice, bailing out the Charlatans in their hour of need. He was a scene stalwart cutting his teeth in Felt, the erratic yet sometimes genius band from Birmingham built around the talented Laurence who would eventually go on to form Denim. Duffy had replaced original keyboard player Maurice Deebank just as the band signed to Creation Records and were working on their first mini album for the label, *Let The Snakes Crinkle Their Heads To Death*, and from there it was just a short jump to Primal Scream where he became their resident wildman, out-misbehaving the rest of the band.

'We weren't running around panicking, thinking that we've got to get someone to replace Rob,' Tim explained. 'We were just thinking that there's four of us, that's it now, we'll just wait until we get some genius whizzkid or whatever. I'm really glad that Duffy came into it, because we never had to rush through a permanent member. We just sort of let it come to us.'

The band never replaced Rob. Eventually they drafted in Tony Rogers as permanent keyboard player, but the core of the band would remain as four, not five.

The band decided not to milk Rob's death at Knebworth in the way that showbizness demands. The usual round of record-selling bullshit and hype from record labels and musicians milking it for every penny wasn't going to happen. There was no dedications of songs to Rob because, as Martin said, from now on everything would be dedicated to him, and they knew that shouting dedications to a field full of people lacked respect.

Tears flowed during the afternoon as friends turned up, upset at having just seen Rob's cremation. It was a demanding and difficult afternoon but the Charlatans played through it. They were a million light years away from the shiny pop group of their first album, and had been forced to grow up in public in a way that few other bands have ever had to before.

Tim was hunched inside his anorak, his stage patter limited to the occasional muttering of 'new one' before the band launched into a track from the upcoming *Tellin' Stories* album.

The set was naturally cloaked with the sadness of the occasion but the crowd was glad that the Charlatans were here at all, and saluted them and their absent friend. The audience was struck by how optimistic, powerful and cheerful the songs sounded; the Charlatans had always written uplifting pop songs and this day of all days they needed those songs to vibe themselves up as much as anyone else. Because they hadn't toured a lot recently it was quite easy to forget just how good they were as a rock & roll band.

The Manics were by 1996 very much in their ascendancy, crossing over into the Oasis 'People's band' fanbase. Knebworth was an awesome bill of post-indie rock, a new generation of powerful bands to firm the spine of British rock. As if to underline how far the groups had moved away from the frugal lifestyles of 1980s indie pop the bands flew in by helicopter; it was the sort of full-on rock & roll swagger that had typified all the boom times in British pop.

After Knebworth things would never be the same again.

'ONE TO ANOTHER' . . . THE CHARLATANS' RALLYING CALL

The first release since Rob's death, and their first single for a year, 'One To Another' was their debut cut from the new album's material and a hint of what was to come. The Charlatans were showing all the signs that they had capped it yet again.

'One To Another' was a killer single, one of the greatest moments in the Charlatans' canon, a rollicking, powerful groove that seemed to hint at the prime-time stomp of the Stones. But this was no retro exercise as the track was powered along with a powerful drum loop provided by Ed from the Chemical Brothers.

The track stank of a dark danger and was a total brute; this was the closest they had got to the fervour of punk rock that lurked in certain members' souls – powerful, incendiary and in yer face, this is the Charlatans' track that you hear everywhere you go.

More like an urban blues than an urban hymn!

Topped off by one of Burgess's best vocals, a sneering heavily compressed power howl that grabbed hold of a melody that burrowed itself into your head.

Great stuff.

Fired by a wave of sympathy towards the band, and combined with their recent high-profile gig at Knebworth and the single's genius anarchic rush of sound, as well as a video that had been finished just a week before Rob's death, this was the band's biggest hit to date, crashing in at number 3 on a 6-week chart run.

When asked by *Vox* if the single's success had helped to get the band back on its feet after all the shit they had been through, Burgess sounded detached, 'It might sound unappreciative but to be honest at that point I didn't give a shit what the single did. My head was somewhere else. Looking back on it, I'm proud. Rob came up with the basic riff and we developed it as a band composition. I think it's a good example of the Charlatans' collective strength – we all needed each other to make it work.'

1997
Still Tellin' Stories

NORTH COUNTRY BOY

1997 was the absolute peak of Britpop, as after Oasis's mass success any old chancer trading on the nostalgia beat was coining it. The Charlatans, being the last true link to the baggy roots of the scene, were the true survivors; and the fact that they were also cutting some of the best material of their career was going to boost their credibility further.

The band's profile had also been raised by the sad death of Rob and, in a similar sort of situation to that which the Manics also found themselves in, they were now far more high profile as a lot of people had been awoken to their existence.

The next single, 'North Country Boy', was the Burgess statement of intent, although its doom and gloom would hardly dent the positive glow that he seemed to perpetually exude. It was a good vibe that he seemed determined to spread to his fellow man in the song's lyrics: 'North Country Boy, what are you sad about, every day you make the sun come out, even in the pouring rain, I'm coming to see yer, and I'll save yer, save yer.'

Recorded a week before Rob died, 'North Country Boy' was one of their strongest singles. A deceptively lazy groove, it captured that Dylanesque mid 1960s sneer and brought it bang up to date. Instead of setting the song in New York in the fevered revolutionary times of Bob Dylan the Charlatans wrote a paean to the north of England, the rusting industrial heartland of the UK as well as a magical place where pop was king.

Mind you, they still flew to New York to film the video and Rob graced the cover with a pastiche shot of himself as Dylan. It was a great shot of him in his favourite Russian hat with guitar held to the camera, aping a shot of prime-time Dylan from his *Nashville Skyline* cover. The video was shot during the crazy 12-hour trip in a classic 1950s diner. New York is such a perfect location for films of all sorts, with its crumbling decadence and concrete bluster, and as the band were trying to capture the intense and yet seedy flavour of Martin Scorsese's stunning *Mean Streets* and *Taxi Driver*, then this was the perfect location.

'North Country Boy' was later used effectively in the great *Twenty Four Seven* film, a gritty reply to *Trainspotting* set in Nottingham about a boxing club that fucks up; the song bursts on to the screen as the club's mentor Bob Hoskins takes a gang of hooligans on the mend for a run on the moors and captures the euphoric escape from the city perfectly, a great moment in the film.

If *The Charlatans* had seemed like the band at their peak, a great album and number 1 to boot, 'North Country Boy' proved that the band were gunning for new highs, as their frontman related to the *NME* when asked if there was a point where everything went right, 'Definitely, yeah. When we did *The Charlatans* album there was such a buzz within the band. We were on such a high. Following on from that we went into the studio and did six tunes and they included "How High", "One To Another" and "North Country Boy", and the other three turned into B sides and stuff, so we knew that we were on to something good. Rob was still alive and it was obvious it was the best thing we'd done. The trouble was that he died before he could see it.'

'COOL BRITANNIA' . . . NEW LABOUR, NEW TOUR AND A NEW KEYBOARD PLAYER

May 1997 was when everything changed – at last the country woke up and kicked the Tory scum out of office and suddenly politics seemed hip and youthful again; there was a brief wave of euphoria and relief, and pop was booming. Britpop was making a big splash around the world and bands were huge in Britain again, the knock-on effect of the Oasis phenomenon had seen several other bands suddenly get huge, Blur having played to 30,000-plus at the Mile End Stadium a couple of years previously was now just another blip on a massive run of successes for British bands.

The Charlatans were perfectly placed and their new sell-out tour was big-time. The band's new mass popularity coupled with a wave of sympathy in the light of the recent cruel events was combining to send things to fever pitch; throw into this already heated cauldron a band wired to prove themselves, one armed with a mighty new album of songs to play, and things were looking like they were going to shoot through the roof.

Up and down the country it was the same story; the best gig for years screamed the punters, and the local press clippings file certainly backs this up with rave review after rave review.

The new tour also saw a new member, keyboard player Tony Rogers.

Tim Burgess was buzzing about him to *Vox*. 'We've found a mad little Hammond player called Tony Rogers who's helping us out at the moment. He's not a session player or anything and he's going to be doing some backing vocals. We didn't advertise, we just found him, so it must be fate or luck. Luck, I think – I don't want to get all spiritual, it's not my thing, man! We've only been playing together for two or three days so I don't know how it's going to pan out. He's a great bloke, but I think we might prefer to keep the core band as a 4-piece now.'

Rogers was never intended to be the 'replacement' for Rob Collins. The band were now shrunk to a kernel of four, more out of a mark of respect for their departed colleague than anything, and in pictures they would appear as a 4-piece, a new, stripped-down Charlatans.

Tony Rogers was yet another Midlands-based player. Playing in

Wolverhampton band Jobe, which he had put together with his brother, they were based in Walsall. They built themselves a studio and recorded demos and although without a big deal they released an album *Rosaries And Ice Cream* on the Viceroy label, but they weren't happy with the production, feeling that it was 'too soft'. Jobe also put out two singles, 'Earth' and 'I Know'. 'Earth' took off in Germany, which made the decision to leave the band a difficult one but fortunately Jobe continued without buckling when Tony left to join the Charlatans.

The Charlatans were looking for a keyboard player from the same neck of the woods, and the grapevine pointed them in the direction of Tony Rogers.

Tony recalled the phonecall that changed his life in *109*, 'I was sitting at home one night and I got a phonecall from a guy called Tim who runs the Varsity in Wolverhampton. We had played there with Jobe two or three times and were building up a bit of a following. He basically said, "Oh, Martin's been in touch from the Charlatans and wants to know if you'd be interested in applying for the band."'

Apparently Rogers' name had been cropping up as being a hot Hammond player as the band had gigged around the country. Blunt rang him and they spent an hour and a half talking music shop on the phone, chewing the fat over influences, etc. It seemed like the right things were said as a few days later Steve Harrison was on the blower giving him a date for an audition.

The audition clicked and he was in.

It must have been a bizarre jump coming from the toilet circuit into the ready-made success of one of the biggest bands in the UK, and Rogers had the usual period of readjustment, as he related to *109*, 'From the time they asked me to join the group to being on *TFI Friday* was about two weeks and my head was totally into getting the parts right. The days of kipping in the band were over! I remember the first couple of gigs we did. We did pre-production in Manchester and I was on stage moving my gear around and a roadie came up and said, "Don't touch that, that's my job," and then it finally kicked in. I don't have anything to do but play!'

Rogers not only brought to the band a keen knowledge of the Hammond, but he also knew his way around a studio, having built his own set-up at home, an added bonus to a band that by now was producing itself full time.

It sounded like he had gelled pretty quick with the band. 'It was like I have found new friends who are on my wavelength,' he chuckled to *109*, a man happy with his life.

'Tony Rogers, our new keyboard player, is something special,' said Martin, 'it's like someone's dealt us a card, a really good one. It's our first piece of good luck for years.'

Things could never be the same as they once were, as Tim points out, 'Rob did have an edge, d'you know what I mean? And going out at night and gigs aren't as unpredictable as they were! Perhaps sometimes we concentrate a little too hard on keeping the spirit of him [Rob] within the group. We're just trying to do what we think is fair to him, to us, his mum and dad. We're not trying to glorify it, but it's stupid not to talk about it. Making the new LP will be our next test, to keep something live that otherwise might die.'

The tour was their first without Collins. Martin Blunt said, 'Obviously it will be hard for us, but we've always found a great adrenaline rush from going on tour and it's no different this time. It's a very big tour for us because of events that have happened and having someone new like Tony on keyboards. The overriding thing is just to do the songs justice. We have been doing everything with a real sense of purpose.'

Rogers filled in well and although he took a step back from his predecessor's powerful playing, he still held the fort.

Burgess was understandably getting bored with the press asking questions about Rob's death. 'We're fed up with talking about it. Not just to reporters and stuff, I mean between ourselves. That's all we seem to do. We had a bit of a wobbler about it the other night because we want to start looking to the future now. We're fed up with reminiscing.'

No wonder; the past was a bizarre mixture of huge success and painful memories. It was like the Charlatans had paid one hell of a price for their success and now they just wanted the slate wiped clean and just to do things like a normal group.

On the tour the band played a 90-minute set with a high percentage of material from *Tellin' Stories*. You could hear all the new flavours of the band's current sound, with those Stones- and Zep-fused riffs c/o Mark Collins driving their sound on. The set-ending 'Sproston Green' was also a reminder of how far they had travelled with its hint of a baggier past – it was like a snapshot from a different era, a time before the going got serious.

BRIXTON

On 17 May the band played another one of their special shows, an all-nighter at the Brixton Academy, a special show in aid of the National Missing Persons Helpline. Brixton Academy was becoming the venue with the flavour, and after years of being sneered at as some sort of big-barn venue in South London with no atmosphere it was now dead cool.

The show was mainly a Charlatans' affair but they were to be joined by several other big names, including Manics frontman James Dean Bradfield playing a solo show, plus Monaco, Peter Hook's latest outfit after New Order, Smaller (featuring Digsy from the Oasis song 'Digsy's Dinner') as well as DJs from the Heavenly Jukebox.

This was all a surprise for the audience who weren't expecting any guests, a great buzz for the pop kids to see this parade of Britpop heroes.

First on, James Dean Bradfield's solo spot included a version of 'La Tristessa Durera' and a singalong version of the classic 'A Design For Life'; Bradfield's appearance at the show was a poignant reminder of absent friends. Monaco didn't play in the end as Peter Hook was ill (Tim was pissed off as he had been looking forward to doing New Order's 'Lonesome Tonight' with a quarter of his all-time favourite band); Hookey, the erstwhile New Order bassplayer, was also a man who had experienced tragedy, following the suicide of vocalist Ian Curtis when they were in Joy Division.

Paul Weller and his band were joined by Noel Gallagher for a rousing 'Shakermaker'; a few months earlier they had played together on the *White Room* TV show to heaps of praise, and now they were onstage in Brixton strumming their way through 'Half A World Away', Noel returning later in the set for the version of 'Shakermaker', ad libbing, 'I'd like to score you lots of coke, and invite you round for tea' . . . cocaine was very hip in 1997.

Before the Charlatans hit the stage the Chemical Brothers ignited the crowd's fire with a set of northern soul and Motown. They played 'Daydream Believer' and Primal Scream's 'Move On Up' before the Charlatans came on, really stoking up the audience, some of whom described it as 'very moving', with everyone singing along.

When the band finally hit the stage, Burgess was the star, swaggering around like a little kid lost inside a pop dream, sleeves of his scruffy pullover pulled down as he waved his hands in the air with that curiously non-committal school of Manc showbiz rabble-rousing. By now the band were adept at playing all the different shades of their sound from the power pop of 'North Country Boy' and 'How High', life affirming tunes with great choruses, to the ballad-style acoustic and harmonica strokes of 'You're A Big Girl Now'.

Weller joined the band onstage to add his chops to 'Can't Get Out Of Bed' and 'Sproston Green'.

Burgess was still quipping the crowd with the mumbled asides that he had always specialised in: 'Today isn't the same as yesterday and not the same as tomorrow.'

Don't worry, he probably hadn't got a clue what he was going on about either.

Brixton was a major step for the band. The mood in the venue was at fever pitch, it was total exhilaration, the band, after years of being nearly but not quite there, were now totally loved. The Charlatans were moving into new territory.

WHAT'S THE STORY? *TELLIN' STORIES*

Released a year after the death of Rob Collins, *Tellin' Stories* was a statement of intent, of a band surviving the cruellest of blows and returning with its best record yet. It was also the band's first self-produced effort, something they felt made the album far stronger.

Something of a watershed in the band's career, *Tellin' Stories* is not only the album that's scarred deep by Rob's death, it was also their last for Beggars Banquet as they were moving to MCA.

Tellin' Stories surprised many people by being a positive, almost euphoric album; they were forgetting that most of the record was laid down before Rob's death, when they were on a high after the success of *The Charlatans*.

Martin Blunt proudly looked upon the new album as 'A record that really does the business. It feels so right and sounds so good. It's like a cross between Dexy's *Searching For The Young Soul Rebels* and *Let It Bleed* by the Stones. That's the spirit behind it.'

The album was drenched in a human warmth, a warmth that was very much one of the Charlatans' key strengths. Doom and gloom was banished as they made a record that reeks of the lust for life. Of course Rob wasn't forgotten as he played on most of the records and his spirit pervades the album. It started off as a group fighting back against career crippling blows and ended up rising above the biggest blow of the lot. With the addition of the Chemical Brothers working on three of the tracks and their own nous for contemporary pop culture the Charlatans had taken their Stonesy rock chassis and made it sound bang up to date.

Again they had pulled off an unlikely coup, with their best album for the third time on the trot.

The publicity blurb that came with the record riffed around this theme. It spat, 'The album is like coming out of the other side of a tunnel, finding that the sun is shining, the kids are shouting and everything is looking up.'

After the doom and gloom, this was the fightback.

'I think it's the first totally Charlatans LP,' Mark Collins explained. 'It's produced by us and we've paid more attention to melodies, structures and arrangements. We were in control, there were no producers. A producer might get your album done 6 weeks earlier but we knew exactly how we wanted it to sound.'

The band were happy to be at the controls of the record.

'I think Flood did a marvellous job on "Weirdo",' said Collins. 'But we didn't feel at all in control on that LP. It wasn't very live sounding, but I think it was a really important LP for us to do cos we're hearing a lot of computer ideas, like on "Weirdo". If we hadn't done "Weirdo" I don't think we could have done "One To Another". You know, getting to grips with sequencers running with a live group. It was the track that pointed us in that direction.'

Just how the hell do you follow *The Charlatans*? For a start here was a band that had broken all the rules by making their best record for their fourth album – that was a feat in itself – but for a fifth album to be any cop? You'd have thought by now the band would have totally shot its collective wad. The Charlatans, as we have noticed, are made of some pretty stern stuff. This was definitely a band that worked better with its back to the wall.

Or, as Martin Blunt pointed out, 'When we started everyone said that we were jumping on the bandwagon. Well, with this album we are driving the bandwagon! There aren't many bands that can say their fifth album is the best one. When we played in Liverpool someone turned round and said that this album is the equivalent of R.E.M.'s *Green* album. It's like the Smiths and the Jam, who got better as well.'

If *Up To Our Hips* was recorded under the shadow of Rob's imprisonment, *Tellin' Stories* was released under the cloud of his death. Like Burgess once said, every Charlatans' record tells a story. Running a strange and sad parallel with the Manic Street Preachers, who were getting over the tragic loss of guitarist Richey Edwards with their best album artistically and saleswise [*Everything Must Go*], the Charlatans were about to do the same.

Recorded in South Wales over several months, the Charlatans made themselves at home in the Monnow Valley Studio. At one point they even built a wall of shame on the studio wall out of clippings from magazines; the collage included pictures of Cameron Diaz, Andy Cole, Eric Cantona and the Wu-Tang Clan, and also in there was a picture of Rob ripped from a newspaper with the caption: 'Rob Collins: he was not wearing a seatbelt.' It was a poignant reminder.

Just working in the studio after the crash was painful enough, but the band had to drive past the car crash site when they travelled to and from it.

One of the problems that groups often face is that after the initial rush of excitement when they first make it large they soon slide into a routine of tour-album-tour-album, and their edge seems to go and the hunger isn't apparent anymore. It can be even more difficult for a band like the Charlatans who arrive on the crest of a pop wave and are then dumped when the fickle finger of fashion points elsewhere.

The feeling was though that the band were going forward instead of looking over their shoulders, and were in fact only just getting into their prime after years of struggle. This was something that Burgess, these days dressed in over-sized parkas and baggy gear, looking like a scruffy, enthusiastic kid fan of rock & roll rather than one of its prime purveyors, reflected upon, 'I don't listen to any of our early albums. I can't face it. I think some groups get it right really early. I don't know how we didn't, but I think that we've started getting it right the longer we've been together.'

As he explained to *loaded* when asked how the band were capable of constantly improving, 'We're slow learners, I suppose. When the Clash got better and stretched themselves on *Sandinista!* it was regarded as a crime. But I think everyone has just wanted us to get better and better. If you're not a fan you wouldn't understand that, but a lot of people have kept the faith, desperately hoping we'd get better! And, touch wood, we have.'

Burgess could definitely sense the direction the band were taking. 'I think the last LP was really slimy, really dirty. It all clicked into place. But by the time we came to this one it was a real group effort. I think some of us twigged quicker than others but being in a gang is a big part of that. I'm a bit suspicious of solo artists. I'd hate to think of me'self as one of those phoneys down the front on me own.'

If anything, this was Mark Collins' album. Dylanesque melodies, Faces' stub-toed riffs and Keef Richards' rhythm lines, the guitar was turning the Charlatans into the sort of good-time rock & roll band that used to stride the land in those hazy days of the early 1970s. The music was getting guitar orientated, built around classic rock & roll riffs.

'Well, I suppose Rob dying gave us the progression to go with the guitar,' Tim pointed out to *109*. 'What else can you do? I mean you can't turn up a dead bloke cos he's not going to be there on the next album. Keyboards are always going to be part of the group, but I don't know how prolific they are going to be any more.'

Mark Collins was now very much at the centre of the Charlatans' sound, his bluesy riffs played on his cool guitar collection: a Les Paul Custom, Gretsch Duo Jet (which he played live), an old Fender Jaguar, for his slide stuff a Gibson SG, and for the pastoral strumming of the title track a Gibson J 200, which he swopped over with his Fender El Rio for thinner acoustic parts. His amp was a pair of the classic Vox AC 30s, one of the most beautiful of guitar amps and a classic British piece of equipment.

'Once I've got the guitar I have a kind of bond with them. It's like having children or something; you can't just pass them on to an orphanage, can you? You have to go and stroke them every now and then and say "I love you,"' he joked. 'I'm a bit of a guitar hoarder but to me, what a guitar looks like is as important as how it sounds.'

Collins was someone who instinctively understood that sound and style in the guitar world are inseparable, and for him the album was marked with Rob's death. 'It's not always easy. There's a lot of memories on the album and at one point I really didn't think we were ever going to get it finished. But I think it's a great album. Maybe in a few years, looking back, I'll remember how I lost a friend during this record and loads of shit went down, but y'know the point is that we've got through it. We've pulled it off, came out fighting.'

The album was only made by the skin of its teeth, as Collins told a guitar magazine. 'The album nearly didn't happen at all. For a while we considered jacking it all in, but then the four of us decided that we had to keep going. We already had so many backing tracks down and we got Martin Duffy in to finish them, but Rob had already played on 90 per cent of the stuff.'

The fact that the album was more guitar heavy was less to do with Rob's death than just the direction that the band were already going in, also due to the way that the band was now writing its songs.

As Mark pointed out, 'The first couple of albums were written as five of us in a room all playing together. I decided that we couldn't carry on like that, so we branched off into two groups for songwriting. Me and Tim do a lot of the songs now.'

This was an unusual turn of events in a group and the sort of friendly compromise that you would expect from a group as laid back as the Charlatans.

Collins and Burgess took their partnership very seriously, and there was none of this knocking out a few riffs on a Tuesday afternoon down the rehearsal room for them.

'We took ourselves off to the Lake District for a couple of weeks,' said Mark. 'We dragged along an 8-track, acoustic guitar, drum machine and bass, along with a record player and lots of records. The main idea was to get inspired and start writing some new tunes for the album.'

Just what sort of records they took with them could be easily guessed from Mark Collins' assessment of the band's current prime influences. 'Me and Tim have been listening to a lot of Bob Dylan, Tim is a huge fan of Dylan's lyrics – well, who isn't? I do like a bit of Keith Richards and I also like a bit of Pete Townshend, Pete's got the most phenomenal right hand on him, I've never seen anything like it. I've been practising, but I just can't get it. Incredible stuff. I want to learn how to play better too. Ron Wood's another hero of mine. I think he's one of the finest slide guitarists ever. Other influences? Jimmy Page, Jimi Hendrix and er, Jimmy Savile,' he joked (hopefully!).

All the classics then, and you can hear their imprints all over the album, although given the Charlatans' own twist. As Jon Brookes explained, 'Our sound is the interplay between the keyboards and the rhythm section and organ; if we go messing with our principles I think we'll become unstuck.'

Coupled to this was a Neil Young influence; as Mark and Tim listened to the guitar-heavy dramatic songs of the Canadian singer-songwriter something struck a chord with them. When *Total Guitar* asked Mark if his influences were a bit old skool and what did he think of some of his contemporaries like, say, Crispian Mills from Kula Shaker, he shot back, clearly not amused, 'You must be joking, I don't feel *any* love from his fingers.'

The rest of the band locked themselves into the rehearsal room, jamming up a heap of bass riffs.

'After two weeks we got together for a week,' Mark said, 'and played everything through to see what we'd got. That's the way we seem to like writing songs at the moment, and I don't know whether that's the reason we're producing more guitar-heavy stuff or whether the guitar playing is just getting better.'

And that coming from the man recognised in his pre-Charlatans days as one of the best guitar players in Manchester.

Apart from Martin Duffy filling in the keyboards at the tail end of the album there was Tom Rowlands from the Chemical Brothers providing the loops on 'One To Another' and adding some textures to 'With No Shoes' and 'Tellin' Stories'.

Tim remembers the Chemicals' creative process behind the title track, 'Originally we had a geezer down to put some strings on that track, but it didn't work out, it sounded a bit stiff. Tom took the best bit – some Indian violin – and looped it.'

One of the ways that the band kept their edge was by remaining just beyond the clutches of fashion; since riding in high on the back of the baggy thang they had remained aloof from that scene. Hardly ones for hanging out at media events, the band had found themselves in the cool long-term position where they still seem to be with their fans; they seemed normal and unobtainable at the same time, cleverly walking the tightrope.

'I don't want to be in that thing when the daily papers slag you off one week,' said Tim, 'and the next, when you've got a massive hit, they're your mates, like these writers who think that they're friends of the stars. I mean, they can call me cunt but as long as the fans don't see me schmoozing with them, then I'm still doing my job right.'

A people's band, an important concept. It was something the Roses and the Mondays had at their peaks, something the punk bands had, something U2 have although they're not a cool band. That's the magic of a band like the Charlatans, to be both cool and a people's band, as Jon Harris from *Select* explains, 'The Charlatans are massive in Scotland and if you can make it big here, you're going to be massive everywhere.'

Tim realised this as well. 'The fans can see that we mean it. You can't get away with nothing in places like Scotland and I said it about two years ago that bands like Elastica couldn't sell out in Scotland because people can see that they are only doing it as a hobby. With us it's real life. Every time we've gone to Scotland we've broken the records for the capacity and we stay true to them by not doing the SEC in Glasgow; we'd rather travel to Dundee and come back and do three nights at Barrowlands. I know that everyone that wants to see us, sees us properly.'

Aaaaah, it's quite quaint, but those old-fashioned values that the Charlatans have always quietly championed have paid off for them.

TELLIN' STORIES – WHAT'S IN THE GROOVES

The thing about the Charlatans is that it's all about subtleties. The music moves on but they never make the mistake of radically kicking the fuck out of their sound, they always play to their strengths, like melody, a tight, hard rhythm section, great guitar licks, a psychedelic touch here and there, and rousing communal choruses. They have always made big music, perfect for stadiums but without all that po-faced idiocy that came with the territory in the 1980s.

As the years rolled by their tastes, especially Tim's, have become more diverse; the vocalist by now was immersed in the Wu-Tang Clan, one of the key outfits in 1990s pop. Wu-Tang are a hip hop collective from New York City organised more like a national music company; after their initial burst of success they seemed to split into smaller sub-groups, putting their full force behind a bewilderingly nicknamed posse of mates building up careers. Their music was fat, heavy dope beats surrounded by the thick dense smog of chong fumes; they captured the leaden-stoned weirdness of recent years better than many and were grabbing a big fat pile of moolah for their efforts – for Tim they were the dons.

He was also listening to a vast array of other music and watching their brilliant voodoo fuse with his own band's muse. 'I was listening to a lot of Ultra Magnetic MCs, A Tribe Called Quest, Led Zeppelin, and *The Second Coming* from the Stone Roses we listened to a lot, you know studied it, understood it, but it weren't quite right although they nearly got there. Erm, Black Grape, that album but, er, mostly Bob Dylan for me . . . We really didn't want any Beatles' influence on the album cos we were bored shitless of the Beatles Beatles Beatles. Paul McCartney's like, fucking know what I mean! [laughs]'

Maybe as a reaction to Oasis's total usurping of the Beatles legend the Charlatans were looking elsewhere. The Beatles may have been a fine pop group in their time, but as a blueprint for eternal pop bands things were getting strictly limiting. The Charlatans had the right attitude to this – the past is cool but let's celebrate the present as well.

The Bob Dylan twist was definitely a growing influence on the band, and you could catch it in Tim's drawl, the occasional keyboard wheeze, the twisting rumbling sneer of the song structures; top-form Dylan was in there everywhere (although Burgess himself once described 'Country Boy' as a cross between the Dubliners and legendary funk bass player Bootsy Collins [Parliament, Funkadelic]!).

'Personally I can't see the difference between Ultra Magnetic MCs and Bob Dylan's *Bringing It All Back Home*,' said Tim. 'There's no difference, it's like someone with loads to say just saying it, and I've got loads to say and even if it doesn't make much sense I'm going to say it! I think "North

Country Boy" says fucking loads, man, even more so than probably "How High". I think it says fucking loads, that tune.'

'How High' was a very personal song and in it Burgess alludes to being a pied-piper figure, inspiring the kids. Not that his message was ever that obvious to impartial observers. 'Yeah, I don't know what it is. I have got one, but I don't know what it is. I don't come up with one and go, "Right, that's what I'm going to say to the people" but I think that every single word from every single song is a message. I don't know where it comes from, it comes into my fucking head from fucking aerials on top of me head or something . . .'

Burgess was still writing lyrics that were on some levels obtuse and other levels his own personal slang, just like Dylan, as Mark Collins pointed out, *'Tellin' Stories* is the most song-y, the most melodic LP we've ever done. And honestly I put that down to Dylan. He's a good guy, Bob. We're trying to get Tim to smoke more cigarettes and, erm, do more things, so he sounds more like Bob actually.'

'I write lyrics to impress the band,' Tim claimed. 'A lot of them might still seem like gobbledygook to some people – they probably are if you don't come from the same town as me. There are others, a song like "High Life", which took me about six months to sing because I felt so much about the words that I didn't want to get the feeling out of me system. But what drives me is the conviction and belief. If I was singing with a little Stylophone in the background, we mightn't have so much attention.'

He talked to Ian Harrison at *Select* about his lyrics. 'I'm dedicated to making stuff as fucking brilliant as our ears hear in other stuff. Like, I really like the words "We Gotta Have Peace" by Curtis Mayfield. If you can say something that's pretty heavy but sounds really happy, that's good.'

Tim was always a big fan of music, from his days of being the scruffy kid down at Omega Music in Northwich buying up his Fall records to being the hip hop aficionado of the late 1990s, he really knew his shit. Music was the main driving force behind all the band and not the usual tittle-tattle that goes around the scene.

'When Rob died we calmed our behaviour down,' explained Tim. 'I don't want to get up to pubescent rock & roll antics. You've got to experience that, but you have to try everything to realise what you are and why you keep doing it, and the biggest reason why we do this is we like making music.'

Tim talked about 'You're A Big Girl Now' to *109*, 'I think it's a progression from "Autograph" and "Tell Everyone"; I mean that tune started out as a daft indie rock song, and I think it was Mark or Jon Boy who said, "It's too fast, it's too jingly-jangly, there's too many parts on it." So we stripped it down and cut it all up, and Mark played it on the acoustic. We just got it miked up right and it's got one of those death-row drum machines in the background, and that was a combination of Mark playing and me doing a guide vocal at our favourite speed which is 90bpm. We do write pretty slow songs.'

Mark Collins spoke about the song to *Total Guitar*, 'The tune was originally a full band thing, but when Tim and I were just going through it in the studio's control room I dropped the tuning to an open G and started playing through the song. The engineer had miked us up in the control room and we just got the sound straight away; we simply overdubbed another acoustic guitar on and then we were there.'

If the band were aiming to make classic albums despite the odds they were certainly succeeding, or as Tim Burgess pointed out, 'We want to make records as classic as possible, like classic period Bob Dylan and the Stones. We want to do that, we want our records to still touch people in 20 years time.'

Burgess explained to *Select* that in some ways the album was a conscious move for the band, an attempt to change their style. 'We wanted to maybe cover our influences a little bit more this time. Martin said that he didn't want to make another record that sounded like the Rolling Stones! We tried to make it sound like the Meters of now, make the groove as important as the guitar.'

The Meters were the classic New Orleans band (they were the backing band on that city's cool cat Dr. John's classic run of albums from several decades ago), they were effectively legendary producer/arranger/songwriter Allen Toussaint's house band in the 1960s, playing on some classic R & B cuts before branching out on their own. The Meters had the groove nailed down tight, with one of the tightest-assed rhythm sections in existence – they have become one of the most sampled bands of all time, and the reader is well advised to buy one of their compilations.

The Charlatans' interest in soul must have come from Martin Blunt, a man whose roots went deep into the soul scene c/o his mod roots, and this interest had helped soak the band with a danceability that had pulsed through their tracks, a driving, propelling bass being one of the prerequisites of classic soul and helped them to avoid the lumpenness that knackers a lot of British bands.

Tellin' Stories went in at number 1, the band's third number 1 of the decade, a feat few other bands have achieved (only the likes of R.E.M. spring immediately to mind), it was claimed rather disingenuously that the album had sold more in its first week than any of the Charlatans' other records had sold but in fact the sales were 69,000, still 14,000 more than Supergrass, the latest hot new band on the block.

The album began in a burst, kicking off with the pure Charlatans' groove of 'With No Shoes', a confident striding boast of a song. 'North Country Boy' (a post-relationship come-down song) was a loose-limbed anthem armed with one of those tunes that just won't shift from your head; the song almost alludes to country rock but is never soporific enough to fall headlong into the worst excesses of the form. 'One To Another' (a song about someone trying to stop their relationship from coming apart at the seams) and the ridiculously catchy title track make it four goodies in a row, as the band crank back into first gear whilst grinding along with that sort of sexy pimp-roll that the Rolling Stones majestically commandeered in their heyday.

This time there are no dips in the album's quality; this is a band that is full-on, strident, confident in its own strengths. Most groups when they get this deep into their careers are really struggling for inspiration, but there's something special at work here, marking the Charlatans as one of the great British pop bands of the 1990s without anyone really realising. In how many pub arguments about the nature of rock & roll this decade does their name come up – not enough! But there are plenty of people buying into their myth at last.

'Get It On', with its nasal voice and harmonica, was hinting at Dylan, and 'Only Teethin' was flavoured with the sweet soul power of Motown.

'You're A Big Girl Now' (riding roughshod on the Who's 'Substitute' riff) and 'How Can You Leave Us' are classic Charlatans, while the upcoming single 'How High' was a great groove with an explosive chorus. The saddest moment on the album is the poignant 'Rob's Theme', an instrumental recorded deep into the night that allegedly features a sample of the dead keyboard player chattering away as a child spookily cropping up in the song. The track was recorded before Rob's death and wasn't a tacky cash-in; this was a band that was far cooler than that and there never was any effort made to capitalise on their missing colleague's death, a tacky state of affairs that is the norm in the sick music business where the dollar nearly always counts far above the feelings of anybody.

The other track that hinted at the tragedy was 'How Can You Leave Us', which, as Burgess explained, was both about coming to terms with their tragic loss, a requiem for Rob, as well as more conventional subject matter. As he told *Vox*, the lyrics weren't directly about Rob. '"How Can You Leave Us" is partly about Rob. We had the title while he was still here, but I finished off most of the words after he'd died, the verses in particular. Martin was really worried about the title of the instrumental "Rob's Theme", thinking that it may be a bit corny or something. It had to be called that though – Rob had been working on it with the engineer on his own late at night for about two weeks. It's actually off a cassette which we'd equalised to sound as much like the rest of the album as we could. Quite amazing really. We've credited it to all of us, because that's the way we've always done things, and Rob's credited even on one or two tracks that he didn't work on. The album sleeve won't say which tracks Rob played on and which Martin Duffy played. Martin Duffy became a friend – he was so respectful, and he added bits and pieces on a lot of the tracks Rob had already worked on just to build things up a little.'

Rob Collins' chaotic life hung heavily over the album, although Tim was keen, as ever, to accentuate the positive. 'We tried to make the album sound as free and positive as possible. I want everyone in the world to know who Rob was. It's a bit of a tall order, but anyone who knew the bloke would understand. I really miss his sense of humour. Going out to the pub just isn't as entertaining any more. Things happened around Rob. I loved the bloke to bits. I still forget sometimes and talk about "us five" rather than "us four". I've never lost anyone like that before.'

Tim told the *Independent*, 'For a few weeks after Rob died we didn't really know what was going on and we just went through every possible emotion you could, but I think we always wanted to finish the album. We knew there was really good stuff in there, and even if we hadn't finished it, I think the record company would have put it out anyway. So it made sense to get the best out of it and we did. And now we can start afresh. It's got to be different now because there's only four of us. We'll all have to stretch our imagination a bit more.'

For Tim the album was some sort of watershed in his life. 'I've been through a lot, y'know what I mean? I got fucking chucked by my girlfriend at the start of the album sessions, and then one of my best friends dies, but through all that we still managed to have a bit of fun . . . it's just what came through. I knew what I wanted to do more than I did on the last LP, then I thought I'd lost it halfway through, but I realised in the end that it was good. It's just taken us ages to realise our own potential.'

The only question mark that remained was would the band be able to repeat this success without Rob Collins, already acknowledged by the band as one of their major songwriters.

At this point in time, it was left to Jon Brookes to comment, 'It's one thing to sell loads of one album but another to sell five that get better and tell a story. Our story. One that's real.'

IF YOU'VE GOT IT, FLAUNT IT BABY

After 'One To Another' crashing in high up the charts at number 12 the band were starting to pick up a whole new generation of fans, vital new blood that was already totally hooked into the zealot-like fanatism that is required to be a follower of the group. By now they were taking the band's success as their own, so it was no surprise to hear chants of 'Number 1, number 1' go up in celebration of *Tellin' Stories'* first of two weeks at number 1 in the album charts that coincided with the tour.

The new fans were in fine fettle, singing along with 'One To Another' and freaking to the climactic finale of 'Get On It', and as ever 'Sproston Green' ended the set, a link from the band's past and a shuddering climax to a show where new songs were easily replacing old ('The Only One I Know' disappearing from the greatest hits package), a great sign for a band's surefire future.

Way Up There fanzine did all the hard work and listed the set the Charlatans were playing on the tour: 'With No Shoes', 'North Country Boy', 'How High', 'Toothache', 'Soul Saver', 'Tellin' Stories', 'Just When You're Thinkin'', 'Just Lookin'', 'One To Another', 'Thank You', 'You're A Big Girl Now', 'Get On It', 'Weirdo', 'Can't Get Out Of Bed', 'Crashin' In' . . . is this their best set yet? It's definitely a great run of quality rock & roll.

'How High' was released on 9 June, lifted from *Tellin' Stories*, and was backed by two new tracks, 'Give Me Rock Steady'/'Down With The Mook' (quite possibly the most ridiculous song title Burgess had come up with so far, a mook being a made up word from Scorsese's classic *Mean Streets*) and 'Title Fight', which was meant to be on *Tellin' Stories* but didn't get finished in time; the track was remixed by Richard March of Bentley Rhythm Ace who had been supporting the Charlatans on tour.

Bentley Rhythm Ace were prime exponents of 'big beat', the post Chemical Brothers huge clanking beat-driven cheeky pop tunes and sample-led dance shit that was busting out of the clubs, especially in Brighton where the Skint label were prime proponents of the form. The Bentleys were easily the most whakoid of the new style, with their frivolous stage props, their funny-when-stoned samples and daft stage wear.

'How High' showed that Burgess had been listening heavily to the Wu-Tang Clan, and if they weren't copping any phat hip hop beats for the single they were certainly paying attention to the lyrics – the title of the song was inspired by the song of the same name by Method Man and Red Man.

'Tim listens to a hell of a lot of hip hop and he's as inspired by that as he is by all that Bob Dylan stuff,' a spokesman for the band told the *NME*.

The video for the single was recorded in Los Angeles in one of those massive concrete drains that cuts across the city, used in countless films, from *Grease* to *Terminator 2*, as Tim told *Vox*, 'It was the chase sequence in *Terminator 2* when Arnie's on the bike trying to save the kid from the liquid man in the juggernaut. It stinks, I'll tell you, and loads of people with dogs live down there.'

By the late 1990s the summer festivals had become the key point of the rock calender; reputations could be made or broken here. Ten years before all the reviews of festivals had been sneering put-downs from the carpet-slippered journos who hate the mud, the hardships and having to watch so many bands! But by 1995 there was a new generation of promoters, bands and journos who were totally clued in to the festival experience and in the post-acid house/baggy culture of the times the dope-smoking masses were totally at home with the semi-stoned hippie ethic of the festivals. By 1997 there were festivals everywhere – ten years before there had only been Glastonbury and Reading, but now there seemed to be a festival every week, with the V festivals in Leeds and Chelmsford, the Phoenix and T In The Park getting added to the agenda.

To be a great festival band in the 1990s would clearly pay great dividends, and the Charlatans had all the things that were critical to being a brilliant festival band. Attributes like a run of catchy singalong singles and a community spirit, bands that were people's bands were always going to score heavily at these huge outdoors events; the feeling of community that superb pop music can bring is the domain of the first-rate live band.

The Charlatans were already regulars on the festival circuit and 1997 was no different from usual. Tim Burgess had done his own fair share of being a punter. 'I went to three Glastonburys before I was in a group, the last time in 1986, when it was New Order, Hüsker Du and the Mighty Lemon Drops,' he told a small local paper, adding, 'since then we've played there three times, and I've been as a VIP one year as well. I never thought I'd get to that from camping with the metal heads, building fires and getting covered in mud.'

Playing the festivals was something that the band treasured. As well as playing T In The Park this year they had been there two years previously.

'We did T In The Park in 1995,' said Tim, 'and we went on before Kylie, and I remember there was this mad ruckus down the front while we were playing and this big cloud of sand in the air. At that point T In The Park was the best gig we'd ever done. Last year we did Knebworth with Oasis cos we're all Led Zep fans! And we did Chelmsford V96, but this year we are only doing two festivals.'

The Charlatans had their festival thing totally worked out, as Tim explained, 'We shorten the set, we take the middle section out. Folk want stuff that they can recognise. They haven't just come for you. There's people there who aren't listening to anything that much.'

That's the festival way. Get in there and grab 'em. And on 12 July that's just what they did at the Glasgow T In The Park.

BACK IN THE USA

That autumn, with the UK well and truly becoming full-on Charlatans territory, they set off to the States for the second time that year to try and make some headway in the world's number 1 rock & roll market.

They still had some sort of following in the US, as a big group of anglophile kids would make sure that they could always sell their shows out, but beyond that the mainstream still looked a long, long way away, although by the back end of 1997 British groups were again breaking out of the underground and making much better headway in the US. Oasis had reached the top 5 with 'Wonderwall' and then watched their album crash in at number 2, the Prodigy and the Spice Girls had both sold even more records. The US was definitely up for it but it still required a lot of legwork.

The Prodigy and the Spice Girls had made it massive without grinding it out on the tour circuit but through a combination of MTV, club support and being in their own weirdly different ways pure pop. Oasis, being far more in the trad band mode, had to tour like fuck to get through, and the Charlatans would have to do the same.

This was something that they weren't prepared to do at all costs, as Mark Collins explained to Paul Moody from the *NME* for yet another piece by the journalist who had been with them since their pre-baggy mod days. 'I've never loved doing big tours. We just go insane after four weeks. The longest tour that we have done over the entire seven years of the Charlatans is five and a half weeks, that was in America in 1992 and after that we said, "Shall we sell another 20,000 records in America or keep our sanity?"'

They opted for the latter but it left them in a cult limbo in the US.

Moody caught up with the band in San Francisco at the legendary hippie joint the Fillmore Theatre, and when the band walked into the venue's lobby who should have their picture on the wall but the Charlatans USA.

'They follow us around everywhere,' grumbled Mark Collins, looking up at the picture of the band dressed in their ridiculous hippie garb complete with daft moustaches.

'Look at the state of them,' mocked Tim Burgess, before adding, 'that'll be us in a couple of years.'

The tour had been the usual mixture of hi jinks and business as usual shows. In Detroit Tim got his second tattoo done, a star on his arm; in New York they played the Roxy and got a buzz from the fact that it was the same venue as the Sex Pistols had played all those years before; in Atlanta they bought a souvenir piece of rubble from the building that was blown up during the Olympics. They quickly slipped into the tour schedule of soundcheck, eat, play, get on the bus, sleep, arrive, soundcheck – it was a never-ending cycle and could drive weaker people totally mad.

As the year drew towards a close the band were on a definite high, though.

'It's a bit like a game of chess,' Burgess told the *NME*. 'In the last year we've just played the queen and it's put us in this brilliant position, and now it's like checkmate.'

Nynex, they fucking sold out Nynex! That's 17,000 pop bunnies crammed into one venue. You gotta be big to even feel that you can pull that damned place off. The huge venue, built in the mid 1990s next to Manchester's Victoria station and the home of the city's ice hockey and basketball teams was custom-built for the big rock & roll shows, replacing GMex, the huge converted old station in the city centre, as the main venue.

Oasis had sold it out and so had the Manics, and so had some vile, lumbering mullet-owning rock pigs and sappy ballad-mongering buffoons.

But the Charlatans, had they got this big?

Damn right they had.

The *NME* asked them if playing such a massive show wasn't a little daunting, but Tim was taking it all in his stride. 'Not really. The one thing that makes me nervous is losing the atmosphere because the place is too big. We want to make sure that they're events . . . that they're special. When we did *Up To Our Hips* we only did four gigs in Britain to support the album, and one of them was at Trentham Gardens, and for a lot of our fans that was one of their favourite all-time gigs, because they travelled in to Stoke and it was a proper away-day party. I don't even know how many people were there, but it was great, and we want to prove that all over again, that we're the biggest secret in Britain.'

Before the gig *Melody Maker*'s Jane Graham (currently producer of the fab Mary Anne Hobbs show on Radio One) spoke to Tim in a piece where he gave a little bit of himself away when, remembering the much-maligned baggy scene of the late 1980s, he went against the grain and spoke positively of the times, 'You know, people are always trying to get us to slag baggy or are using it to slag us. I actually think a lot of good came from it; it did change minds, it was about attitude and honesty. When I think back to that time, I wish I'd said more then, I wish I'd been more outspoken about what I believed cos I really think that it could have gone further, got better instead of fizzling out. I hate it when that happens.'

Tim was talking with the hindsight of someone who had gone through a life-changing experience and come out the other side and, as one of the scene's prime movers, it was rare to see someone like him give the heavily criticised scene support.

Jane remembers how Tim was disappointed with the end result of baggy. 'He was let down by how corporate things got; he looked on himself as a pioneer, not as a follower, he really wanted to be a righteous figure. He was really into Shaun Ryder, I think he wished he could be more like that, and I think he really admired the way that Shaun Ryder could write such great lyrics.'

The problem with Tim is that he's too nice; he just couldn't piss people off, a rare quality in the ego-driven, belligerent world of rock.

'He's so charming,' Jane notes, 'in some ways he's like a little boy.'

It's that beguiling mixture of innocence in a cynical world yet streaked with a hooligan charm that gave him that delinquent edge in his teens that made him the sort of frontman that people could identify with.

'When I interviewed him,' says Jane, 'his mother and dad were there. They were really proud of him, he's a total spit of his mum. They kept telling stories of what he was like as a kid and he was just giggling!'

Burgess, ever the music fanatic, spent hours talking about the tunes that were firing his soul, in Jane Graham he found a fellow Dylan fan and impressed her with tales of spending 400 quid on Dylan bootlegs (as well as buying heaps of other stuff one afternoon: on the Chocolate Watch Band, garage psychedelia and Gram Parsons (who virtually invented country rock with the Flying Burrito Brothers), his taste as eclectic and all-consuming as ever) and tales of trying to learn the harmonica to emulate his tousle-mopped hero . . .

'The impression I got was that now that Rob had gone all the mania had gone out of the band's lives. The death of Rob had calmed the band down. They weren't a bunch of kids in a band any more, they were adults with kids and houses. The vibe had changed around the band, although Tim seemed to be eternally boyish. They seemed really laid back; they talked about Rob a lot and it was all tales of the chaos that surrounded him,' said Jane.

These stories would usually be of Rob getting pissed and egging people into causing trouble; he was the ringleader, the agent provocateur.

The band mightn't have been having big-time japery on the road any more but their wry sense of humour was still apparent. Checking into hotels under various aliases they must have been sniggering their way across the foyer: Tim checked in as Hank Williams, Mark as Nobby Stiles or Bobby Charlton, Tony Rogers as Tony Ferino.

'Apart from that they weren't into that smash the hotel up sort of stuff at all,' explains Jane. 'During the interview Tim spilt coffee on the bedroom floor and wiped it up.'

Not that remarkable in real life but in the 'I am God' lifestyle of rock & roll, truly revolutionary!

The permanently upbeat, impeccably mannered Burgess with his semi out-of-it manner could have been accused of being a hippie, an accusation the ex punk found hard to swallow. 'You know I'm not walking around looking at the stars all the time. I don't go looking for guidance from some outside force all the time. I just have respect for other people. It's not like I'm really happy and self satisfied all the time, that sounds really pathetic.'

In the interview Burgess felt that rock & roll was jaded. 'There's not as many great characters in music as there once was. People still want to be Sly Stone and Brian Wilson [the Beach Boys], but they shut up and let themselves be mothered by the record company and do what they're told to get their gold-star badge. That's why I love Jon and Martin being in the band.

I always miss them when they're not there cos they think of things and see things in a way that I never would.'

Rob's death was, obviously, still hanging over Tim. 'When Rob died, lots of things in my life just stopped. And I thought about them for a while, then I began to take some tentative steps forward again, and now I'm sprinting. It made us all think, why are we doing this? Is this the greatest love of our lives? Could it ever become embarrassing?'

Jane found Tim completely unjaded by his stardom. 'He can't believe his luck, he's not like Liam Gallagher, he seems totally egoless. Someone came in and put the Charlatans on the jukebox and he was very embarrassed.'

Still the fan, Tim refused to diss Ian Brown who had just gone on record slagging him off, claiming that Brown's family would laugh at Tim every time he appeared on TV. The band may have been hurt by Brown's comments but they were still fans of the Roses and weren't prepared to get into a public slanging match; it just wasn't their way. After years of struggle, death, and pain, a few stray comments weren't going to faze them.

If 1997 had been a year of consolidating their triumph then the Nynex show and the sold-out 6 December concert at London's Docklands Arena represented flexing of muscle for the band. The previews of the gigs expressed shock and surprise at how the so-called runts of the litter had suddenly got so big without their permission. But the Charlatans had been big for a long time and now they were just making sure that people knew about it; even a band with their lack of ego needed occasionally to affirm their status, and in the brand new empire of Britpop where big was best, it was no good pretending that you were just ambling along any more.

Never before had they played such massive gigs as the main act. Trentham Gardens had been a great moment, but that was to only 4000 people, and since then Oasis had shifted the goalposts a long way with their mega shows – no longer was a 10,000 capacity show a mega gig but a rite of passage.

Pre these big shows the Charlatans played a couple of gigs in Belfast and Dublin, supported by Bentley Rhythm Ace.

For Tim Burgess the Nynex gig was one of his top 3 favourite gigs that he ever played (the best gig that he had ever been to apparently was a Saint Patrick's Day Pogues show at Brixton Academy – 'They came onstage all wearing American police uniforms,' he remembers, 'and there were a load of mad Celtic fans there as well,' as you would expect and, at their peak, Pogues gigs were always mad, ribald celebrations of getting pissed, punk rock and Irish folk music; his other all-time favourite gig was New Order at Heaven in 1983-1984, one of the first shows that they played), along with Reading and Trentham Gardens. After the Nynex gig Tim felt 'freaked out' and slipped off home to have a small party with six friends; in complete contrast, after the Docklands show they had to leave the venue with a police escort.

Opening, as usual, with 'With No Shoes' and 'North Country Boy', the band shot through a set stuffed full of classics, including 'One To Another', 'Weirdo' and 'The Only One I Know'. Worries that their less than heavy sound may get lost in the huge cavernous space of the Nynex centre were swiftly dispelled. Surprising everyone apart from themselves, the Charlatans fitted easily into the huge hall; the stage, decked out in Christmas lights, was a typically homely touch, making something as cold and mean as a stadium show seem like a pleasant jaunt.

Things might have been going really well and most of the band might have been on a high but Martin Blunt still had his feet on the ground. 'No matter how good things might look on the surface, everything is always a constant struggle, against the odds. Against everything,' he pointed out to the *NME*.

'TELLIN' STORIES' AS A SINGLE

Squeezing a bit more life out of the album, on 20 October they released the fourth single off the album, the title track.

Building up on the loop provided by the Chemical Brothers with a light acoustic feel the single eventually kicks in with one of those choruses that you take for granted will do the business. In the context of the album the track isn't an automatic choice as a single, although when you pull it out on its own it makes complete sense.

Coming off an already released album affected its sales and it didn't chart high like the previous three singles, going in at a still respectable number 16, and despite a *Top Of The Pops* appearance, it crashed out of the 40 altogether the following week.

This time instead of having a band member leering out from the sleeve they had used the infamous Christine Keeler on a chair shot.

The single's three B-side tracks included 'Keep It To Yourself' (an acoustic workout) and 'Clean Up Kid' (trad old-skool Charlatans in a near return to baggy shock) and were also, incidentally, the first co-credits for keyboard player Tony Rogers. The single's video was live footage shot at that year's Phoenix festival. The third track was 'Thank You', a live cut culled from their Phoenix festival set, Martin Blunt's poignant thank you to the fans.

MELTING POT

The Charlatans' innings on Beggars Banquet came to an end with the release of the *Melting Pot* compilation, a 17-track collection of hits, misses, rarities and other bits and bobs. *Melting Pot* was the Charlatans putting the breaks on their career and having a good sieve through all their tunes – whether it's the end of part one or the beginning of part two remains to be seen.

At least this compilation was put together by the band themselves, instead of being hacked out by some gimp at the label trying to impose a point of view on the history of the band. After entering their tenth year the group who few would ever have expected to have made it this far had plenty of songs to choose from. It checkpointed their variation in style and made a mockery of that bold claim that they 'were always playing "The Only Song That I Know" '. Because the band chose the tunes and are a bunch of awkward sods, this greatest hits record is anything but, although it's an interesting potted history of the group.

Kicking off with 'The Only One I Know', their first release on Beggars Banquet and their first top-10 hit, it showed a sparkling, optimistic young band on the cusp of pop greatness; it was an effortless summer hit and sounds great today with its (still) regular plays on Radio One.

The next track, 'Then', was the follow-up single and demonstrated that the band weren't just one-hit wonders; this and the *Some Friendly* album proved that the band were going to have staying power. 'Opportunity Three' from the following EP makes the compilation, as does 'Over Rising', showing a band moving and starting to stretch its sound.

'Weirdo', the first appearance here by Mark Collins, was the band at their wildest, and their favourite instrumental 'Theme From "The Wish"' as well as the US version of the classic 'Sproston Green' pretty well round up *Melting Pot*'s cull from the band's early years.

The mid period is well represented by the Chemical Brothers' mix of 'Patrol', marking the band's exploration into the groove, a groove that they would master and make their own. The first signs of a new maturity was the run of singles 'Can't Get Out Of Bed', 'I Never Want An Easy Life', 'Jesus Hairdo', 'Crashin' In' and 'Just Lookin'', showcasing a new, rawer Charlatans. 'One To Another' still sounds like a monster, one of their best ever records, and 'North Country Boy' is as charming as ever.

The album is great driving music; cranked high in a car and with a load of mates it's a superb soundtrack to the 1990s, a rip-roaring ride through the decade. It shows a band that is one of the best of their era, always keeping their garage edge and shit-tight rhythm section, and never falling into the flaccid laziness that ruins some of their contemporaries.

1998
Just When You're Thinkin'
Things Over

POP LIFE NOW

In many ways the initial rush when a group makes it is the most exciting part of their career. After all the pain, the trials and the tribulations, the Charlatans have become survivors, with hardly anyone seeming to notice how they have arrived as one of the most respected bands now in the country.

The Roses and the Mondays had long ago buggered off, leaving the Charlatans as the authentic last link with the original scene. At last this was something that Tim was beginning to come to terms with, 'I loved both of those groups, and I was really sad when the Roses broke up – I saw it as a real waste of talent. But at least Mani's in Primal Scream now. I haven't heard the album yet, but I trust them.'

Now their gigs could easily be sold out several times over, the people are definitely down with the band, and the days of worrying whether fashion had excluded them are over. Even *Top Of The Tops* has become a regular jaunt, as Tim pointed out, 'It's long and it's boring, it always is and it always will be . . . but it's still the best show to do. And bands always get treated the same on *Top Of The Pops* whether they are starting out or they are number 1, which is cool. My favourite *Top Of The Pops* appearance was in 1994 for "Can't Get Out Of Bed". Before then we had struggled and that single was a breakthrough, plus there was the fact that Rob had been out of prison for just days and then he was on *Top Of The Pops*, which was pretty weird.'

The 1990s saw British pop culture totally awash with drugs music that was selling in massive quantities, virtually created to smoke dope to.

When asked if they used drugs to aid the creative process, Tim replied, 'Well, they can help, but obviously not when you are on them, cos you're out of control. Sometimes the day after an E, when you're in a beautiful mood, it's good. I like the drugs. I've got no problem with them at all. I like taking uppers when we put the backing track down, then get into a smoking mood while we overdub, and then get into a straight mood when we're mixing.'

Mark Collins told Johnny Cigarettes at the *NME* that there had been a chemical rush to his good times, a rush that now was totally under control. 'We aren't that big on drugs any more as a band. I was a bit of a coke fiend in America. Mind you, I can only smoke it now, because my nose is so fucked!'

He may have been tongue in cheek here, but there was a definite swagger about pop stars and their drug intake in the mid 1990s. Drugs were big news in the new generation of groups, and the music press was littered with interviews with bands all trying to have the most outrageous drugs claims. Like it was outrageous any more as, for most of the musicians, like most of their fans, drugs were very much a fact of life; as Noel Gallagher told the press, taking drugs was like having a cup of tea. It was bizarre that the media could still find any sensation in something that it seemed nearly everyone did. Drug use was now totally casual; it wasn't a case of rock & roll rebellion, it was something that all your neighbours in your seedy block of flats seemed to spend all their time and money doing.

In the gradual slump of pop from the mid 1990s' white heat of creativity to the latest depressive flavour, certain pop bands held the line with their own style and sound. The Charlatans were one of the few bands who remained a constant, ever improving and maturing, and avoiding some of the pratfalls that were destroying some of their contemporaries . . .

AND FINALLY

1998 for the Charlatans was a low-key year. They built their own studio deep in the countryside near Northwich and started working up material for another album. Lying low after years of non-stop work is important for any band, and after the long and tiring road that they had travelled along, the break was welcome for the band.

The tracks that your author has heard and the rehearsal-room jams are great loose loping songs that sound like they are deeper into the classic mid 1960s Dylan and the Band country. They sound like a band totally relaxed with what it is and what it does; they sound like people who know each other inside out playing their way around one another.

At some point before the millennium there will be a new album, one that Steve Harrison feels will finally be the record that establishes the group as the truly worldwide band that they have constantly hinted at being. The fact that they are finally on a big worldwide label that has the muscle to make this happen is a deciding factor in this new-found optimism.

The pop scene may be entering one of its creative troughs but bands like the Charlatans are already too big to be affected by this, and their explosive show at the V98 festival in Leeds and Chelmsford when they played their first-ever headline gig in front of a reverential audience of thousands, is rock solid proof that the band definitely have what it takes for the big breakthrough.

Those gigs were certainly the best I've seen them play, tight and mean. Tony Rogers' Hammond playing was a revelation and, mixed up high, his chops dominated a confident and assured set. There was real magic in the air as a great British rock & roll band played through a never-ending heap of fantastic hits and a few half-forgotten songs.

Steve Harrison's bold prediction for world takeover didn't look like the hot air of hype that evening!

The Charlatans, the true survivors of the UK 1990s pop scene, were staring at the future with a new and defiant optimism.